GRAMMAR
WITH A PURPOSE

GRAMMAR
WITH A PURPOSE
A Contextualized Approach

Myrna Knepler

Northeastern Illinois University

MAXWELL MACMILLAN
International Publishing Group

Associate Director/Editor: Mary Jane Peluso/Maggie Barbieri
Production Supervision: Editorial Inc./Ann Knight
Text Design: Ezra Holston
Cover Design: Marysarah Quinn
This book was set in 10½ × 12 Meridien Light by V & M Graphics, Incorporated; printed and bound by R.R. Donnelley & Sons. The cover was printed by Phoenix Color Corp.

Library of Congress Cataloging-in-Publication Data

Knepler, Myrna.
    Grammar with a purpose : a contextualized approach / Myrna
Knepler.
      p. cm.
    ISBN 0-02-365240-3
    1. English language — Textbooks for foreign speakers. 2. English
language — Grammar — 1950— I. Title.
PE1128.K55 1990   89-22152
428.2'4 — dc20   CIP

Collier Macmillan Canada, Inc.

Credit lines appear on pages vii–viii, which constitutes an extension of the copyright page.

Printing: 1 2 3 4 5 6 7   Year: 0 1 2 3 4 5 6

Maxwell Macmillan
ESL/EFL Department
866 Third Avenue
New York, NY 10022

Printed in the U.S.A.

ISBN 0-02-365240-3

PREFACE

Grammar with a Purpose: A Contextualized Approach is planned to help ESL students who already know a good deal of English but who need help in producing the kind of sophisticated and flexible language they need for full participation in college or professional life.

Grammar with a Purpose presents the regularities in English in ways that are simple enough to be helpful yet are truthful to the complexity of language in use. It tries to guard against misleading students with overly simplified explanations about how English works. Advanced students are done a disservice when they are given easy "rules" — "rules" that they soon find out do not apply to the language they hear and read.

Examples and exercises are always presented in a context. Mature students do not need to be presented with textbook language about lives of imaginary "Mr. and Mrs. Browns." Many sections in this book use short pieces of high-interest professional writing (Maxine Hong Kingston and Andy Rooney), newspaper and magazine articles, charts, and graphs as the basis for examples and exercises. In other sections, exercises are constructed around topics likely to turn up in students' own conversations — getting an education, leaving home, choosing a job, understanding cross-cultural differences.

ACKNOWLEDGMENTS

Marjorie Fuchs, Edward Tosques, Bernard Susser, Becky Lamaitre, and Peggy Lindstrom read the manuscript in various stages of its development and gave me many helpful suggestions for which I am grateful. Mary Jane Peluso, my sponsoring editor, has given enthusiastic support throughout the long process of writing. I want to extend my thanks to her and to other members of the ESL staff at Maxwell Macmillan for their support. I am particularly indebted to Ann Knight of Editorial Inc. for her skillful help in the editing and production process, always given with great patience and good humor. My daughter Elinor and especially my husband Henry spent many hours proofreading with me. I thank them.

Text Credits

Pages 14−15 "Querencia," by Suzannah Lessard from The Talk of the Town, *The New Yorker*, September 26, 1977. Reprinted by permission, © 1977 The New Yorker Magazine, Inc. Page 23 Excerpt from "The Kitchen" from *A Walker in the City*, copyright 1951 and renewed 1979 by Alfred Kazin. Reprinted by permission of Harcourt Brace Jovanovich, Inc. Page 31 "Dolphin Brain Studies Shed New Light on Mental Skills," by Erick Eckholm, *The New York Times*, August 31, 1986. Copyright © 1986 by the New York Times Company. Reprinted by permission. Page 66 Excerpt from *The Hidden Dimension* by Edward T. Hall. Copyright © 1966 by Edward T. Hall. Reprinted by permission of Doubleday, a division of Bantam, Doubleday, Dell Publishing Group, Inc. Page 83 Excerpt from "American Space, Chinese Place," by Yi-Fu Tuan, *Harper's Magazine*, July, 1974. Pages 111−112 From *The Concise Columbia Encyclopedia*, copyright © 1983, Columbia University Press. Used by permission. Page 126 Mihaly Csikszentmihalyi and Eugene Rochberb-Halton, "Object Lessons," from *The Meaning of Things: Symbols in the Development of the Self*, p. 78. Copyright © 1981, Cambridge University Press, New York. Page 128 John Joyce, "What is the Order of Things?" from The Observer section, *Chicago Tribune*. © copyrighted the Chicago Tribune Company, all rights reserved, used with permission. Pages 138−139 Excerpts from *The Woman Warrior: Memoirs of a Girlhood Among Ghosts*, by Maxine Hong Kingston. Copyright © 1975, 1976 by Maxine Hong Kingston. Reprinted by permission of Alfred A. Knopf, Inc. By permission of Schaffner Agency. Pages 164−165 Excerpts from "Dictionaries," and "Spelling" reprinted with permission of Atheneum Publishers, an imprint of Macmillan Publishing Company, from *And More by Andy Rooney*, by Andrew A. Rooney. Copyright © 1982 by Essay Productions, Inc. Page 195 Excerpts from "What a Difference a Book Makes," Carol Levin's review of *Books That Made the Difference* by Gordon and Patricia Sabine in *Psychology Today*, October 1983. Reprinted by permission of the publishers. Pages 209−210 Excerpts from *Miss Manners' Guide to Rearing Perfect Children*, by Judith Martin, reprinted with permission of Atheneum Publishers, an imprint of Macmillan Publishing Company. Copyright © 1984 by United Feature Syndicate, Inc. Page 228 Excerpt from "Fear of Dearth," by Carll Tucker, *Saturday Review*, October 27, 1979. Pages 229−230 Excerpt "It is an ultimate kitchen gadget . . . a human hand," from *Capon on Cooking* by Robert Capon. Copyright © 1983 by Robert Farrar Capon. Reprinted by permission of Houghton Mifflin Company. Page 309 From *Newsweek*, March 31, 1986. Page 319 "Changing Attitudes Towards Women's Roles," chart adapted from *The Sunday New York Times*, November 23, 1986. Copyright © 1986 by The New York Times Company. Reprinted by permission. Pages 322−323 Excerpts from "Halfway to Dick and Jane," by Jack Agueros from *The Immigrant Experience* edited by Thomas C. Whaler. Copyright © 1971 by Thomas C. Whaler. Reprinted by permission of Doubleday, a division of Bantam, Doubleday, Dell Publishing Group, Inc. Page 355 "The First Year," chart adapted from *The New York Times*, May 5, 1987. Copyright © 1987 by The New York Times Company. Reprinted by

TO THE TEACHER

Grammar with a Purpose is designed to be useful to the many different kinds of classes labeled upper-intermediate. Its form is modular, designed to provide maximum flexibility. Rather than grouping all the verb tenses or modal auxiliaries in a single place, it spreads the treatment of such difficult-to-learn items through ten well-planned chapters. After completing the introductory chapter and Chapter 1, a teacher might choose to work through the remaining chapters in the order in which they appear, or he or she might teach relevant sections in sequence from a number of different chapters. In classes with limited time, "Check Yourself" and "Practicing Your Skills" exercises can be used as pre-tests to identify problems that need class treatment or assignment for guided self-study.

The following easily identifiable sections appear throughout the book:

Time and Tense
This section begins each chapter and focuses on the use of one or more verb tenses in context.

Using Modals
Modals and modal-like forms often have multiple meanings whose implications are elusive even for advanced students. Students are helped to understand these meanings through the use of a wide selection of examples and exercises.

Finding Out About...
This section deals with a variety of grammatical points often relating to other items in the chapter.

Little Words
Short words such as determiners and prepositions are among the most difficult for ESL students to master. This section focuses on gradually increasing the accuracy with which students use these forms.

Sentence Sense
In Chapters 1–6 students are introduced to the sentence patterns that occur again and again in English and are encouraged to expand skeleton sentences with modifying words and phrases. In subsequent chapters, students learn to combine simple sentences in increasingly complex and sophisticated ways.

Checking it Over
These sections, which occur at the end of each chapter, teach proofreading skills and help students integrate grammar points taught in earlier chapters with more recently learned material. Designed primarily for self-study with teacher guidance, answers are provided for most exercises.

A variety of exercise types are used throughout the book.

Practicing Your Skills

These exercises follow most explanatory sections and are designed to provide controlled practice of the structures that have just been taught. Only one answer, or in a few cases a limited number of answers, is correct. Teachers should note errors for immediate correction or indication that the material needs to be re-explained.

Using Your Skills

These exercises are open-ended and are designed to allow students to rehearse the expression of their own thoughts in contexts similar to those they might encounter outside of class. Any answers that communicate meaning appropriately should be acceptable whether or not students are using forms they have just been taught. Teachers are advised to ignore, at least for the moment, errors that do not impede communication.

Ask and Answer

Students work in pairs alternately asking and responding to question cues.

Check Yourself

These exercises can be used in a variety of ways depending on the composition of the class, the time available, and the teacher's style. In classes using the material in sequence, the "Check Yourself" exercises at the end of a section alert students and teachers to gaps that need to be filled before moving on.

When dealing with material that students have no doubt been taught but may not have mastered, such as the formation of questions and negatives, "Check Yourself" exercises appear as pre-tests. Teachers with limited time who are using the book for a selective review of grammar problems may use the other "Check Yourself" exercises in this way also.

Some exercise types appear less frequently. "How it Sounds" gives students practice in distinguishing between utterances that are frequently confused such as *can* and *can't* and alerts them to reductions that appear in normal rapid speech. "Looking at Forms" assures that students can identify the forms that they will be studying, for example the different kinds of nouns examined in Chapter 1. "Checking Your Accuracy" asks students to do guided error analysis of work they have done previously.

CONTENTS

CHAPTER 7

CHAPTER 8

WORKING TOGETHER

WORKING TOGETHER

Perhaps this is your first day of class. You came in the door, looked around, and took a seat. Maybe the person sitting next to you is someone you have never seen before. Perhaps you exchanged greetings; perhaps you said nothing.

Take a moment and look around at your classmates. These are the people you will be working with in this class. You will be doing the exercises together, exchanging papers, and helping one another to learn. As advanced students of English, you have knowledge that you can share with others. Sharing that knowledge will also help you to learn.

Now, look at the two people sitting closest to you. Tell them your name and find out their names. If you already know the students next to you, exchange names with the nearest strangers.

Use this space to write the names of two of your classmates.

_____   _____

GETTING TO KNOW ONE ANOTHER

Talk to one of the people that you exchanged names with. Ask him or her any of the following questions you feel comfortable asking. In some cases you might want to tell your partner about yourself before asking a question.

Example

I came here from Thailand a year ago. Where are you from?

The following are possible subjects for questions.

1. country of origin
2. location of country
3. home town (size and location)
4. interesting facts about country
5. native language(s)
6. feelings about speaking English
7. reason for coming to school
8. length of time at this school
9. field of study
10. current courses in addition to this one
11. current job
12. future job plans
13. spare-time activities and interests
14. interests that you might have in common

CHECKING IT OVER

All of the following questions were asked by students in a class like this. Each of the questions was understood and answered. However, each question contains one or two small mistakes. Correct each sentence. Then, explain your corrections.

1. Did you finish~~ed~~ high school? _After_ did, _we use the base form of the verb._
2. What your native language is? _____
3. How long you live in this city? _____
4. When are you started at this school? _____
5. What kind books read you in your spare time? _____
6. Do you driving to school or taking bus? _____
7. The weather in your country warmer is as Chicago? _____
8. How old did you start to learn English? _____

FORMING QUESTIONS

Imagine one of your classmates is being interviewed over the telephone. You can hear the answers but not the questions. Write the question you think the interviewer asked. When you have finished, check your questions for mistakes.

1. _____ _How old are you?_ _____   **1.** I'm 33.
   2. I'm divorced.
   3. Greek.
   4. Greece.
   5. Reading detective novels and playing soccer.
   6. In high school in my country.
   7. Probably computer science.
   8. Almost a year now.
   9. Fun, but hard work.

■■■■■■ *Softening Questions*

Often when we ask questions of people we want to get to know better, we put our questions in a softened, less direct form. Direct questions are efficient in getting information quickly and satisfying our curiosity about the new person, but they may not seem as polite or friendly.

Direct (more efficient)	*Softened (more friendly)*
What's your name?	My name's Jenny. What's yours?
How do you spell your name?	Would you mind spelling your name for me?
What's your address?	Do you live far from here?
What's your native language?	I see you've got a Korean-English dictionary. Is Korean your first language?
What are you interested in?	Everyone's talking about the Bears. I don't understand American football. How about you?
How long have you lived in Chicago?	Is this your first winter here?

Often we give information about ourselves before asking someone a friendly question. Friendly questions usually allow a person to answer in more than one way. Often extra words like *would you mind* are added in order to soften questions.

USING YOUR SKILLS

Take five of the questions you wrote down earlier and rewrite them in softened form. What changes did you make?

About You and Your Progress in Learning English

The next few pages contain two sets of questions to help your teacher find out about you, about your goals in learning English, and how far along you have come in meeting those goals. Some of the questions may be discussed in class. Your teacher may want you to write answers to some of the questions on separate sheets of paper.

ABOUT YOURSELF

Some questions may not apply to you or your situation. If you see a question that you cannot answer, write NA (not applicable).

1. What is your full name? (Write your family name last.)
2. What name would like your teacher and classmates to call you?
3. What country are you from?
4. What is your first language?
5. What is your major (possible major)?
6. What activities do you like to do in your spare time?
7. What subjects do you like to talk about with friends?
8. What subjects do you like to read about?
9. What is your present job?
10. What job would you like to have several years from now?

LANGUAGE LEARNING QUESTIONNAIRE

If you are using this book, you are probably a fairly advanced learner of English. However, in any advanced class individuals will vary in skills. You may be good at reading English but feel less comfortable about speaking it. The student sitting next to you may be a better speaker than reader.

You probably have a good idea of your own strengths and weaknesses. Answering some of the questions that follow will help your teacher to know how to help you.

1. Describe what you believe is important about your previous experiences in learning English. Indicate whether you learned English primarily in school or primarily by talking with English speakers. About how old were you when you began to learn? Tell what has helped you most in learning.

2.   When do you use English outside of class? At work? At home? With friends? Estimate the percentage of time you spend speaking English. Are there any ways you could increase your opportunities to speak?

3.   Which of the following skills in English are easy for you? Fairly easy? Which skills do you need to work at the most?

understanding informal conversations

understanding formal lectures and presentations

speaking with friends in informal situations

speaking in more formal situations: school or work

understanding newspapers and magazines in English

reading for study or work

writing informally

writing for school or work

4.   What are your long-term goals in learning English? What do you hope to be able to do when you have achieved your long-term goals?

5.   Learning a language well takes a long time. Probably you won't be able to achieve all your goals by the end of this course. Which goals are most important to you? What are three specific goals you hope to achieve by the time this course is over?

ABOUT THE CLASS

After answering so many questions, you probably have some of your own. Write out ten questions about this class that you want to ask your teacher. The following are suggestions for questions.

1.   material to be covered in class
2.   normal class procedures
3.   homework (What kind? How often?)
4.   use of dictionaries
5.   other books or materials needed
6.   attendance policy
7.   policy on late work
8.   tests (What kind? How often?)
9.   grading
10.   opportunities for additional help
11.   suggestions about how to study effectively

CHAPTER 1

An Introduction to Tenses

> **1.** The student often *writes* to her friends. (simple present tense)
> **2.** She *is writing* a letter now. (present progressive tense)
> **3.** She *will write* several more. (future tense)
> **4.** She *wrote* several letters last week. (simple past tense)
> **5.** She *has been writing* for an hour. (present perfect progressive tense)

Each of these sentences uses a different tense of the verb *write*. The tenses of English are formed with main verbs like *write* or a combination of main verbs and auxiliary verbs like *is*, *has*, and *will*. (Auxiliary verbs are also called helping verbs.)

The tense of a verb usually tells you the time when something happened. The tense of the verb may also give other important information. For example, it can tell you if something that started in the past is still happening at the present time. Sentence 5 tells you that the student is still writing.

Tense and time are not really the same thing. Time exists in the real world independent of language. No matter what language we speak, we all understand that yesterday is past and tomorrow is in the future.

Tense is the way many languages express time, but it is different from language to language. Your own language and English may have different tenses to express similar ideas about time, while similar tenses may have different meanings. Your language may not show tenses when it is necessary to do so in English. Or your language may show the tense of a verb when English does not.

Forming and Using Tenses

Because the formation of verb tenses in English usually follows regular rules, it is fairly easy to learn which verbs or combinations of main and auxiliary verbs are used to form the tenses you need. Knowing which tense to use to express a particular meaning is more difficult, even for advanced learners of English. Often more than one choice of tenses is correct for any situation. In some cases, sentences with different tenses will have similar meanings. In other cases, their meanings will be significantly different.

Because you must consider meaning when choosing which verb tense to use, there are no rules that will help you 100 percent of the time. As you continue to use English and listen to other people's responses to what you say or write, your ability to choose the right tense will improve. Each chapter will give guidelines on using the verb tenses of English to say what you mean.

■ *Main Verbs and Auxiliary Verbs*

It is useful to distinguish between main verbs and auxiliary verbs in English. In the first three paragraphs, the main verbs are underlined twice and the auxiliary verbs are underlined once.

MARTA CASTRO

1   Marta Castro, the student on my left, is from Brazil. Her first language is Portuguese, but she also speaks Spanish and a little Italian. She enjoys learning languages. She studied English in high school for several years but did not have very many chances to practice until she came to the United States six months ago.
5   She has been studying at this school for only a few months. She says that her English is not very good, but it sounds good to me. She wants to improve her English very rapidly.

When she was a child, Marta lived in a small village about a hundred miles from Rio, but her parents had moved to the city by the time she started high school,
10   and they have lived there ever since.

Marta is single now but thinks she will not be single five years from now. When I asked her, "Do you plan to have children?" she said that she didn't know.

PRACTICING YOUR SKILLS

Continue underlining the main and auxiliary verbs. Check your answers on page 426.

Marta is the first person in her family to study in a foreign country, and she misses her family a lot. Right now she is living with her cousins. She hopes her sister will come
15   to the United States next year and they can share a small apartment.

This semester Marta is taking a biology course, a math course, and two English courses. She wants to major in biology and to go to medical school. After graduating from med school, she will be returning to Brazil to practice medicine in a small town like the one she was born in.

■ *Points to Remember About Verbs*

1. Every sentence has at least one main verb.
2. All tenses except the simple present, the simple past, and the imperative tense are formed with a combination of a main verb and one or more auxiliary verbs. Since there are not many auxiliary verbs, the best way to recognize them is to memorize them.

   Auxiliaries Used in Forming Tenses

   be (am, are, is, was, were)

   have (have, has, had)

   Auxiliaries Used in Forming Questions and Negatives

   do (do does, did)

   Note: *be*, *have*, and *do* can also be used as main verbs.

   Modal Auxiliary Verbs

   will, would, can, could, may, might, shall, should, must

3. Infinitives (to + verb) and *-ing* verbs used without auxiliaries (gerunds) cannot be used as the main verbs of a sentence. The first paragraph in the story about Marta Castro contains two examples of infinitives (*to practice*, *to improve*), and one example of a gerund (*learning*).

USING YOUR SKILLS

Write a few short paragraphs introducing the classmate you interviewed earlier (page 2).

After you have finished writing, underline all the main verbs in your essay twice. Underline all the auxiliary verbs once. Be sure that every sentence has a main verb. Do not underline infinitives or gerunds.

The Simple Present Tense

Forming the Simple Present Tense

For almost all verbs the simple present tense has two forms—the base form and the base form with an *-s* or *-es* added.* (The base form is sometimes called the simple form or the dictionary form.) The choice of the base or the base + *s/es* form depends entirely on the subject of the sentence. In the simple present tense, verbs must agree with their subject (subject-verb agreement).

The third-person singular form of *have* is *has*.

Subject	Base + s/es	
He		
She	writes	
It	addresses	letters.
The student		

Use base + *s/es* when the subject of a sentence is a third-person singular pronoun—*he, she, it*—or a singular noun.

Subject	Base	
I		
You		
We	write	
They	address	letters.
Her friends		

Use the base form of the verb after the pronouns *I, you, we,* and *they*, or after plural nouns.

Forming the Simple Present with be

As you have probably realized, the most common verb in the language—*be*—is an exception. *Be* has three forms in the simple present tense: *am, is, are.* None of these forms is the same as the base.

I *am* here.	He She It The student *is* here.	You We They The students *are* here.

*See page 420 for information on adding *-s* or *-es*.

PRACTICING YOUR SKILLS

A. Complete the following sentences in your own words. Use the simple present tense. Be sure that the verb you use agrees with the main subject of the sentence.

1. Their idea _is interesting_ .
2. My ideas _are good too_ .
3. The students at this school _are indisciplined_ .
4. A woman that I know _is very jalous_ .
5. A typical student in my country _is always on time_ .
6. The men in my country _are good workers_ .
7. The women in my country _start to working very young_
8. People in the United States _like fast food_ .
9. My parents _are not from the same village_
10. My friend's parents _is from Paris_ .
11. The classes that I am taking this term _have very good teachers_ .
12. The English language _is the business language_
13. My first language _is french_ .
14. Languages throughout the world _are all beautiful_ .

B. Write out ten of the sentences, underlining the verbs you used and circling the main subjects.

Example

Their (idea) is ridiculous.
      S   V

■■■■■ *How to Find the Main Subject*

Because verbs must agree with their subjects, it is important that you know how to find the main subject of a sentence. If you have difficulty identifying the subject of any sentence, follow these directions step by step.

First, find the verb.

The school _has_ several hundred students.
          V

The students at this school _come_ from many different countries.
                              V

Next, ask a question beginning with *who* or *what*, followed by the verb phrase.

What has several hundred students?   The *school*.

Who comes from many different countries?   The *students*.

The answer to your question will be the subject.

CHECK YOURSELF

Circle the subject of each verb in the essay on Marta Castro. Check your answers on page 426.

PRACTICING YOUR SKILLS

The following sentences come from students' essays about schools in their own countries. Fill in the blanks with the correct simple present form of the verb. Remember to make verbs agree with subjects. (This exercise is more challenging if you cover the base forms of the verbs in the right-hand margin and try to guess the word used.) Check your answers on page 426.

1. In Vietnamese schools, when the teacher
_____*arrives*_____ the students _____*stand up*_____   arrive / stand up
and _____*say*_____ "Good morning, Teacher."   say

2. In Korea, the class _____*has*_____ a leader. The   have
leader _____*controls*_____ the students and   control
_____*helps*_____ the teacher. When the teacher   help
_____*stands up*_____ the leader _____*stands up*_____   stand up / stand up
also and _____*says*_____, "Pay attention." Then the   say
leader _____*bows*_____ to the teacher.   bow

3. When a Korean student _____*answers*_____ the   answer
teacher's questions, she _____*stands up*_____ and she   stand up
_____*uses*_____ very polite language.   use

4. Students in Korea _____*come*_____ to class and   come
_____*open*_____ their textbooks before the teacher   open
_____*arrives*_____. They _____*close*_____ their   arrive / close
textbooks and _____*leave*_____ only after the teacher   leave
_____*leaves*_____ the room.   leave

5. In my country, Colombia, the relationship between
students and teachers _____*is*_____ like the   be
relationship between parents and children. In the United

States, the students and teachers _____try_____   try
to be friends.

6. In Thailand, students _____say_____ "Teacher"   say
when they _____are_____ a question. It   ask
_____is_____ more respectful not to use the   be
teacher's name.

7. In my country, students _____are_____ not active   be
in class. Only the teacher _____talks_____. The   talk
students _____are_____ usually afraid to say   be
something wrong.

USING YOUR SKILLS

A.   Rules about classroom procedures vary from country to country. Construct several sentences describing typical classroom procedures in your home country.
B.   Write a paragraph either describing classroom behavior in your country in detail or comparing one aspect of classroom behavior in two countries you know.

Accuracy focus: When you have finished writing, check to see that all verbs agree with their subjects.

PRACTICING YOUR SKILLS

The simple present tense is often used when we want to define an unfamiliar word or idea.

The following paragraph in the *New Yorker* by Suzanne Lessard, a contemporary American writer, defines the word *querencia*. Fill in the blanks with the correct form of the missing verb: base or base + *s/es*. See answers on page 426.

QUERENCIA

1   *Querencia* _____is_____ a Spanish word that   be
_____means_____ affection for the place one*   mean
_____calls_____ home and the sense of well-being   call
that that place _____gives_____ one. It   give
5   _____is_____ an offshoot of the verb *querer*, ["to   be
love"] "to desire," and can be applied to the contentment of

One: a pronoun meaning he or she (used only in formal writing or speech)

a wild animal in its haunts as well as to the comfort felt by
a person in familiar surroundings. It ___means___   mean
the sense of being nourished by a place in which you
10 ___belong___. Narrowly defined, the word   belong
___applies___ to the immediate environs in which   apply
a person ___lives___, but one can apply it to   live
home in a larger sense without vitiating its meaning. . . .
We ___live___ in a world awash with people   live
15 torn from their *querencia* who ___face___ the   face
enormously difficult task of cultivating another. A person
might find *querencia* in more places than one, but not in
many more. Once found, it cannot be lightly discarded,
because lack of *querencia* is a kind of starvation.
20 *Querencia* ___nurtures___.   nurture

VOCABULARY

haunts: familiar places
immediate environs: places close by
vitiating: weakening
nurtures: provides food or other nourishment

USING YOUR SKILLS

Define a word from your own language that cannot be easily translated into
English.

▬▬▬▬ *Common Uses of the Simple Present Tense**

1.   Use the simple present tense to talk about facts, ideas, or beliefs that are true
not only at the present moment but for an extended period of time.

Water *freezes* at 32 degrees Fahrenheit.

Customs *vary* from country to country.

A bird in the hand *is* worth two in the bush. (proverb)

---

*The use of the simple present tense with nonaction verbs (She *understands* the situation now) is
discussed in Chapter 2. The use of the simple present to talk about scheduled events in the future (My
plane *leaves* at 3:15 tomorrow) is discussed in Chapter 3.

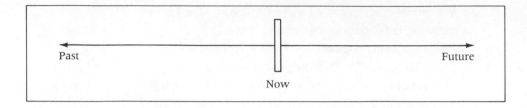

2. Use the simple present tense to talk about repeated or customary actions or situations.

    In my country, people *eat* their largest meal in the middle of the day.
    In the United States, I usually *have* a sandwich for lunch.

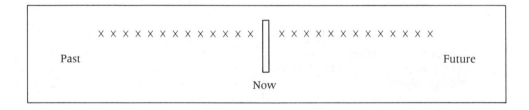

3. The simple present tense is sometimes used to create a sense of immediacy. Newspaper headlines are often in the simple present tense even when the events they describe took place in the past.

Plane Crashes,
Seven Injured

QUESTIONS FOR DISCUSSION

Here are some proverbs that many English-speakers know. Try to decide what they mean. (Sometimes more than one meaning is possible.) Which proverbs do you believe? Do any contradict one another? Can you think of situations in which people would be likely to say one of these proverbs?

1. All that glitters is not gold.
2. Don't count your chickens before they're hatched.
3. Don't put all your eggs in one basket.
4. It's no use crying over spilt milk.

5. When the cat's away, the mice will play.
6. People who live in glass houses shouldn't throw stones.
7. Absence makes the heart grow fonder.

USING YOUR SKILLS

A. Select a proverb from your own culture and, with the help of your classmates and your teacher, translate it into English in a way that makes its meaning clear. (You may have to change some of the words for your translation.) Explain the meaning of your proverb by talking about the circumstances in which people would be likely to use it.

B. Answer in complete sentences using the simple present tense.

1. What are some things that you do every weekday?
2. Is your routine the same on weekends? What do you do on weekdays that you don't do on weekends? What do you do on weekends that you don't do on weekdays?
3. What are some places that you go to from time to time?
4. What foods do you eat often? Occasionally?
5. What kinds of clothes do you usually wear?
6. How many meals do people usually eat in your country? When do they usually eat their largest meal? What kinds of foods are customarily served at each meal?
7. What sports do people play in your country? Which sports do people watch?
8. How do people usually greet one another in your country? Do they usually shake hands, smile, kiss, or bow? What do they usually say when they see a friend?

C. If English-language newspapers are available to you, copy ten headlines from a city or campus newspaper. If they contain a verb, is the verb in the simple present tense? Note: You will notice that headlines frequently leave out words to save space. In a few cases, headlines do not contain a verb (particularly the verb *be*) when the verb is not necessary for understanding the message.

USING MODALS: AN INTRODUCTION

The Modal Auxiliaries

A small but important group of verbs called modal auxiliaries are often used with other verbs to modify or add to the meaning of the main verb. The nine common single-word modal auxiliaries are

will	would	may	might	must
can	could	shall	should	

In addition to the nine single-word modals, a number of two- or three-word expressions such as *ought to*, *had to*, *had better*, *be able to*, and *would like to* are used like modals to modify or add to the meaning of the verbs that come after them.

Forming Sentences with Single-Word Modals: Points to Remember

1. Single-word modals have only one (base) form. None of them has a base + *s/es* form. That means that they look and sound the same with third-person singular subjects as with other subjects.

   I *can* speak Portuguese.

   He *can* speak Portuguese.

2. The verb that comes directly after all the single-word modals is also the base form.

   He might *understand* Spanish.

   She should *have* tried to talk to him.

3. The next word after a single-word modal cannot be *to*.

4. You can form negative sentences for the nine single-word modals simply by adding *not* (*n't*) directly after the modal.

   She *couldn't* speak his language.

5.   You can form questions by moving the modal in front of the subject.

Can they speak Portuguese fluently?

CHECK YOURSELF

The following sentences come from essays in which students were asked to give advice to another student who was having trouble learning a language. You should have no problem understanding what the sentences mean. However, each sentence contains one or two small mistakes. Find each mistake and correct it. Check your answers on page 426.

1.   He must to try to listen to people speak the language as much as possible.
2.   She should talks with as many people as she cans.
3.   He no must be embarrassed to make mistakes.
4.   She might had got help with her problems sooner.
5.   How he can study if he doesn't understand the directions?
6.   Who he should talk to if he needs help? He must to find out.
7.   He not will stop trying even when he gets discouraged.
8.   He should listening to cassette tapes every day.
9.   He can't to expect to learn everything in one year.

PRACTICING YOUR SKILLS

What advice would you give to a student beginning to learn a language? Complete the following sentences in your own words.

1.   You should _____.
2.   You might _____.
3.   You shouldn't _____.
4.   You can _____.
5.   You must _____.
6.   You must not _____.
7.   You could _____.

Choosing the Right Modals to Say What You Mean

Although it is easy to learn the rules for forming sentences containing modals, it is harder to choose which modal auxiliary or modal expressions you need in order to say what you mean.

Modals add many different meanings to sentences. Some modals add meanings that relate to ideas like ability, possibility, or necessity. Some modals and modal expressions are used as softeners to make sentences more polite. One modal (*will*) is used to talk about future time.

Almost every modal has more than one meaning.

Examples	*Meanings*
He *can* speak my language.	He is able to speak it.
	He has permission to speak it.
He *could* speak my language.	He was able to speak it in the past.
	It is possible that he speaks it now.
He *must* speak my language.	He probably speaks it now.
	It is necessary for him to speak it.

Maybe you are wondering how English speakers are able to understand one another when they use modals. Most of the time the meaning of the modal is clear from the context—the other things the person is saying and doing—but sometimes even English speakers are uncertain.

Since understanding the meaning of modals and modal expressions is difficult, the best way to learn how to use them is to study only a few meanings at a time and to understand the context in which each modal is used. We will be working on one or two different meanings of modals in most of the chapters that follow.

Expressing Ability: *can, be able to*

Examples	*Comments*
She *can* read Italian well.	The modal auxiliary *can* is used to talk about the ability to do something in the present.
She *is able* to speak Italian, but not as well as she *can* read it.	The modal expression *be able to* is also used to express ability in the present.
She *will be able to* speak Italian better after she returns from Rome next year.	*Will be able to* is used to talk about ability in the future.

ASK AND ANSWER

Interview your classmates. Find out if there are classmates who can do any of the following things. Write down their first names if they answer yes.

Example

Ask: Can you _____?

Are you able to _____?

1. whistle _____
2. whistle a tune _____
3. whistle the national anthem of your country _____
4. play a musical instrument _____
5. drive a car _____
6. change a flat tire _____
7. use a computer _____
8. write a computer program _____
9. say an English proverb _____
10. play chess _____
11. count to 100 by fives _____
12. count backwards from 100 by fours _____
13. write with your left hand _____
14. spell your name backwards _____
15. touch your toes without bending your knees _____

PRACTICING YOUR SKILLS

A. Construct five sentences about things you can do (are able to do) now.
B. Construct five sentences about things that you can't (cannot)* do now, but would like to be able to do in the future.

Cannot is usually spelled as one word. *Can't* is used in most speech and in informal writing.

HOW IT SOUNDS

In normal rapid speech it is sometimes difficult to distinguish between *can* and *can't*. The most important difference is in the vowel sound. The vowel sound in *can* is like the vowel of *pin*. The vowel sound in *can't* is like the vowel in *cat*.

Listen for differences in these two sentences:

She *can* teach tonight.

She *can't* teach tonight.

Your teacher will say either the positive or negative form of each of the following sentences using normal rapid English. Raise your thumb in the air if you hear *can*. Turn your thumb downward if you hear *can't*.

1. She (can / can't) teach Spanish.
2. He (can / can't) type 50 words a minute.
3. She (can / can't) explain the exercise.
4. They (can / can't) cook Chinese food.
5. I (can / can't) carry a tune.
6. We (can / can't) help you with that problem.
7. They (can / can't) see you right now.
8. She (can / can't) see the blackboard.
9. You (can / can't) turn on a red light.

FINDING OUT ABOUT

Different Kinds of Nouns: An Introduction

LOOKING AT FORMS

The following paragraph by Alfred Kazin, a New York writer, describes the most important room in the apartment of his childhood and his mother who worked there as a dressmaker.

Kazin's paragraph contains more then 80 nouns. You probably can recognize most of them. Read through the paragraph and write the letter *N* under each noun. The first sentence has been done for you. Check your answers on page 426.

THE KITCHEN

1   In Brownsville tenements the kitchen is always the largest room and the center
of the household. As a child I felt that we lived in a kitchen to which four other rooms
were annexed. My mother, a "home" dressmaker, had her workshop in the kitchen. She
told me once that she had begun dressmaking in Poland at thirteen; as far back as I
5   can remember, she was always making dresses for the local women. She had an innate
sense of design, a quick eye for all the subtleties in the latest fashions, even when she
despised them, and great boldness. For three or four dollars she would study the fashion
magazines with a customer, go with the customer to the remnants store on Belmont
Avenue to pick out the material, argue the owner down—all remnants stores, for some
10   reason, were supposed to be shady, as if the owners dealt in stolen goods—and then
for days would patiently fit and baste and sew and fit again. Our apartment was always full of women in their housedresses sitting around the kitchen table waiting for a
fitting. My little bedroom next to the kitchen was the fitting room. The sewing machine,
an old nut-brown Singer with golden scrolls painted along the black arm and engraved
15   along the two tiers of little drawers massed with needles and thread on each side of the
treadle, stood next to the window, and the great coal-black stove which up to my last year
in college was our main source of heat. By December the two outer bedrooms were closed
off, and used to chill bottles of milk and cream, cold borscht, and jellied calves' feet.

VOCABULARY

Brownsville: section of New York City
tenement: a run-down apartment building
remnants store: store that sells leftover pieces of fabric
annexed: attached
innate: inborn
argue the owner down: argue for a lower price
shady: dishonest
stolen goods: stolen products
baste: sew with large stitches that can be easily removed
treadle: foot pedal to start and stop the sewing machine
borscht: beet soup

■■■■■■ *Identifying Nouns*

How did you know which words were nouns? Probably most of the time you made the right guesses without thinking why. However, when you are not sure if a word is a noun or not, there are several kinds of clues that might help you.

1.   Meaning: Most nouns talk about persons (*mother*), places (*bedroom*), or things (*machine*). Some nouns refer to ideas, qualities, or concepts (*subtleties, boldness*).
2.   The plural of many (but not all) nouns ends in an added *-s* or *-es*.
3.   You may have noticed that certain little words like *a, the, my, her,* or *our* often occur before certain kinds of nouns. These words always tell you that a noun will be coming soon. We will be learning about this type of little word (determiners) in the next section of this chapter and in several of the following chapters.

LOOKING AT FORMS

A.   Look at "The Kitchen" again. Find some nouns that end in an *-s* or *-es* that was added to the singular form. (Remember that not all words that end in *-s* or *-es* are nouns. Present-tense verbs that agree with third-person singular subjects also end in *-s* or *-es*.)
B.   Find some nouns that are preceded by the little words *a, the, my, her,* or *our.* Write both words.
C.   Take one or two paragraphs from a piece of writing you have done yourself. Identify all the nouns.

■■■■■ | Identifying Different Kinds of Nouns | ■■■■■

Sometimes it is important not only to know that a word is a noun but also to know what kind of noun it is. Is it a proper noun or a common noun? If it is a common noun, is it countable or not?

Let's begin by dividing nouns into two groups: proper nouns and common nouns.

Proper Nouns

Proper nouns almost always refer to specific persons, places, or things. They begin with a capital letter.

LOOKING AT FORMS

A. Find all the proper nouns in "The Kitchen." Check your answers in the chart on page 426.

B. Write down 12 proper nouns that you use frequently, for example, your first and last names; names of streets, neighborhoods, towns, cities, countries, universities, businesses; and brand names of products. Remember to use a capital for the first letter.

Common Nouns

Common nouns do not refer to specific persons, places, or things.

Common nouns can be divided into two groups: countable nouns and mass nouns. (Mass nouns are also called noncount or uncountable nouns. See page 70 for more information on mass nouns.)

COUNTABLE NOUNS

Examples	*Comments*
a kitchen two kitchens	Most countable nouns refer to persons, places, or things that we can picture in our mind. We can count how many there are.
a subtlety	A few countable nouns refer to ideas.
several subtleties	Countable nouns are either singular or plural.

MASS NOUNS

Examples	*Comments*
milk heat	Mass nouns usually refer to things that do not have a definite shape.
boldness	Many mass nouns refer to ideas or qualities.
	Mass nouns are always singular.

LOOKING AT FORMS

All the proper nouns and mass nouns from "The Kitchen" are listed below. Some singular and some plural countable nouns are also listed. Find five more singular countable nouns and five more plural countable nouns and write them in the appropriate column.

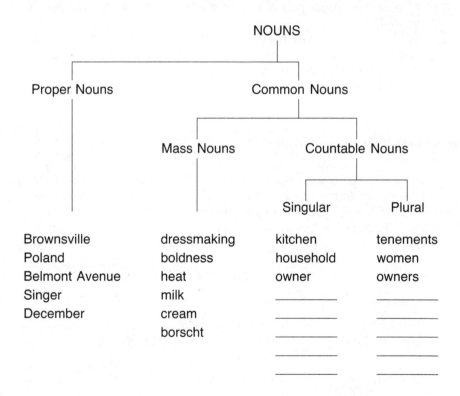

	NOUNS		
Proper Nouns	**Common Nouns**		
	Mass Nouns	**Countable Nouns**	
		Singular	**Plural**
Brownsville	dressmaking	kitchen	tenements
Poland	boldness	household	women
Belmont Avenue	heat	owner	owners
Singer	milk	_____	_____
December	cream	_____	_____
	borscht	_____	_____
		_____	_____
		_____	_____

Countable Nouns: Singular and Plural

SINGULAR

Examples	Comments
a kitchen	Countable nouns are either singular or plural.
her watch an idea a good example the child	Singular countable nouns must be preceded by little words called determiners. Some common determiners are *a (an), the, my, her, this. A (an)* can only be used with singular nouns.

PLURAL

Examples	Comments
kitchens her watches three different ideas many good examples	Most plural nouns are formed simply by adding *s/es* to the singular.
the children three deer several hypotheses	Irregular plurals are formed in a variety of different ways.

CHECK YOURSELF: PRETEST

Write the plural form of each noun without looking in a dictionary. Check your answers on page 427. If you made any mistakes, review the explanations on the following pages.

1. a baby	**5.** a phenomenon	**9.** a fish	**13.** a tooth
2. a foot	**6.** a series	**10.** a hypothesis	**14.** an analysis
3. a duty	**7.** a library	**11.** a woman	**15.** a man
4. a wife	**8.** a stimulus	**12.** a nucleus	**16.** a crisis

1. babies 5. phenomena 9. fishes ? 13. teeth
2. feet 6. series 10. hypotheses 14. analyses
3. duties 7. libraries 11. women 15. men
4. wives 8. stimuli 12. nuclei 16. crises

Forming Noun Plurals*

1. Adding -es

a. If the singular noun ends in *sh*, *ch*, *z*, or *x*, add -es to form the plural

watch   watch*es*   dish   dish*es*   box   box*es*

b. Most nouns that end in *o* add -es to form the plural.

hero   heroes
tomato   tomato*es*   *but* piano*s*, radio*s*

2. Changing a letter and adding -es

a. If the singular noun ends in *y* and is preceded by a consonant, change the *y* to *i* and add -es.

baby   bab*ies*   duty   dut*ies*
Do not change if the *y* is preceded by a vowel: boy   boy*s*

b. If the singular noun ends in *fe* or *f*, the plural ending is usually -ves.

wife   wi*ves*
calf   cal*ves*   *but* roof   roof*s*, belief   belief*s*

3. Plural nouns that do not end in *s*.

a. *People* and *police* are plural. Other words must be used for the same meaning in the singular.**

A person is . . .   People are . . .
A police officer is . . .   The police are . . .

---

*Only the most common irregular plurals are listed here. Check a dictionary if you are not sure of the spelling of an unfamiliar word.

**The singular form (*a people*) is used occasionally to mean a nation. *A people must preserve its culture and language.*

b.   A few nouns have the same singular and plural forms.

a deer, a sheep, a fish   three deer, two sheep, five fish

a series   many series

a species   several different species

c.   A few very frequently used nouns have kept the irregular plural forms used by English speakers many hundreds of years ago. You probably have learned these already, but don't forget the following plurals.

man   men   woman   women   child   children

mouse   mice   tooth   teeth   foot   feet

4.   Borrowed words
Some words, borrowed from Latin or Greek and found mostly in scientific and academic writing, have kept their foreign plurals. Learn only the ones you need to know for school or work. Add others you come across in your reading.

us → i

stimulus   stimuli   bacillus   bacilli   radius   radii

nucleus   nuclei   syllabus   syllabi/syllabuses

is → es

analysis   analyses   basis   bases   crisis   crises

diagnosis   diagnoses   thesis   theses   hypothesis   hypotheses

parenthesis   parentheses   synopsis   synopses

um → a

bacterium   bacteria   stratum   strata   datum   data

curriculum   curricula

on → a

criterion   criteria   phenomenon   phenomena

a → ae

formula   formulae/formulas   vertebra   vertebrae

ex, ix → ces

index   indices/indexes   appendix   appendices/appendixes

■■■■■■■ *Points to Remember*

Remember that most countable nouns have regular plurals (*-s* or *-es*). Many students make more mistakes by forgetting to add *-s* or *-es* to regular plural nouns than they do by forgetting the spelling of irregular plurals.

CHECKING FOR ACCURACY

Write a paragraph describing the most important room in the place where you are now living. Try to make a reader see the room and the activities that take place in it through your description.

Accuracy focus: After you have written your paragraph, check it as carefully as you can for subject-verb agreement and the correct use of noun plurals.

LITTLE WORDS

An Introduction

Advanced students of English sometimes feel frustrated when they make mistakes with little words like *a, the, in, at, to,* or *of.* These words look as if they should be easy—after all, they are so short. However, many learners find that these short words are the hardest to learn—at least to learn well. How do you know when to use *a* and *the*? How do you know when to use *of* and when to use *from*?

To give you a sense of how often little words occur in English, read the following selection from *The New York Times* story by Erik Eckholm about dolphins, intelligent animals that live in the ocean. Determiners (words used before nouns, like *a, the, their,* and *some,* and prepositions (words like *of, at, in, on, to, from*) are printed in boldface type.*

---

*The 12 most commonly used words in written English are: *the, of, and, a, to, in, is, you, that, it, he, for.*

DOLPHINS

What's **on a** dolphin's mind? **The** playful demeanor **of** dolphins and **the** relative ease **with** which they and **their** whale cousins can be trained have long raised speculation **on the** intelligence **of** marine mammals.

Many observers think they perceive humanlike qualities **in** dolphins, and **some** scientists place **their** mental skills somewhere between those **of** dogs and chimpanzees, which are considerable **by** animal standards.

But new research **on the** structure **of** dolphin's brains, conducted **by** scientists **at the** New York Aquarium **at** Coney Island, suggests how futile it may be to rank marine mammals **on an** animal I.Q. scale. **Some** scientists have found **the** friendly creatures to have brains that are **in some** ways **as** advanced but very different **from** those **of** land mammals.

VOCABULARY

mammal: animal that feeds on mother's milk when young
marine mammal: mammal that lives in water
demeanor: behavior
futile: useless
I.Q.: abbreviation for intelligence quotient, a measure of intelligence based on tests

◼◼◼◼◼ *Why Little Words Are Hard to Learn*

1.   Little words tend to have many different meanings, and their meanings tend to be dependent on the context they are used in. Does the preposition *in* have the same meaning in each of the following contexts?

The letter is *in* the drawer.

I live *in* Chicago.

Don't be *in* such a hurry.

She has fallen *in* love.

A dictionary may not help you to understand little words. Most little words are more connected to the grammar of a language than to its vocabulary.

2.   Little words are less likely than larger words to have exact equivalents in your own language. If you look them up in a bilingual dictionary, you may not find a definition that will help you. Your language may not use words like *a* and *the* to announce nouns. It may not use prepositions like *of*, *on*, and *at*. Or it may use these words in different ways.
3.   Little words are often hard to hear in normal spoken English. When English speakers speak at a normal, rapid speed, the little words are said very, very quickly, and their sounds change slightly.

HOW IT SOUNDS

Listen to your instructor say the following sentences, first very slowly, stressing each word equally, and then at normal speed, stressing only the words in capital letters. What happens to the little words? Do they sound the same?

THE DOLPHIN DIVED INTO THE OCEAN.
The DOLPHIN DIVED into the OCEAN.
IT SWAM TO A PLACE IN FRONT OF A LARGE ROCK.
It SWAM to a PLACE in FRONT of a LARGE ROCK.

What You Can Expect to Learn About Little Words

There are no rules that will tell you which determiner or preposition to use 100 percent of the time. Sections in this chapter and in most of the following chapters will give you guidelines that will help you choose the word you need most of the time.

Concentrate on progress and don't worry about perfection in using determiners and prepositons. Going from 70 percent accuracy to 90 percent accuracy is good progress and should increase your confidence in your ability to use English.

Determiners

One important group of little words is called determiners. A determiner is a signal that a noun will follow later in the sentence. Determiners are closely related to the nouns that come after them.

a marine *mammal*

this kitchen

the dolphin

her busy *workshop*

many places

our small, crowded, but happy, *home*

A, an, *and* the

Three determiners, *a*, *an*, and *the*, are among the most frequently used words in English. *The* is called the definite article. *A* and *an* are usually called indefinite articles.

CHECK YOURSELF: PRETEST

Although all of the following sentences are understandable, each contains one mistake in the use of articles. Correct each error you find. Check your answers on page 427.

1. A egg has approximately 80 calories. *an*
2. She is lawyer. *a*
3. The carrots are my favorite vegetable.
4. I'm not afraid of an insects.
5. We live in small apartment. *a*
6. How did you like a movie we saw last night? *the*
7. Shut a door right away. *the*
8. The Brazil is the largest country in South America.
9. The football is my favorite sport.
10. Money can't buy the happiness.

The Indefinite Article: *a, an*

Distinguishing between a *and* an

We have been talking about *a* and *an* as two words, but it is more accurate to say they are one word with two different forms.

A is used when the next word begins with a consonant sound.
An is used when the next word begins with a vowel sound.*

a child	an only child
an owner	a store owner

*Most words beginning with vowel sounds begin with the letters *a, e, i, o, u*. However, in a few words these letters represent different sounds, and in a small number of other words the beginning consonant letter is not pronounced.

an uncle	*but* a university, a union (first sound is /y/)
an owner	*but* a one-hour program (first sound is /w/)
a home	*but* an hour (*h* is not sounded)

PRACTICING YOUR SKILLS

Add *a* or *an* before the following names of occupations and professions.

1. __a__ computer programmer
2. __an__ artist
3. _____ office manager
4. _____ electrician
5. _____ police officer

6. _____ union organizer
7. _____ manager
8. _____ accountant
9. _____ instructor
10. _____ commercial artist

11. _____ mechanic
12. _____ tax accountant
13. _____ travel agent
14. _____ associate professor
15. _____ elementary school teacher

USING YOUR SKILLS

A. Construct five sentences telling about the occupations of some of your relatives or friends, and one sentence about your present or future occupation.

B. Explain an occupation or profession to someone who is interested but does not know very much about it. Explain the daily routine, training, normal salary and benefits, and advantages and disadvantages.

SENTENCE SENSE

Basic Sentence Patterns in English

There are millions of possible English sentences. The last sentence you heard is probably a sentence you have never heard before. The next sentence you say might be one you have never said before.

Although there are millions of different sentences, there are a few sentence patterns that are used again and again in English. In fact, most simple English sentences belong to one of six common sentence patterns. Most of the sentences people create are made by adding words to modify the basic parts of one of these six patterns or by combining patterns together.

Pattern 1	subject	+ verb		
	BABIES	CRY.		
Pattern 2	subject	+ verb	+ object	
	BABIES	MAKE	SOUNDS.	
Pattern 3	subject	+ linking verb	+ noun	
	BABIES	ARE	PEOPLE.	
Pattern 4	subject	+ linking verb	+ adjective	
	BABIES	ARE	CUTE.	
Pattern 5	subject	+ verb	+ object	+ object
	PARENTS	GIVE	BABIES	LOVE.
Pattern 6	subject	+ verb	+ object	+ object complement
	PARENTS	CONSIDER	BABIES	GENIUSES.
	PARENTS	CONSIDER	BABIES	WONDERFUL.

Pattern 6 is much less common than the others.

Headline English: Sentence Pattern 1

Yankees Win
Shuttle Flies
Drought Continues

Sentence Pattern 1   subject   + verb
                      BABIES   CRY.

It is possible for a sentence in English to have only two words: a subject and a verb. One place you are likely to see such short sentences is in newspaper headlines. Headline writers want to save space. They print only the most important words in a message.

S(ubject)	V(erb)
SCHOOL	OPENS.
PRESIDENT	SPEAKS.

Of course most sentences contain many other words. We will call these additional words *modifiers*, since their purpose is usually to modify or to give additional information about the essential parts of a sentence such as the subject and the verb.

The city's first new public elementary SCHOOL in ten years OPENS tomorrow in a ceremony to be attended by the mayor and several other public officials.

Even though we have added many new words, the most important words in the sentence are still the subject and the verb: SCHOOL OPENS.

CHECK YOURSELF

Find the subject and the verb in each of these sentences. Write them in headline form (subject and verb only). Check your answers on page 427.

1.   During the first few weeks of life, children sleep most of the day.

       _____CHILDREN_____   _____SLEEP_____
              s   v

2.   At six months many children cry at the sight of a stranger.

       _____Children_____   _____cry_____
              s   v

3.   The vocabulary of the average child grows rapidly in the second year of life.

       _____Vocabulary_____   _____grow_____
              s   v

4.   Around the time of their first birthday, babies usually stand upright while holding on to a chair or to their parents' hands.

       _____Babies_____   _____Stand_____
              s   v

USING YOUR SKILLS

Expand each of the following headlines into a sentence of ten words or more by adding modifiers. Your may change the tense of the verb. Compare your sentences with those of your classmates.

1.	PRESIDENT SPEAKS.	**5.**	TEAM WINS.
2.	ECONOMY GROWS.	**6.**	FACTORIES CLOSE.
3.	SPRING COMES.	**7.**	VOLCANO ERUPTS.
4.	TOURISTS ARRIVE.	**8.**	PEOPLE WORK.

CHECKING IT OVER

Changing Subjects from Singular to Plural

PRACTICING YOUR SKILLS

The paragraphs that follow tell about the development of speech in a typical child.

It is also possible to use a plural subject and write about children in general without changing the meaning of the essay.

Rewrite, changing *child* to *children* and *baby* to *babies* each time those words appear. This change will force you to make many other changes. For example, you will need to change most verbs to make them agree with their new plural subjects, and you will have to eliminate the indefinite article *a, an* before plural nouns. Underline each word you change. The first sentence is done for you. Check your answers on page 427.

Babies growing up anywhere in the world *learn* whatever language is spoken around *them* in the first few years of *their lives*.

HOW A BABY LEARNS LANGUAGE

1   A baby growing up anywhere in the world learns whatever language is spoken around him in the first few years of his life. Long before he enters school, a child knows the sounds of his mother tongue, and the rhythm and melody unique to that language. He understands many of the words he hears adults say. More amazingly, a young child
5   knows how to put the words he knows together to form completely new sentences. We can say that a child of four or five already knows the grammar of his own language. Of course, he cannot talk about the rules of grammar, but he is already able to do something much more important. He is able to use the grammar of his language to express his thoughts.
10   A child goes through certain predictable stages in learning his first language. The stages are the same for a child who hears Chinese spoken around his crib as they are for a baby who hears English, Spanish, or any other of the world's 4,000 or more languages. A baby in Beijing learns Chinese in the same way and at about the same age as a baby in New York City learns English or a baby in Mexico City learns Spanish.
15   In the first few months of life, a baby growing up anywhere in the world makes the same kinds of sounds. He cries and makes sounds to show happiness and displeasure. The very first noises a baby makes are not related to the language he hears his parents speaking. Even a deaf child makes these same sounds. But soon a child begins to distinguish between the sounds that are part of his language and those that are not. He

20 keeps the sounds he needs and discards those that he does not need. Even though a baby may not say his first word until around the time of his first birthday, by that time he already is beginning to sound like a speaker of his native language.

■ *Points to Remember*

Contemporary writers in English often find if convenient to use a plural subject when writing about customary or typical behavior, especially when they are talking about both females and males. If that way writers can avoid referring to a person as either *he* or *she* when that person's sex is unknown or not important to the meaning of the passage.

USING YOUR SKILLS

A. Write a paragraph telling about a typical high school student in your country. Use a singular subject—either *he* or *she*.

B. Rewrite your paragraph changing the subject of your first sentence to *most high school students in my country*. Remember that you will have to change the verbs in most sentences to agree with your new plural subjects.

Revising and Proofreading

When you write down your ideas, you have an opportunity that you don't have when you speak. Writers have the time to revise their work by changing and rearranging words and sentences until they are satisfied that they have expressed themselves as well as they can. Writers can add additional details that give life to a paragraph or take away words and sentences that no longer seem necessary. Experienced writers write and rewrite work that is important to them. Often a professional writer will revise a short essay several times.

■ *Revising*

The first time you read over your own writing you should concentrate on content. You want to make sure that you have expressed your ideas in a way your readers will understand. Ask yourself these questions as you read.

1. Have I left out details that my reader needs to know?

   When we are writing about a subject we know well, it is easy to forget that our readers may not know everything that we do. Good writers think about what their readers already know and what they need to be told.

2. Have I organized the ideas in my writing in the most effective way?

   Usually when we write down ideas for the first time, we are not able to put them in the most logical order or the order that will be easiest for our readers to understand.

Tips to Help You Revise

1. Slow down your reading. Try to focus on one idea at a time.
2. Try to imagine that you are reading someone else's writing and not your own.
3. Try to ask questions that your readers might ask. Have you provided the answers?
4. Try to think of at least one other way of organizing the information you have written. Experiment with moving a sentence from the beginning of your essay to another section. You may decide that your original organization is the best one, but it is useful to consider alternatives.

USING YOUR SKILLS

Find one or two more short pieces of writing that you have done for this class or for another class. Read them again to determine if they contain sufficient details and are organized in the most effective way possible. Rewrite a piece of writing that you think you can improve.

Proofreading to Find and Correct Errors

After you are satisfied that you have expressed your ideas in the most effective way you can, you need to read your work again. This time try to find and correct small errors that you might have overlooked while concentrating on writing your ideas down. Read your work at least one more time in order to eliminate as many small errors as you can.

Tips for Proofreading to Correct Errors

1. Read as slowly as you can, looking at each word. Many people find it helpful to read their work aloud or to read silently while trying to hear the words as they read.
2. Focus on your own mistake patterns. Look especially hard for mistakes you tend to make. For example, if you know that you have difficulty remembering to make verbs agree with their subjects, proofread your work one more time, looking at subject-verb agreement only.

Proofreading Symbols

Many teachers use proofreading symbols to help you identify the errors you need to correct. Sometimes teachers will write the correct form next to the symbol; at other times you will be asked to find the corrections on your own.

Examine the corrections made in sentences from a short essay a student wrote about high school in her country.

1. In Korea, teachers very strict because they want students learn more.   *are* / *to*
2. My country have a compatitive college entrance examination, and all students wants to go to good college.   *s-v/sp competitive* / *s-v / a*
3. Most high school students each week have 52 hours. of class.
4. Isn't that to much?   *sp too*
5. All students bags is very heavy because they carry many books.   */s-v are*

Some Proofreading Symbols and Their Meaning*

Symbol	Meaning	What you should do
?	I'm not sure I understand what you mean.	Rewrite the section. You may want to check the new version with your teacher first.

*Additional symbols are presented in Chapters 2 and 3.

id	Idiom. I understand your meaning, but your idea is expressed differently in English.	Try rewriting or check with the teacher.
sp	Spelling error	Check the dictionary. If you have misspelled a frequently used word, add it to your spelling list.
^	Word(s) missing	Are there some words that you often leave out or put in when you don't need to? Work on the "Little Words" sections in this book to improve your accuracy.
ᵔ	Take out letter or word	
ℵ	Word order incorrect	Word order helps establish the relationship between ideas in English. Learn word-order patterns that help you say what you want to say.
S–V	Subject-verb agreement error	Locate the verb and the subject. Check for agreement.

USING YOUR SKILLS

A. If your teacher uses proofreading symbols to help you correct your work, be sure you understand them. Look over your corrected papers and ask any questions you need to ask about the symbols used.

B. Two students wrote paragraphs translating and explaining proverbs from their countries. Although their explanations are clear, each paragraph contains several errors. Find the errors and correct them.

FATHER IS MOUNTAIN; MOTHER IS WATER

There *are* ~~is~~ many old proverbs that the older people in Vietnam uses. One that I like is "Father is mountain; mother is water." It mean that the father and mother are the two peoples most important in a family, but that they has different roles. The father is the head of family and he work to suport his wife and childrens. The mother is one who carry the children and bring them to life. She sacrifice a great deal for her family.   *s-✓*

ONE MOMENT OF TIME IS WORTH
A POUND OF GOLD

"One moment of time is worth a pound of gold" is Chinese proverb. It tell people that they must treasure time and uses it carefully, because the life of person is finite and valuable. If person lose gold, he can to get it back again, but if he lose time he will never get back it.

CHAPTER 2

The Present Progressive Tense

Forming the Present Progressive Tense*

The present progressive tense of all verbs is formed with the present tense of *be* (*am, is, are*) and base + *-ing*.

Subject	be	base + -ing
I	*am ('m)*	*writing.*

Subject	be	base + -ing
He	*is ('s)*	*writing.*
She		
It		
The student		

Subject	be	base + -ing
They	*are ('re)*	*writing.*
You		
We		
Students		

When writing in the present progressive tense, it is sometimes necessary to make small changes in the spelling of the base before adding *-ing*.

CHECK YOURSELF: PRETEST

Write the base + *-ing* form of the following verbs. In most cases you will have to change the base slightly before adding *-ing*. Check your answers on page 428. If you made more than one mistake, review the rules that follow.

1.	sit	**4.**	boil	**7.**	try	**10.**	offer	**13.**	help
2.	come	**5.**	run	**8.**	argue	**11.**	start	**14.**	dream
3.	tie	**6.**	plan	**9.**	choose	**12.**	sob	**15.**	open

*Also called the present continuous tense.

▬▬▬▬ *Points to Remember: Spelling Changes*

1. If the base form ends in *e*, drop *e* before adding *-ing*.

    hope   hoping

2. If the base ends in *ie*, change *ie* to *y* before adding *-ing*.

    die   dying   lie   lying

3. Double the last letter of one-syllable words when the base ends in one vowel and one consonant.

    stop   stopping   hop   hopping

    Double the last letter of two-syllable words only when the louder sound is on the last syllable.

    beGIN   beginning
    preFER   preferring

    but

    LISten   listening

▬▬▬▬ *Using the Present Progressive Tense*

1. The present progressive is the tense we usually choose to talk about actions that are taking place at the moment we are speaking or writing. Usually the action is limited in time — it has a clear beginning and end.

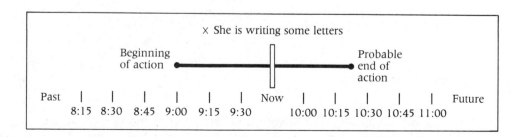

She *is writing* some letters.

2. Contrast the use of the present progressive tense to talk about actions of limited duration with the use of the simple present tense to talk about time- less or repeated activities.

Present Progressive Tense	Simple Present Tense
The baby *is sleeping* now.	The baby *sleeps* a lot.
The phone *is ringing*.	The phone *rings* every time I start to study.

3. The present progressive tense may also be used to talk about activities that are not in progress at the moment of speaking or writing. In many of these cases the simple present could also be used. The choice of the present prog- ressive often shows that the activities will continue for a limited period of time, or are exceptional in some way.

Present Progressive Tense	Simple Present Tense
I'*m writing* a book. (I should finish it next year.)	I *write* books. (my profession)
We *are living* with my sister until we find our own apartment.	We *live* with my sister. (perhaps a more permanent arrangement)
She *is taking* an extra course this semester.	Usually she *takes* four courses.

4. The present progressive can be used to talk about future planned actions.*

   She *is working* in a law office next summer.

CHECK YOURSELF

Before continuing, check your understanding of the use of present progressive and simple present tenses by choosing the correct form. Check your answers on page 428.

*See also Chapter 3, page 98.

1. Please be quiet. I (study) _I'm studying_ now.
2. I usually (study) _study_ in quiet places.
3. Look out the window. It (rain) _It's raining_ hard.
4. It usually (rain) _rains_ a few times in February.
5. Can I call you back? The other phone (ring) _____.
6. I usually (leave) _____ work earlier, but one of the other employees is sick, and I (work) _I'm working_ later this week. I (do) _am doing_ his work as well as my own. (intention)
7. It is so late today that I (take) _I'm taking_ a taxi home. Most of the time I (take) _take_ the bus, but it (run) _runs_ only until midnight.

PRACTICING YOUR SKILLS

A. Take a moment to observe how you are sitting at this very moment. Do not change your posture.

How are you sitting? Describe your position in the present progressive tense.

Some possibilities: toward the front (back) of the chair; with your back straight (curved); with legs stretched out in front of you (crossed at the ankles) (crossed at the knees) (one leg curled under you); with your right (left) hand (both hands) in your lap (on the arm of the chair) (in the bend of the opposite elbow) (touching your face).

How do you usually sit? Describe your position in the simple present tense.

B. A teacher or student walks across the front of the room, either naturally or in an accentuated manner. How is s/he walking? How does s/he usually walk? How do you usually walk?

Some possibilities: (very) (quite) (fast) (slowly); with a long (short) stride; with head (down) (up) (forward); one or both hands (in pocket) (swinging at sides).

USING YOUR SKILLS

Find a place where you can observe a lot of activity but have the privacy to sit and write while you observe (a library, a cafeteria, a desk by a window). Write a long paragraph describing the activities you see. You will probably use the present progressive tense in many of your sentences.

■■■■■■■ *Use of the Simple Present Tense with Nonaction Verbs*

I understand the problem now.

Not: ~~I am understanding the problem now.~~

Some verbs are never used with progressive tenses. Other verbs are used in progressive tenses only when they have special meanings. Verbs that are not used with progressive tenses usually refer to mental activities, attitudes, emotions, or long-term conditions or states.

Study the following groups of common nonaction verbs, also known as stative verbs. Note how the two present tenses are used in the sample paragraphs that follow each group.

✗ ■■■■■■■ *Common Verbs That Are Not Usually Used in Progressive Tenses*

Group 1. Verbs referring to states of being

be	look ("seems to be")	resemble
seem	appear ("seems to be")	

Now I *am* certain that the baby *is* sick. He *seems* restless, *looks* pale, and *appears* to be in pain. I *am taking* him to the doctor right away.

Group 2. Many verbs referring to mental activities

know	remember	mean
understand	forget	think ("believe")*
recognize	believe	doubt (question about)

I *know* you *are thinking* about the problem now. I *understand* what you *mean* when you *say* that it is difficult to solve. You *are telling* me that you don't *remember* all the details at this moment. That *is* OK because everyone *forgets* details. I *think* that we all *recognize* the difficulties you *are experiencing* now.

*Think (meaning "consider") is used in the progressive tenses. I *am thinking* about (considering) the answer I should give her.

Group 3: Many verbs referring to attitudes and emotions

want	love	dislike
prefer	hate	miss
need	like	appreciate

Sometimes it *is* difficult for me to know what I *want*. I *think* I *prefer* my new part-time job to my old full-time one, but I *am* not sure. Of course, I *am making* less money now that I *am working* less. I *miss* some luxuries. You *know* that I *like* to eat out with friends and I *hate* to cook or eat alone, but restaurants *are* too expensive for me right now. However, life *is* not too bad. Right now, I *need* the time to study more than I *need* the money.

Group 4. Some verbs referring to the senses

see*	sound
taste ("have a flavor")	hear*
smell ("give out a smell")	

The food *smells* wonderful and *tastes* delicious.

Group 5. Verbs expressing possession or relationship

possess	contains
have ("possession")	consists of
own	includes
belong	depends on

Because we *are asking* for a loan to buy a house, the bank *wants* us to list everything of value our family *possesses*. That *includes* furniture and cars. Though we don't *have* a lot of money, we *own* two cars. The old gas-guzzler in the driveway and the new subcompact both *belong* to us. It *is* not unusual for a family in the United States to have two cars. It *depends on* where they live.

---

*A few sense verbs have special meanings in progressive tenses: *see* (meaning "to visit or have an appointment with"): She *is seeing* her adviser this afternoon. *Hear* (meaning "be in communication with"): You will *be hearing* from us soon.

Group 6. Verbs of measurement

weigh ("have weight")   fit

cost   equal

measure ("have length")

I can't *decide* which coat to buy. Both *fit* well. The brown one *weighs* a little more than the other, but the lightweight one *is* just as warm and more comfortable. However, it *costs* a little more than I *want* to pay.

PRACTICING YOUR SKILLS

A.   Construct several sentences expressing your opinions about some current television shows. What shows do you watch? What do you like/dislike about them? Do the shows you like have anything in common? If the shows are in English, do you usually understand most of the language?

B.   Describe a food you like and one you dislike. How does each taste, look, smell?

C.   What factors do you consider when you buy something for yourself or another person? Think about something you need to buy. Construct sentences telling about your purchase using the following verbs in the simple present tense.

1.   want   **3.**   own   **5.**   depend on   **7.**   fit
2.   need   **4.**   have   **6.**   cost

D.   Write several paragraphs of your own using as many nonaction verbs as possible. You may use the sample paragraphs as models.

CHECK YOURSELF

Fill in the blanks with either the simple or present progressive form. In a few cases either tense is correct. Check your answers on page 428.

Dear Ming,

1   I'm sorry I haven't written you sooner. You
_____*know*_____ me well and ___understand___   know / understand
how I __hate_____ to write letters even though   hate
I _____love_____ to talk. I __miss_____   love / miss
5   you and I ____think_____ about you a lot.   think

Most of the time, I ___am___ happy here — be

and I ___m'making___ new friends and ? — make

___m' discovering___ new things. It ___is___ — discover / be

exhausting to have to speak English all the time, though.

10   Sometimes I ___appear___ to be shyer than I — appear

really am. I can't speak when I don't ___understand___ — understand

what people are saying. Sometimes I don't even

___recognize___ words I ___know___, — recognize / know

especially when people ___say___ them fast. — say

15 Many English words ___sound___ so different — sound

than they ___look___. Sometimes I — look

___forget___ a word, and when I — forget

___remember___ it, the conversation — remember

___is___ already over. But, I — be

20 ___am trying___ hard, and I ___know___ — try / know

my English ___is improving___. I ___spend___ — improve / spend

almost all my time with English speakers and with other

students who don't ___speak___ our language. — speak

Even with my friends from home, I ___try___ — try

25 to speak English some of the time.

This semester I ___'m living___ in a dormitory, — live

although I ___'m thinking___ about getting an — think

apartment next year. My dorm room ___is___ — be

very small but modern and convenient. The nicest thing

30 about my room ___is___ that it — be

___has___ a big window. When I (?, ing) — have

___study___ there ___are___ always — study / be

something interesting to look at. Right now, a bright-colored

bird ___is hopping___ from tree to tree, and a cat — hop

35 ___is watching___ it closely. I can also — watch

___see___ students on their way to class. — see

That ___reminds___ me that I have to go to class, — remind

too. I'll write to you again soon.

Your friend,

40   Mae Soo

USING YOUR SKILLS

Write a letter similar to one you might write to a good friend in another country. Tell your friend about your present life and your activities. You will probably use either the simple present or the present progressive tense in most of your sentences.

Accuracy focus: When you have finished writing, check the form and use of verbs in each sentence you wrote.

USING MODALS

Asking Permission to Do Something

May, can, and *could* are used to ask permission.

Examples	*Comments*
May I use your telephone?	Some people believe that using *may* to ask permission is more polite than using *can* or *could*. However, educated speakers of English probably use *can* or *could* as often as they use *may*.
Can I borrow your class notes?	
Could I make an appointment to see you?	

ASK AND ANSWER

With a partner, experiment with asking for and either giving or refusing permission in a variety of situations. One person should take the role of teacher, classmate, friend, or stranger, as appropriate. Refusals should include a reason and/or an alternative suggestion. Here are some possible roles and subjects.

student-student

look at your class notes
share your book
borrow your dictionary
sit next to you
ride home with you

student-teacher

                    write in pencil
                    use a dictionary during the exam
                    turn in the assignment tomorrow
                    type single-spaced
                    leave class when I finish the exam
                    make an appointment to see you

between friends

                    have another cup of coffee
                    borrow your car
                    see what is on Channel 2
                    look at the other section of
                    the newspaper

with strangers

                    make an appointment to see the doctor
                    talk to the person in charge of returns
                    talk to the insurance claims adjuster
                    talk to your supervisor
                    talk to the person in charge
                    pay with a personal check
                    park here for just a moment

USING YOUR SKILLS

Write out four short dialogues (4–8 lines) about asking permission. In two of your dialogues, permission should be given and in two others permission should be refused politely. Each dialogue should have a different set of characters and a different setting. Add phrases to make your dialogues seem more natural.

Requesting Someone to Do Something

Examples

Would you turn down the radio please?

Could you help me with the assignment?

Can you speak more slowly?

Will you repeat the question for me?

Comments

Would, could, can, and *will* are all used to ask someone to do something.

An affirmative reply might be simply to do the requested action.

Could you help me with the assignment?

No, I'm sorry, I'm really very busy now, and I just don't have the time. Perhaps tomorrow.

A polite refusal often includes an apology and a reason for refusing.

ASK AND ANSWER

With a partner, practice making requests and replying to them. Practice both consenting to and refusing requests.

Example

Would you/Could you/Can you/Will you?

say your name for me again, slowly

spell your name for me

say that one more time, please

speak a little louder

explain the assignment to me

do the assignment for me

give me change for a dollar

lend me $20

give me your address

let me borrow your car

move a little closer

wait for me after class

USING YOUR SKILLS

Write two short dialogues (4–8 lines) about requesting someone to do something. Include both consenting to and refusing the requests.

FINDING OUT ABOUT. . .

Questions, Negatives, and Short Answers

CHECK YOURSELF: Pretest

Even advanced learners of English occasionally make mistakes in forming questions and negatives. Before continuing with this section, check your ability to identify and correct errors in the formation of questions, and negatives. Check your answers on page 428.

1. I like it not when people don't look at me when they are talking.
2. Like you it when people look directly at you?
3. In some cultures people stand very close to one another when they are talking, do they?
4. I no can understand why people move their hands like that when they are talking.
5. What gestures does people in your country use frequently?
6. At what time is said "Good afternoon"? said
7. He don't wave his hand at me when he sees me in the halls.
8. Do you can show me the way people greet an acquaintance in your country?
9. In my country a person doesn't talks like that to a stranger.
10. It can be difficult to understand other people's customs, can it?

■■■■■■ *Reviewing the Formation of Negatives, Yes/No Questions, and Short Answers*

SENTENCES WITH *BE* OR AUXILIARY	SENTENCES WITHOUT *BE* OR AUXILIARY
Sentences with the auxiliaries *be* or *have*, modal auxiliaries, and sentences in which *be* is the main verb use either the auxiliary or *be* to form negatives, questions, and short answers.*	Sentences with no auxiliaries (simple present and simple past tense) use *do* to form negatives, questions, and short answers. The main verb is in the base form.** *Does* — simple present tense, 3rd person singular only *Do* — simple present tense other persons *Did* — simple past tense all persons
Negatives	*Negatives*
Add *not [n't]* or auxiliary. It is*n't* polite to shake hands in other cultures. They are*n't* shaking hands now. People may *not* shake hands each time.	Add the appropriate form of *do* + *not [n't]* before the main verb. The main verb is in the base form. A woman *doesn't* always shake hands. Women *don't* always shake hands. They *didn't* shake hands when they saw each other.

*If there is more than one auxiliary, the first auxiliary is used to form negatives and questions.

**When *have* is the main verb, speakers of British English use it to form negatives and questions. American English speakers use *do*.

American English	*British English*
She *doesn't* have any ideas.	She *hasn't* any ideas.
Does she have any ideas?	*Has* she any ideas?

Yes/No Questions	Yes/No Questions
Put *be* or auxiliary in front of the subject.	Put appropriate form of *do* in front of the subject. Main verb is in base form.
Short Answers	*Short Answers*
Use *be* or auxiliary. *Is* it polite to shake hands in your culture? Yes, it *is*. No, it *isn't*. *Are* they shaking hands now? Yes, they *are*. No, they *aren't*. *Should* they shake hands? Yes, they *should*. No, they *shouldn't*.	Use appropriate form of *do*. *Do* people usually shake hands? Yes, they *do*. No, they *don't*. *Does* a person usually shake hands when introduced to someone? Yes, they *do*. No, they *don't*. *Did* they shake hands when they met? Yes, they *did*. No, they *didn't*.

ASK AND ANSWER

In pairs or small groups, construct several questions about how friends, acquaintances, and family members usually greet one another in your partner's country. Ask about verbal and nonverbal behavior.

Examples

Do new acquaintances shake hands? Bow? Kiss one another when they meet? How about friends? Family members?

Teacher's note: Pair students from different countries if possible. If not, students from the same country may work together to construct questions a newcomer to their country might ask.

USING YOUR SKILLS

A. Most of the time we describe ourselves by using affirmative statements. We can also draw a portrait of ourselves by telling what we don't look like, what we are not interested in, what we don't want to be or don't like to do. Construct sentences for a portrait of yourself. Use both affirmative and negative statements.

1. Your appearance.
2. Your personality characteristics: extroverted, introverted, athletic, sedentary, strong-willed, easily diverted, hard-working, laid back, vain, modest.
3. Conversational roles you usually (don't) enjoy: telling jokes, talking with people about serious problems, teaching people how to do something.
4. Sports you are (not) interested in
5. Music you (don't) like
6. Things you (don't) know how to do
7. Jobs you (never) want to have

B. Write a paragraph describing the physical characteristics (appearance, voice, gestures) of a close friend or a relative. Write for someone who has never seen the person you are describing. Make your description detailed enough for your reader to recognize that person in a crowd. Use both affirmative and negative statements in your paragraph.

■■■■■■■ *Incomplete Questions*

Questions without a subject or auxiliary are normal in informal conversation.

Example

Taking any other classes this semester? (Are you taking any other classes this semester?)

ASK AND ANSWER

A. Take turns asking your partner the following informal questions (without subject or auxiliary). Add others if you can. Your partner should answer the questions using short answers.

1. Know the assignment for tomorrow?
Yes, I do.
or
No, I don't.

2. Understand the assignment?
3. Have another class after this one?
4. Going to the science building?
5. Eating lunch in the cafeteria?
6. Know someplace else to eat?

7. Having lunch with anyone?
8. Mind if I have lunch with you?
9. Like music?
10. Going to the concert this weekend?
11. Know if any tickets are left?

B. Incomplete questions are not appropriate in writing or formal spoken language. Make the questions in the previous exercise more formal by adding a subject and auxiliary.

Example

Do you know the assignment for tomorrow?

Forming Negative Questions

Note how negative questions are formed.

Sentences with be *or Auxiliary*	Sentences without be *or Auxiliary*
Is*n't* it polite to shake hands in your country?	*Doesn't* a woman usually shake another woman's hand in your country?
Are*n't* they shaking hands?	*Don't* young people usually shake hands when they are introduced?
Should*n't* two old friends shake hands every time they meet?	*Didn't* they shake hands when they were introduced?

Using Negative Questions

Negative questions often have a different meaning from affirmative questions.

1. Negative questions are often used when people believe they already know the answer. Affirmative questions are used when people do not know the answer.

Negative Question

Don't we all *know* what to do when we are introduced to a stranger?

(Meaning: I think we know what to do.)

Affirmative Question

Do we all *know* what to do when   (Meaning: I'm not sure we know
we are introduced to a stranger?   what to do.)

2.   Negative questions are often used to make suggestions, informal offers, or invitations.

Don't you *want* to call home before we leave? Your family might be worried.

Don't you *want* another cup of coffee? I have some made.

Wouldn't you *like* to come with us? We'd like you to.

3.   In some cases a negative question will express surprise and occasionally irritation that something is not as expected.

Isn't Ann spelled with an *e*? I thought it always was.

Didn't you *proofread* your essay before you turned it in?

4.   The answer to a negative question is the same as the answer to an affirmative one—according to the facts and not according to the form of the question.

Doesn't water freeze at 40 degrees Fahrenheit? No, it *doesn't*. It freezes at 32 degrees Fahrenheit.

Isn't one inch equal to approximately 2.54 centimeters? Yes, it *is*.

ASK AND ANSWER

A.   The following negative questions contain assumptions that are false. Take turns asking your classmates the questions and calling on anyone who can provide the correct information. Check your answers on page 428.

1.   Isn't English the only official language of Canada?

Example

No, it isn't. Both English and French are official languages.

2.   Aren't dolphins land mammals?
3.   Isn't a dolphin's brain just like a human brain?

4. Don't most babies say their first word around the time of their second birthday?
5. Don't most North Americans show they are listening to someone by lowering their eyes respectfully?
6. Don't people all over the world shake hands when they meet a good friend?
7. Isn't Canada the third largest country in the world in area?
8. Don't most Canadians live in the northern part of the country?
9. Don't the words *stationery* and *stationary* mean the same thing?
10. Isn't Jones the most common last name in the United States?

B. When using recipes it is sometimes necessary to convert metric weights and measurements (grams, kilograms, liters, deciliters) to the system used in the United States (pounds, ounces, gallons, quarts, pints, cups, teaspoons, and tablespoons).

Work in pairs or small groups. One person should ask the following questions about weights and measures used in cooking. (Not all questions contain accurate information.) Another should respond with the appropriate short answer and correct the information when necessary. (The chart on the following page gives the information needed to convert from the metric to the U.S. system.)

	Answer	*Correct Information*
1. Isn't 1 kilogram the same as 1,000 grams?	*Yes, it is.*	
2. Isn't 1 kilogram the same as 1 pound?	*No, it isn't.*	*1kg = 2.2 lb*
3. Don't 100 grams equal 3.5 ounces?		
4. Don't 2 cups equal 5 deciliters?		
5. Doesn't 1 cup plus 1 tablespoon equal ¼ liter?		
6. Doesn't 1 tablespoon of liquid weigh ⅛ ounce?		
7. Aren't 4½ cups of liquid equal to 1,000 grams?		
8. Isn't 1 tablespoon the same as 3 teaspoons?		
9. Don't 2 quarts weigh more than 2 liters?		
10. Isn't ½ deciliter more than ¼ cup?		

C. Review some of the previous lessons. Write out some questions you have about English grammar. If you really don't know the answer at all, use regular question form. If you think you know the answer but want to be sure, write negative questions.

Spoon-Cup/Ounce-Gram Equivalents

American Spoons and Cups	Liquid Ounces	Liquid Grams
1 tsp (teaspoon)	⅙	5
1 Tb (tablespoon)	½	15
1 cup (16 Tb)	8	227
2 cups (1 pint)	16 (1 pound)	454
4 cups (1 quart)	32	907
6⅔ Tb	3½	100
1 cup plus 1 Tb	8½	250
4⅓ cups	2.2 pounds	1,000 (1 kilogram)

Cup-Deciliter Equivalents (1 deciliter equals 6⅔ tablespoons)

Cups	Deciliters	Cups	Deciliters
¼	0.56	1¼	2.83
⅓	0.75	1⅓	3.0
½	1.13	1½	3.4
⅔	1.5	1⅔	3.75
¾	1.68	1¾	4.0
1	2.27	2	4.5

Gram-Ounce Equivalents

Grams	Ounces	Grams	Ounces	Grams	Ounces
25	0.87	75	2.63	100	3.5
30	1.0	80	2.8	125	4.4
50	1.75	85	3.0	150	5.25

▬▬▬▬ *Forming Tag Questions*

Notice how questions can be formed by adding a question tag (*be* or auxiliary and subject pronoun) to a statement. When there is no auxiliary or *be*, an appropriate form of *do* is used.

1.   When the statement is affirmative, a negative tag is used.

It's polite to shake hands when introduced, *isn't it*?
They shook hands when they met, *didn't they*?

2.   When the statement is negative, an affirmative tag is used.

They aren't shaking hands now, *are they?*
A woman doesn't always shake hands, *does she?*

3.   The question tag for *I am* is *aren't I,* for *I'm not* is *am I.*

I'm right, *aren't I?*
I'm not late, *am I?*

4.   *There* can be used in question tags.

There's something wrong, *isn't there?*
There's nothing wrong, *is there?*

5.   Sentences beginning with *that* substitute *it* in the question tag.

That's OK, *isn't it?*

PRACTICING YOUR SKILLS

A.   Practice adding question tags to the following statements until you can do them quickly without error.

1.   You spell your name with a *y,* _____ *don't you* _____?
2.   The library closes soon, _____?
3.   It isn't open this evening, _____?
4.   Tomorrow isn't the first of the month, _____?
5.   You're not leaving right after class, _____?
6.   I'm usually on time, _____?
7.   You can come with us, _____?
8.   You will come with us, _____?
9.   The first letter of people's names is capitalized, _____?
10.   You capitalize names of countries and nationalities too, _____?
11.   Singular countable nouns need to be preceded by a determiner, _____?
12.   Mass nouns are not usually preceded by determiners, _____?

B.   With a partner, take turns asking and answering the questions above. Add others.

■■■■■■ *Using Tag Questions to Confirm Information*

1. People often ask tag questions when they did not completely understand something or have forgotten something that someone told them. In those circumstances a tag question may seem more polite or less embarrassing than a more direct question.

    You said your name was Frederick, didn't you?

    You asked us to read pages 110–113, didn't you?

2. When tag questions are used to confirm information we have forgotten or were never sure of, they are usually said with a rising intonation.

    _____/

    You're from Colombia, aren't you?

ASK AND ANSWER

By now you probably know a little bit about most of your classmates, but you may have forgotten some of the information people told you earlier. Construct several tag questions to help gather information you have forgotten or are uncertain about.

Examples

Ivette, you spell your name with two *t*'s, don't you?

Alejandro, you aren't majoring in business, are you?

■■■■■■ *Using Tag Questions to Start Conversations*

1. Tag questions can also be used when we already know an answer or when the answer is self-evident.

    It's really raining hard, isn't it?

    There are a lot of people at this party, aren't there?

    This kind of tag question is frequently used as a way of starting a conversation with someone you do not know well. People will answer and then have the opportunity to continue the conversation with comments or questions of their own.

2. Conversational tag questions usually have falling intonations, like statements.

We've had a lot of snow this winter, haven't we?

ASK AND ANSWER

With a partner, practice asking and responding to tag questions that you might ask in the following situations.

1. first day of class (to a person sitting next to you)
2. while waiting in a line (at the supermarket, movie, cafeteria)
3. at a large party
4. when there is a (slightly) new or unusual circumstance to comment on (weather, traffic, new clothing, haircut, change in the room)

USING YOUR SKILLS

If you are now in a country where English is spoken outside the classroom, listen to people using tag questions for small talk. When do people use them? What are they usually talking about? Write down in your notebook any tag questions you hear. Bring your notes to class for discussion.

Reviewing Information Questions*

In our discussion of information questions, we will be using examples referring to nonverbal communication. Before continuing, read the following selection about that topic.

---

*Information questions cannot be answered *yes* or *no*. Information questions begin with words like: *who, what, why,* and *how.*

In speech, *yes/no* questions and information questions have different intonation patterns. The voice goes up in pitch toward the end of a *yes/no* question.

Are they talking now?

Information questions have the same intonation pattern as statements; the voice goes down in pitch.

How often do they talk?

When most of us think about communication with others, we think mostly about verbal communication: words and sentences. In the following excerpt from *The Hidden Dimension* by Edward T. and Mildred Hall, the authors talk about an important form of communication that takes place without words.

NONVERBAL COMMUNICATION

1   [Nonverbal communication] is the first form of communication you learn. You use this preverbal language, consciously and unconsciously, every day to tell other people how you feel about yourself and them. This language includes your posture, gestures, facial expressions, costume, the way you walk, even your treatment of time
5   and space and material things. All people communicate on several different levels at the same time but are usually aware of only the verbal dialogue and don't realize that they respond to nonverbal messages. . . .

      Few of us realize how much we all depend on body movement in our conversation or are aware of the hidden rules that govern listening behavior. But we know
10   instantly whether or not the person we're talking to is "tuned in" and we're very sensitive to any breach in listening etiquette. In white middle-class American culture, when someone wants to show he is listening to someone else, he looks either at the other person's face or, specifically at his eyes, shifting his gaze from one eye to the other.

15   If you observe a person conversing, you will notice that he indicates he's listening by nodding his head. He also makes little "Hmm" noises. If he agrees with what's being said, he may give a vigorous nod. To show pleasure or affirmation, he smiles; if he has some reservations, he looks skeptical by raising an eyebrow or pulling down the corners of his mouth. If a participant wants to terminate the con-
20   versation, he may start shifting his body position, stretching his legs, crossing or uncrossing them, bobbing his foot or diverting his gaze from one eye to the other. The more he fidgets, the more the speaker becomes aware that he has lost his audience. As a last measure, the listener may look at his watch to indicate the imminent end of the conversation.

VOCABULARY

breach: break
etiquette: manners, rules for polite behavior
terminate: end
diverting: turning away from
gaze: look
fidgets: makes quick, nervous movements
imminent: will happen soon

■■■■■■■ *Questions with* when, where, why, *and* how

To form information questions with *when, where, why,* and *how* (*how much, how many, how often*), add the question word before a *yes/no* question.

SENTENCES WITH *BE* OR AUXILIARY	SENTENCES WITHOUT *BE* OR AUXILIARY
Yes/No *Question*	Yes/No *Question*
Are they listening?	*Do* we use nonverbal communication?
Information Question	*Information Question*
When Where are they listening? Why How	When Where *do* we use nonverbal communication? Why How

PRACTICING YOUR SKILLS

Supply the appropriate question word: *when, where, why, how.*

1. _____ often do people use nonverbal communication?
   Answer: Every day of their lives.

2. _____ do people learn nonverbal communication?
   Answer: Before they learn to speak.

3. On _____ many different levels do people communicate at the same time?
   Answer: On several different levels.

4. _____ do people use nonverbal communication?
   Answer: To tell others what they feel.

5. _____ does an American look when he wants to show he is listening to someone?
   Answer: At the other person's face, or specifically at his eyes.

6. _____ does a listener look at his watch?
   Answer: When he wants to end a conversation.

7. _____ does a listener look at his watch?
   Answer: To indicate that the conversation will be over soon.

■■■■■■■ *Forming Questions with* who(m), whose, which, *or* what

The formation of information questions with *who(m)*, *whose*, *which*, or *what* depends on whether or not the question word represents the subject of the sentence.

1.   When *who(m)*, *whose*, *which*, *what* do not represent the subject, *do*, *did*, or *does* or a change in word order is needed to form questions.

   Examples

   Which gestures *do* people *make* to show that they are listening?

   Whose face is the listener watching?

2.   *Who*, *whose*, *which*, or *what* can also represent all or part of the subject of a sentence. In this case, *do* is not used and the order of subject and verb is not reversed.

Examples	*Comments*
Children learn nonverbal communication.	*Who* is used only with people. A singular verb (learns) is used even when the expected answer (children) is plural.
Who learns nonverbal communication?	
His eyes are looking straight at me.	*Whose* replaces a possessive noun (the teacher's, Mr. Jordan's) or possessive pronoun + a noun (his eyes).
Whose eyes are looking straight at me?	
A smile shows pleasure or affirmation.	*What* usually replaces a nonhuman noun (a smile).
What shows pleasure or affirmation?	
The rules of nonverbal language are hidden.	*Which* can be used with or without a noun.
Which rules are hidden?	*Which* usually replaces a specific group of people, places, or things.
Which are hidden?	

PRACTICING YOUR SKILLS

Construct ten questions of your own about nonverbal communication. You may ask questions whose answers can be found in the reading on page 66, or other questions you would like to discuss.

QUESTIONS FOR DISCUSSION

A.   Nonverbal behavior varies from country to country. Describe what is done or not done in your country.

1.   How far apart do people stand when talking with a friend?
2.   Are people supposed to look directly at the person they are talking to, or should they lower their eyes or look away?
3.   Do people nod their heads up and down to show agreement? If not, what do they do?
4.   What do people do to show that they are listening?
5.   What do people usually do to show that they are ready to end a conversation?

B.   In your country, how does nonverbal communication change when two women are speaking? Two men? A man and a woman? When one of the speakers is older or has more prestige than the other?

USING YOUR SKILLS

Prepare a questionnaire with ten questions about nonverbal communication. Include both *yes/no* and information questions. If possible, use your questionnaire to find out about nonverbal communication in another country. Try to ask at least two people from the same country. Then report your findings to the class.

Mass Nouns

Although most English nouns are countable (one chair, two chairs), there are many nouns that cannot be counted. These mass (uncountable) nouns are always considered singular.

Examples	*Comments*
Dressmaking is a difficult skill.	The indefinite article *a/an* is never used with mass nouns. The definite article *the* is seldom used with mass nouns.
Cream has more calories than milk does.	

Identifying Mass Nouns

It is impossible to memorize all the mass nouns in English. However, you should know the ones you use often. Since many mass nouns fall into categories with similar meanings, you can often guess whether an unfamiliar word is a mass noun. Remember, however, there are exceptions.

Some other languages use countable and mass nouns in ways similar to English. If you speak one of these languages, of course, it will be easier for you to identify them. However, since individual words may be countable nouns in one language and mass nouns in another, you still must take note of differences.

Categories of Mass Nouns

Common mass nouns are listed below. Add other words that you use frequently.

1. *Objects that have no definite shape.* These are easier to measure than count.

Liquids	*Gases*	*Small particles*	*Names of materials*	
coffee	air	ice	aluminum	steel
cream	fog	rice	cotton	wood
ink	oxygen	sand	iron	wool
milk	smoke	snow	leather	
rain		sugar	nylon	
tea			plastic	
water			silk	

2. *Abstract ideas, concepts, or qualities.* *

beauty	freedom	knowledge	progress
boldness	happiness	loneliness	success
cold	health	love	thoughtfulness
confidence	(im)patience	misery	timidity
courage	infinity	nature	trouble
(dis)honesty	intelligence	peace	violence
eternity	justice	poverty	wisdom

3. *Fields of study, activities.*

Field of Study	Activities	
computer science	dancing	swimming
economics	football	teaching
mathematics	learning	traveling
music	running	

4. *Some nouns can be mass or countable depending on their meaning.*

Mass	*Countable*
Iron is a strong, malleable material.	I need an *iron* to press my shirt.
I like to have a lot of *room* to work in.	There are three *rooms* in our apartment.
Experience is the best teacher.	My first trip to the hospital was an unpleasant *experience*.
She cooked *chicken*.	She cooked a *chicken*. (a whole chicken)
I don't have much *time*.	I tried to call you three *times*.

5. Some mass nouns are often used with countable classifying words such as (a) piece(s) of, (a) slice(s) of, (a) cup(s) of, (a) pound(s) of, (a) quart(s) of.

Examples

Several *pieces of* furniture are broken.

Four *slices of* bread are toasted, one *slice* is not.

We need a *quart of* skim milk.

I ordered three *cups of* coffee.**

*A few abstract nouns are countable: an *idea*, two *ideas*, a *subtlety*, several *subtleties*.

**People sometimes say: "I ordered three coffees," meaning three cups of coffee.

6. *Miscellaneous mass nouns.* Some other mass nouns do not fall easily into categories. Learn the ones that you use frequently. Write down others as you come across them in your reading. The following common words are mass nouns in most or all contexts:

advice	goods	mail	politics
baggage	hair	mankind	property
clothing	homework	merchandise	research
education	housework	money	traffic
equipment	information	nature	transportation
furniture	luggage	news	(un)employment

PRACTICING YOUR SKILLS

A. Construct several sentences of your own whose subjects are mass nouns referring to liquids, gases, or collections of small particles. Remember that the verb should be singular and you should not use an article before the mass noun.

Example

Water boils at 212 degrees Fahrenheit.

B. Construct several sentences telling what materials some of the objects in your classroom are made of. What materials are your clothes made of?

C. Construct five sentences telling about five different fields of study that you know about or would like to know about.

D. Construct five sentences telling about five different activities you either participate in or like to talk about.

E. Construct ten additional sentences using mass nouns from the preceding lists.

USING YOUR SKILLS

A. Select five abstract mass nouns that represent qualities you admire in a person and five nouns that represent qualities you do not admire. Write them in rank order.

QUALITIES I ADMIRE MOST

1. _honesty_
2. _humour sense_
3. _generosity_
4. _happiness_
5. _(liable)_

QUALITIES I ADMIRE LEAST

1. _stupid (?)_
2. _jealousy_
3. _nosy_
4. _slow_
5. _serious_

B. Write or tell about the kind of person you would like to be, using mass nouns from your list.

C. Select five abstract nouns and give one- or two-sentence definitions telling what each means to you. Your definitions may be different from those in a dictionary. For example, in a line from a popular song, *freedom* is defined as "another name for nothing left to lose." In a popular cartoon, *happiness* is defined as a warm blanket.

Example

To me, freedom means . . .

D. Do you usually shop for yourself? For yourself and others? Do you like to buy food and other commodities in small quantities or in as large a quantity as possible? For example, do you usually buy a quart of milk or a gallon? A pound of coffee or several pounds? Talk about your shopping habits. Use classifying words when appropriate.

CHECKING FOR ACCURACY

You have already realized that it is impossible to tell 100 percent of the time if a particular noun is a countable or a mass noun. However, paying attention to the nouns that you use frequently will help increase your accuracy when using nouns. Some dictionaries will indicate whether a noun is countable or not.

Look at essays you have written for this class or another class. Find examples of both countable nouns and mass nouns in your work.

LITTLE WORDS

Quantity Words Used with Countable and Mass Nouns

Numbers tell exactly how many things, people, places, or ideas we are talking about. Quantity words like *much*, *many*, *some*, *several*, and *a lot of* are often used to tell approximate quantities or amounts.

Exact	*Approximate*
There are exactly 36 chairs in this room.	There are *a lot of* chairs in this room.
There are three other courses you can take after this one.	There are *a few* courses you can take after this one.

Some quantity words can be used only with plural countable nouns. Other quantity words can be used only with mass nouns. Some quantity words can be used with both.

With Plural Countable Nouns	*With Mass Nouns*	*With Both Plural Countable Nouns and Mass Nouns*	
many several cars few chairs a few	(not) much* a great deal of traffic little furniture a little	some** cars (not) any** chairs a lot of traffic lots of furniture	

━━━━━━ **Much *and* many**

Examples	*Comments*
Are there *many* cars on the road? There aren't *many* cars now. There are *many* cars on the highway during rush hour.	*Many* is used with plural countable nouns (cars) in questions and affirmative and negative statements.

*Used chiefly in negative statements and questions.

**Some* is used in affirmative sentences. *Any* is generally used in negative sentences.

    There's *some* coffee in the pot.

    There isn't *any* coffee left.

Both *some* and *any* can be used in questions. *Any* is generally used when the answer is unknown. *Some* is often used when the expected answer is *yes,* or in making offers.

    Do you have *any* time? (I don't know.)

    Do you have *some* time? (I hope you do.)

    Would you like *some* coffee? (offer)

Is there *much* traffic now?

No, there's not *much* now.

There's *a lot of* traffic late in the afternoon.

Much is used with mass nouns (traffic). Usually *much* is used only in questions or negative statements. *A lot of (lots of, a great deal of)* is substituted in affirmative statements.

ASK AND ANSWER

With a partner, practice asking and answering questions about your home countries or regions. Use *much* or *many* in questions. Answer in complete sentences. Use *a lot of* before mass nouns in affirmative answers.

Here are suggested topics. (You may add your own.)

climate: snow, rain, good weather, sunny days

resources and economy: oil, coal, forests, lakes, minerals, jobs, (un)employment, industry, factories

quality of life: recreational and cultural opportunities (parks, theaters, museums, concerts), pollution, good food, safety, variety of interesting people, distinctive customs, standard of living

■ Few, a few, little, a little

Few and *a few* are used with countable nouns. *Little* and *a little* are used with mass nouns. Note the differences in meaning.

Many successful people have *a few* close friends. (A factual statement.)

Many successful people have *few* close friends. (*Meaning:* They don't have as many friends as they should.)

Most students have *a little* money.

Most students have *little* money.
(*Meaning:* They have less money than is desirable.)

PRACTICING YOUR SKILLS

Fill in the blanks with *a few, very few, a little, very little.*

1. It's hard for me to choose a course for next semester. I have to work during the day, and there are _very few_ classes given in the evening.

2.   I was able to buy a new bike, because I made _a little_____ money at my part-time job.

3.   I believe it's better to have _very few_____ good friends than many ac-quaintances.

4.   I need _____a little_____ more time to finish the exam. May I stay for five more minutes?

5.   The only thing I don't like about my job is that I make _____little_____ money.

6.   My roommate is terribly shy. He's made _very few_____ friends.

7.   Can you wait for me? It will take only _____a few_____ minutes for me to finish.

USING YOUR SKILLS

A.   Give a quick description of your kitchen and its contents. Approximately how many kitchen drawers and cabinets are there? How many knives, forks, and spoons in each drawer? How many shelves in your refrigerator? How many ice cube trays? How much butter, milk, cream, and yogurt do you have in your refrigerator? Since you probably do not know exact numbers, use quantity words.

B.   Think of a very busy and crowded place you know well—one that is often full of people, noise, and activity: an airport, a football stadium, a central market or shopping center. Write a paragraph describing what it is like to be in the center of such a place at its busiest time. Try to make the reader feel the rush of activity. Your description will probably involve the use of quantity words to describe how many people and things you can see, touch, or smell, how much noise you hear, and how much excitement you feel.

   Accuracy focus: Proofread for use of quantity words.

C.   Write about the same place at a time when it is empty or almost empty—the football stadium after the game is over or the market at midnight. Even if you have never been to the place when it is empty, try to imagine what it would look like and feel like at a time when there are few people and little or no activity.

   Accuracy focus: Proofread for use of quantity words.

CHECK YOURSELF

   Only three of the following sentences are correct. The others contain errors in the use of nouns or quantity words. Find and correct the errors. Check your answers on page 429.

1. In the past several years, most countries in the region have made a great deal of progress in solving economic problems.
2. Newspapers in the region publish a few news about industrial development.
3. There is not some information about the economy in the foreign press, however.
4. Much new factories were built near the major cities recently.
5. There are many research on pollution and other undesirable effects of industrialization. There is a lot (great deal)
6. Because of the development, there is not much unemployment in the central part of the country.
7. Unfortunately, several areas in the north and a little places near the border are still underdeveloped.
8. There aren't much natural resources in all parts of the country.
9. Many equipment is scarce in rural areas.
10. The government has built several new roads through the mountains.
11. However, transportation are still a problem in isolated sections.

Possessive Determiners*

An important group of determiners express possession or other relationships.

SINGULAR DETERMINERS

Examples

my	hair	
your	notebooks	
his	mouth	
her	ears	
*its***	cover	

Comments

Like other determiners, the possessive determiners, *my, your, his, her* . . . , are related to the noun that follows them.

PLURAL DETERMINERS

Examples

our	crowded kitchen
your	turn
their	money

That must be *your* notebook. *My* notebook has *my* name on *its* cover.

---

*Also called possessive adjectives. Be careful not to confuse possessive determiners (*my, your, his, her*) with the pronouns *mine, yours, his, hers*. Determiners are always related to a noun that comes later in the sentence. Pronouns are used to substitute for a noun.

**Do not confuse *its* with *it's (it is)*.

━━━━━━━━━ *Points to Remember*

1.   The same possessive determiners are used before singular and plural countable nouns and mass nouns.

    her jacket   *her* jackets   *her* hair

2.   When talking about parts of the body, people generally use the possessive determiner, not an article.

    She combed *her* hair.
    Not: ~~She combed the hair.~~

PRACTICING YOUR SKILLS

A.   Construct several sentences using possessive determiners to describe possessions you, your family as a whole, or individual members of your family value. What things would you or your family be willing to give away if you moved to a smaller apartment? Which would you keep?

B.   Use possessive determiners to give a brief physical description of yourself. Imagine that you are on the telephone describing yourself to someone who is going to meet you at the airport but has never seen you before.

    Example

    My hair is . . .   *My* eyes are . . .

C.   Give a brief but exact physical description of two other members of your family; one male and one female.

    Examples

    My brother . . .   *His* hair is . . .
    My aunt . . .   *Her* eyes are . . .

USING YOUR SKILLS

    What characteristics do you share with other members of your immediate family? In what ways do you differ from other members of your family?

    Example

    My hair is darker than that of other members of *my* family. *Their* hair is light brown, but *my* hair is chestnut.

The Definite Article: *the*

In Brownsville tenements *the* kitchen is always *the* largest room and *the* center of *the* household.

The definite article *the* is used four times in the first sentence of Alfred Kazin's description of his family's kitchen on page 23. *The* is the most frequently used word in English.

Like other determiners, *the* is always related to a noun following it. (In most cases *the* is not used before proper nouns. However, there are many exceptions. See Chapter 3, pp. 111–117.)

THE WITH COUNTABLE NOUNS

Examples

The owner of *the* remnant store.

The owners of *the* remnant stores.

Comments

The can be used before singular and plural countable nouns.

THE WITH MASS NOUNS

Examples

Money can't buy happiness.
(a general statement)

The money that I earned last summer was spent on tuition. (a specific quantity of money)

The happiness that I felt when I got my first paycheck was clear to everyone in my family. (Happiness is connected with a specific occasion.)

Comments

The is not used with mass nouns like *money* or *happiness* when the reference is general.

The is used with mass nouns only when the reference is specific.

LOOKING AT FORMS

A.   Circle all occurrences of the definite article *the* in "The Kitchen" (page 23). How many times did you find *the*? Find the noun that follows each *the*. Identify three definite articles that introduce singular countable nouns. Identify three that introduce plural countable nouns. Do any introduce mass nouns? Check your answers on page 000.

B. Look at two pieces of writing you have done for this class. Circle all occurrences of *the*. Find the nouns that they introduce. If you are not sure whether you have used *the* appropriately, check with your teacher.

Choosing *a/an*, *the*, or No Article*

Choosing to use *a/an*, *the*, or no article before a noun depends partly on the kind of noun it is and partly on the meaning you want to convey.

	a/an	*the*	No Article
Singular Countable	*a* store *an* animal	*the* store *the* animal	
Plural Countable		*the* stores *the* animals	stores animals
Mass		*the* happiness (specific only)	happiness

▪▪▪▪▪ *Points to Remember*

1. The indefinite article *a/an* is used only with singular countable nouns. All singular countable nouns must be preceded by an article (*a/an*, *the*) or another determiner such as *my*, *your*, *this*.
2. The definite article *the* is used with both singular and plural countable nouns. *The* is used with mass nouns only when they refer to something specific.
3. Plural countable nouns and mass nouns can be used without articles or other determiners such as *my*, *your*, *this*.

*If your own language uses articles similar to *a/an* or *the* before nouns, your job in learning to use them in English will be simplified. However, other languages with articles may not use them in exactly the same way as English does. You need to make a note when you come across differences.

If your own language does not have articles, it will be harder for you to learn to use them accurately. There are no rules that can tell you what to do 100 percent of the time, but if you follow the guidelines in this chapter and check your written work carefully, your ability to use articles accurately should improve rapidly.

4.   In many cases the choice of whether to use *a/an, the,* or no article at all depends on (1) the meaning you want to express and (2) what you expect your listener or reader to know.

Examples	*Comments*
A dressmaker makes clothes for women.	*A/An* is used before a singular countable noun (dressmaker). No article is used before plural countable nouns (clothes, women). The speaker is making a generalization. The reference is to any dressmaker and to clothes and women in general.
The dressmaker makes *the* clothes for *the* women in *the* neighborhood.	*The* is used when the reference is to a particular dressmaker, particular clothes, and a particular group of women in a particular neighborhood.
(In Brownsville tenements) *The* kitchen is always *the* largest room in *the* house.	The author is referring to a particular kind of kitchen found in apartments like the one he knew as a child.
Please put *the* book on *the* desk. (the book we can both see on the only desk in the room) Galileo proved that *the* earth revolves around *the* sun.	A speaker or writer uses *the* when he or she believes that the listener or reader will know what or who is being referred to.
She would study the fashion magazines with *a* customer, and go with *the* customer to the remnant store on Belmont Avenue.	Often *a/an* is used the first time something is mentioned. *The* is used later.

LOOKING AT FORM AND MEANING

The following is a continuation of *The New York Times* article on dolphins found on page 31. It compares the dolphin's brain with the brain of other animals and that of humans.

1   In terms of the organization of its circuitry, the dolphin's brain is simple, more like a hedgehog's [brain] than a human's [brain]. Hedgehogs are among the most "primitive"

living land mammals, and are thought to share many traits, including brain structure, with ancient mammals. Instead of being divided into many different specialized areas, as in

5 higher land mammals, the cortex of the brain in dolphins, as in hedgehogs, is relatively uniform throughout, the researchers have established.

Despite their "primitive" qualities, though, the brains of dolphins and whales evolved in a rare manner. In sharp contrast with a hedgehog, the dolphin brain has a large cortex comparable in size to that in higher primates, an "advanced" trait normally

10 associated with higher intelligence.

This unusual combination of simplicity and size gives dolphins their own special kind of intelligence. The scientists draw an analogy with a large simple computer that has the same internal units repeated over and over. Sheer size allows the processing of more information than would be the case with a smaller computer, but far less flexibility

15 than a machine with more varied internal components.

VOCABULARY

circuitry: connections between brain cells
hedgehog: small mammal with spines on back, similar to a porcupine
cortex: part of brain responsible for higher reasoning
relatively uniform: fairly similar in all parts
comparable: similar
higher primates: the most highly developed mammals — apes and humans
trait: a quality characteristic of someone or something
analogy: comparison
components: parts

1. Underline all occurrences of *a/an* and *the* in the preceding passage.
2. Write down each occurrence of *a/an* and its related noun in the second paragraph. What kind of noun (singular countable, plural countable, mass) follows?
3. Write down each occurrence of *the* and its related noun in the first paragraph. How many are followed by singular countable nouns? By plural countable nouns?
4. The last sentence of the first paragraph refers to *the* researchers. The second sentence of the third paragraph refers to *the* scientists. Would the meaning be different if no article were used?
5. The last sentence in the second paragraph refers to "*an* 'advanced' trait." Would the meaning be different if *the* were used? Check your answers on page 429.

PRACTICING YOUR SKILLS

A. In the following paragraph Yi-Fu Tuan writes about the typical American home and American ideas about space. Fill in the missing *a/an* or *the* when required. If no article is needed, write ∅.

1   Americans have __*a*__ sense of __∅__ space, not of __∅__ place. Go to __an__ American home in __∅__ exurbia, and almost __*the*__ first thing you do is drift toward __the__ picture window. How curious that __the__ first compliment you pay your host is to say how lovely it is outside his house! He is pleased that you should admire his vistas.
5   __The__ distant horizon is not merely __a__ line separating __the__ earth from __the__ sky; it is __a__ symbol of __the__ future. __The__ American is not rooted in his place, however lovely: his eyes are drawn by __the__ expanding space to __a__ point on __the__ horizon, which is his future.

VOCABULARY

exurbia: suburban area far from city
vistas: views
horizon: line between earth and sky

Check your answers with the author's original on page 429. Some of your answers may be different from the ones given but may be reasonable alternatives. Discuss these with your classmates and teacher.

B. In the second paragraph of his essay, Yi-Fu Tuan describes the traditional Chinese home, contrasting the Chinese concept of place with the American concept of space.
Again fill in the blanks with either *a/an, the,* or ∅. Check your answers on page 429 and discuss alternative answers with your teacher and classmates.

1   By contrast, consider __the (a)__ traditional Chinese home. Blank walls enclose it. Step behind __the__ spirit wall and you are in __a__ courtyard with perhaps __a__ miniature garden around __a (the)__ corner. Once inside his private compound you are wrapped in __an__ ambience of __∅__ calm beauty, __an__ ordered world of __∅__ buildings, __∅__
5   pavement, __∅__ rock and __∅__ decorative vegetation. But you have no distant view: nowhere does __∅__ space open out before you. Raw nature in such a home is experienced only as __∅__ weather, and __the__ only open space is __the__ sky above. __The__ Chinese is rooted in his place. When he has to leave, it is not for __the (a)__ promised land on __the__ terrestrial horizon, but for another world altogether along __the__ vertical, reli-
10   gious axis of his imagination.

VOCABULARY

ambience: atmosphere
vegetation: plants
terrestrial: of the earth

USING YOUR SKILLS

A.   Copy two short paragraphs from a newspaper or book. Note the author's use of *a/an* and *the*. Are there cases in which another choice could have been made? Check your ideas with your classmates and teacher.

B.   Look at two short essays you have written. Which nouns are preceded by *a/an* or *the*, which by no determiner (∅), and which by another determiner? Are your choices correct? Could you have made other correct choices? Work with your teacher or another classmate if you are not certain.

Note: Remember that learning to use articles is one of the hardest tasks in English if your own language does not have similar words. Concentrate on improving your accuracy by checking your written work carefully by yourself and with the help of your teacher.

SENTENCE SENSE

Headline English: Sentence Pattern 2

Sentence Pattern 2   Subject   + verb   + object
                     BABIES   MAKE   SOUNDS.

One very common sentence pattern in English has three main parts: a subject, a verb,* and an object.

S(ubject)   V(erb)   O(bject)

PEOPLE   SPEAK   LANGUAGES.

STUDENT   MEETS   FRIENDS.

*Verbs that appear with objects are called transitive verbs. Verbs that do not usually appear with objects (Sentence Pattern 1) are called intransitive verbs. Many verbs in English can be either transitive or intransitive, depending on meaning.

    She walked   to the park. (Pattern 1)
    S   V(ERB-INTRANSITIVE)
    She walked   the dog   to the park. (Pattern 2)
    S   V(ERB-TRANSITIVE)   O(BJECT)

PEOPLE throughout the world SPEAK more than 4,000 different LAN-GUAGES belonging to a number of different language families.

Every Friday before classes begin, the tall, slender Korean STUDENT with the shy smile MEETS two old FRIENDS from his home town for a cup of coffee and a chance to talk about news from home.

▄▄▄▄▄▄ *Finding the Object*

To find the object of a sentence, ask a question beginning with *who(m)* or *what* and add both the subject and the verb.* Your answer will always be the object of the sentence.

What do *people speak?*	Answer: *languages*
s v	O(BJECT)
Who(m) does the *student meet?*	Answer: *friends*
s v	O(BJECT)

CHECK YOURSELF

Find the subject, verb, and object in each of these sentences and write them in headline form. (Check your answers on page 000.)

1. In addition to words of greeting, people from all parts of the world use certain gestures to greet friends and acquaintances.

PEOPLE	*USE*	*GESTURES*
s	v	o

2. In India, people touch their hands together in front of their chests as a gesture of greeting.

People	Touch	hands
s	v	o

3. They also incline their upper bodies slightly forward toward their joined hands.

they	incline	bodies
s	v	o

Whom is used in formal English when it stands for the object of a sentence. In informal English, *who* is used for both subjects and objects.

4.   In the United States, young people do not always shake hands when introduced to a person of their own age.

_____ *people* _____   _____ *shake* _____   _____ *hands* _____ .
           s   v   o

5.   However, for a formal introduction, especially to someone older than he is, a young American man usually extends his right hand for a handshake.

_____ *man* _____   _____ *extends* _____   _____ *hand* _____ .
           s   v   o

6.   After a long separation, an American woman often hugs good friends to express her joy at seeing them again.

_____ *Woman* _____   _____ *hugs* _____   _____ *friends* _____ .
           s   v   o

7.   Except for a handshake or an occasional pat on the back for an old friend, American men do not usually touch male friends when greeting them.

_____ *men* _____   _____ *touch* _____   _____ *friends* _____ .
           s   v   o

USING YOUR SKILLS

Expand each of the following headlines into a sentence of 12 words or more. You may change the tense of the verb.

1.   PRESIDENT MEETS MINISTER.
2.   CONGRESS PASSES LAW.
3.   FIRE DESTROYS BUILDING.
4.   POLICE ARREST CRIMINAL.

5.   COMPANY SELLS STOCK.
6.   TEAM WINS GAME.
7.   STAR RECEIVES AWARD.
8.   MOTHER KISSES CHILD.

Expanding the Noun Phrase

Nouns are often preceded by other words that modify or describe them.

(Determiner)	(Adjective)	(Adjective)	(Noun modifier)	Noun
a	large	intelligent	sea	mammal
our	battered	old	kitchen	table
the	elegant	French	fashion	magazines

In a noun phrase, the single words that modify a noun will come before it. If there is a determiner, it will come at the beginning of the noun phrase. (A determiner is necessary when the noun is a singular countable noun.) Other words — usually adjectives — follow.

Notice that the adjective is the same for both singular and plural nouns.

Many nouns can be used like adjectives to modify or describe other nouns. When nouns are used as modifiers, they almost always go immediately before the noun.

Order of Adjectives

the   big   red   shiny   new   foreign   sports   cars

When more than one adjective is used in a noun phrase, the adjectives usually appear in a particular order. You probably can recognize that

the   elegant   new   French   fashion   magazines

sounds better than

the   French   new   elegant   fashion   magazines

Although there is some variation in the order of adjectives in English, the usual order is (1) adjectives that give opinions, (2) physical description (size, shape, age, color), (3) origin, and (4) material.

ADJECTIVES

| Determiner | Opinion | Physical Description | | | | Origin* | Material | Noun Modifier | Noun |
		Size	Shape	Age	Color				
the	beautiful			new	black		ebony	coffee	table
my	precious	tiny				Mexican	silver		earrings
a		tall	slender	young		Korean			student

*Note that adjectives indicating country of origin are capitalized.

PRACTICING YOUR SKILLS

A.   Construct sentences using some of the following adjectives. Check the meaning of words you do not know in a dictionary.

Opinion: attractive, appealing, fascinating, terrible, disgusting, ugly, pleasant, congenial, superb, satisfactory, mediocre, boring, irritating

Size: vast, huge massive, minuscule, average, short

Shape: circular, square, rectangular, curved, angular, stocky

Age: old, modern, contemporary, recent, ancient

Color: white, purple, blond, brunette

Origin: French, Greek, foreign

Material: metal, plastic, wood (wooden), cotton, silk, wool (woolen), nylon

B.   Fill in the blanks by adding modifiers to the following sentences. Compare your answers with those of your classmates.

1.   The _____ _____ dancers hear the _____ _____ _____ music.

2.   I like to wear my _____ _____ sweater with my _____ _____ pants.

3.   There is a _____ _____ vase on the _____ _____ table and a _____ picture on the _____ _____ wall behind it.

4.   The _____ _____ parent hugged the _____ _____ child.

USING YOUR SKILLS

A.   Adjectives help us to describe people, places, and things in ways that make listeners or readers see what we see. They can also provide important details on the sound, taste, smell, or feel of things.

In your own writing you may want to limit yourself to one or two adjectives before each noun. However, it is valuable to practice writing and understanding sentences with many adjectives. In the following exercises, begin by trying to pack as many adjectives as possible into each sentence. Then edit your sentences, keeping only the adjectives you think are the most descriptive.

1.   Describe the shape, color, size, and general appearance of a room that you know well.

2. Describe the most important piece of furniture in that room.
3. Describe an object in that room that you think is particularly striking or interesting.
4. Describe a piece of clothing that you feel comfortable wearing. Describe the texture of the clothing as well as size, shape, and color.
5. Describe the taste, smell, and appearance of a food you enjoy eating.
6. Describe part of a natural scene—trees, flowers, grass, sky, and clouds.
7. Describe part of an urban scene—buildings, streets, people, and traffic. Include sounds and smells when possible.

B. Write a paragraph describing a possession of yours that you value highly even though it may have no value to anyone else, for example, a favorite picture, book, or piece of clothing or jewelry. Try to describe the object as clearly as a photograph would and to make the reader understand the feelings you have about it.
C. Write a paragraph about a place that makes you feel happy or sad, comfortable or uncomfortable. Try to make the reader see the place as you see it. Choose details that emphasize the mood you want to create.

CHECKING IT OVER

More on Subject-Verb Agreement

Reviewing What You Have Learned

1. In most tenses the main verb or the auxiliary must agree with its subject.*

    I write home often.   *I am* writing a letter now.
    He writes home often.   *He is* writing a letter now.

2. Don't be confused by words that appear before or after the subject. See pages 12 and 13 for directions on how to identify the real subject.

    The *dolphins* in the experiment *are* intelligent.
    (The subject is *dolphins*, not *experiment*.)

    My cousin's *friends live* near the university.
    (The subject is *friends*, not *my* or *cousin* or *university*.)

*When modal auxiliaries (*can, could, will, would, may, might, shall, should, must*) are used, the next verb is in the base form. In the simple past tense (Chapter 4), subject-verb agreement is necessary only with the verb *be*.

3.   Remember that mass nouns are considered singular.

The *news* from home *is* good. (*News* is a mass noun.)

CHECK YOURSELF

Some of the following sentences are correct; the others have an error in subject-verb agreement. Find the correct sentences. Then correct the others. Check your answers on page 430.

1.   The rooms in the back of the house next to the kitchen is small.
2.   The furniture seem old but comfortable.
3.   Their mother's sewing machine is in the extra room.
4.   She don't usually shake hands when she meets someone.
5.   Her gestures are very bold.
6.   The brain of a dolphin are not divided into specialized areas.
7.   Honesty is a quality I admire in people.

◼◼◼◼◼ *Special Cases of Subject-Verb Agreement*

1.   *Compound subjects.* When a sentence has two or more singular subjects, use a plural verb.

My older *brother* and my *cousin are* studying abroad.

2.   *Collective nouns.* Certain nouns, called collective nouns, refer to groups of people: family, government, team, class, union, Congress, club, orchestra.

In American English these collective nouns are almost always used with singular verbs. In British English, a plural verb is often used.

American: My family *is* moving to a new apartment.
British: My family *are* moving to a new apartment.

3.   *Delayed subjects after* there + be, here + be. The verb *be* must agree with the subject that follows it.

There *is* a framed *picture* of my sister on the wall above my desk.
There *are* also several *pictures* of my mother.

In speech, *here** is often used with a delayed subject when we are showing or giving something to someone.

Here *is* a *picture* of my family.

Here *are* the *keys* to the car.

PRACTICING YOUR SKILLS

Find the subject and add *there is* or *there are* to form a complete sentence. Write your answer in the space provided.

1. _____*There are*_____ some photographs that are very important to me in my apartment.
2. _____ a picture of my brothers and some friends.
3. _____ two pictures of my parents on my desk.
4. _____ my best friend from high school and my oldest friend.
5. _____ my high school class in another photo.
6. _____ my school's soccer team the year I was captain.
7. _____ pictures that I took of my cousins on my last trip home.
8. _____ several other people in the background.
9. _____ my whole family at my sister's wedding.
10. _____ dates written on the back of each photo.

USING YOUR SKILLS

A. Do you have some photographs in your room that are important to you? Describe them to the class. If you have some photos that you can bring to class, show them and tell about them.

B. Write a paragraph describing a place that does not look the way if usually looks. Use *there is* or *there are* in several parts of your description.

Here are some suggested topics.

A Garden in Wintertime

A Busy Market or Store before It Opens

A Large Office Building Late at Night

*In informal speech, *here's* and *there's* are sometimes used with plural subjects. "*There's* two ways to pronounce that word." "*Here's* ten dollars."

In addition to describing the scene, try to capture the mood of the place. Does it make you feel, happy, sad, lonely?

Subject-Verb Agreement with Indefinite Pronouns

The following indefinite pronouns are used with singular verbs even when talking about more than one person or thing.

anyone	everyone	someone	no one
anybody is . . .	everybody is . . .	somebody is . . .	nobody is . . .
anything	everything	something	nothing

Examples

Everyone in the picture *is smiling*.

No one in my immediate family *lives* with me now.

Everything there *reminds* me of home.

Agreement with Other Pronouns or Possessive Determiners

Not all English-speakers agree on what to do when other pronouns or possessive determiners follow an indefinite pronoun used to talk about both men and women.

There are three possibilities:

1.   Use the masculine form only. This usage is traditional but strikes many English speakers as unfair or inaccurate.

Everyone in the picture is wearing *his* best clothes.

2.   Use both the masculine and feminine forms. This usage is more accurate for referring to mixed groups but can produce awkward sentences.

Everyone in the picture is wearing *his or her* best clothes.

3.   In informal English, many people use the plural pronouns (*they, them*) and possessive determiner (*their*).

Everyone in the picture is wearing *their* best clothes.

PRACTICING YOUR SKILLS

Complete the following sentences in your own words. Use the present tense (simple present or present progressive).

1. No one in the building . . .
2. The football team . . .
3. The players . . .
4. Nothing in my kitchen . . .
5. Somebody in my family . . .
6. Everything in the room . . .
7. My mother and father . . .
8. My first class . . .
9. Anyone in a foreign country . . .
10. Nobody at work . . .

Some Additional Proofreading Symbols

Note the proofreading symbols used to indicate errors in a composition a student wrote.

I am sitting in the library, looking out the window. It is winding outside and the branches of the trees *wf windy* are blowing. Many students are hurry inside to get out *wm vb hurrying* of the wind.

I usually do my homeworks in the libary because it *pl homework* is quiet, and I can sit in a nice place near a windows. *pl window* I going to school full-times this semester. At first it *vb I am going pl time* was hard, but now I think that I am succeed at learning *vb succeeding* English and my life is more fully than before. I am knowing *wf full tn I know* many interesting peoples and I am having many story *pl people tn have* to tell you when I am seeing you again. *tn see   pl stories*

Symbol	Meaning	What to do
pl	Error in noun plural	Check to see if noun you need is a singular or plural countable noun or a mass noun. Then check for appropriate form.
wm	Word meaning. The word you have used does not have a meaning that is appropriate in this context.	Check the dictionary.

wf

The meaning is correct
but you have used the
wrong form of the word
e.g., *succeed* for *successful*.

Use a dictionary that lists different forms
of each word in each entry.

vb

Error in verb form

Check a dictionary or the appropriate
chapter in this book.

tn

Error in verb tense

Check to see if the tense used is
appropriate to the meaning you want
to express.

USING YOUR SKILLS

Proofreading symbols are used here to show several mistakes in a letter written by a student to a friend who was also studying in a foreign country. Rewrite the letter, correcting the mistakes.

Dear Sompron,

I think it is a good time to write to you about my life in Chicago. I am knowing that you are live away from home, too, and that you sometimes feels homesick just like me.

As I write letter. I am sitting the library of the University and looking out of the windows. is raining, but not very hardly. Many student are running into the buildings to get out of the rain, but a few is walking slowly in the rain. They seems to like the rain weather, just like you and me. Do you remember our walks in the rain?

I am liking the university better. Most of the time I am very busy with my school works so I don't have time to be boring. In my classes I have many classmate from many country: China, India, Korea, Vietnam, and Mexico. I have some freinds to talk to, even though sometimes we are not understanding each other when we talk, and we must use our hand to help explain something.

Please write me. I want to receive your new very much. I hope you are enjoyable and happy. I promise to write a letter to you again next months. I have many story to tell you yet.

Love,
Pornswan

tn tn

s-v

∧ ∧

∧ wf

pl

s-v

wf

tn

pl wf

pl pl

sp

tn

pl

pl

wf

pl pl

CHAPTER 3

TIME AND TENSE

Talking About the Future

Four different ways of talking about future time are discussed in this chapter.*

In many situations, more than one way of talking about future time is correct and appropriate. However, there are times when English speakers are more likely to choose a particular form to express a particular meaning. There are also cases in which one choice may sound wrong or be very unusual.

The Future with going to

Probably the most common way to talk about future time is to use the present tense of the verb *be* (*am, is, are*) + *going to* and the base form of the main verb. This way of talking about the future is especially common in spoken English, but it is also used in writing.

Be + *going to* + base is often used when people talk about their own specific future plans or intentions.

Subject	be	going to	Base		Contracted forms
I	*am*	*going to*	*meet*	my friend after work.	I'm *going to*
He	*is*	*going to*	*wait*	for me in the lobby.	He's *going to*
We	*are*	*going to*	*have*	dinner together.	We're *going to*

In normal rapid speech, the *be* verb is sometimes difficult to hear, and several different short words may sound like a single word.

We are going to visit our relatives on the East Coast next summer. (The first four words of this sentence may sound like "wergonna" when spoken quickly.)

*Additional ways of talking about future time are found in Chapter 9.

PRACTICING YOUR SKILLS

A.   Tell the class two things you intend to do later today, three things you plan to do next week, and four things you intend to do later in the year. Use *be + going to* + base.

B.   When a new class begins, many teachers will talk about plans for the rest of the term. They usually expect students to ask them questions about those plans. Write out ten questions that you might want to ask a teacher the next time you begin a class. Use *be + going to* + base.

Examples

Are we *going to write* a term paper?

How many pages of reading *are* you *going to assign*?

Is there *going to be* a final exam?

▬▬▬▬▬ *The Future with* will

Subject	will	Base		Contracted forms
I	*will*	*return*	your book tomorrow.	I*'ll*
We	*will*	*give*	you a raise soon.	We*'ll*
It	*will*	*turn*	cold in October.	It*'ll*

Will + base is used in many of the same situations as the *going to* future. However, most English speakers choose *will* to express promises, offers, or predictions.*

I*'ll return* your book before class tomorow. I *won't forget.* (promise)

We*'ll pay* you minimum wage at first, but we*'ll give* you a 10 percent raise after three months. (offer)

It*'ll turn* cold before the end of October. (prediction)

---

*Occasionally *shall* is used to express future time after *I* and *we,* especially by speakers of British English. The contracted form of *shall* is the same as of *will* — *'ll.*

PRACTICING YOUR SKILLS

On the first of January, some people like to make New Year's resolutions. These are usually promises to improve or change themselves in some way: lose weight, get more exercise, study harder, be a better person. Many people forget their New Year's resolutions before the end of January.

Imagine it is the first day of a new year. Make some resolutions for yourself. Be as specific as possible. It is easier to keep a specific resolution like "I will proofread my homework twice before I hand it in" than a general one like "I will try to write better."

■■■■■■■■ *Using the Present Progressive Tense to Talk about Future Time*

The present progressive tense is often substituted for the *going to* future in talking about future plans or intentions.

Examples

I'*m meeting* my friend after work. (I'*m going to meet* my friend after work.)

We'*re having* a short quiz next week. (We'*re going to have* a short quiz next week.)

Do not use the present progressive to talk about the future

1.   when talking about events that clearly do *not* involve human planning or intention

It is going to snow tomorrow.

Not: ~~It is snowing tomorrow~~.

2.   with most nonaction verbs (see pages 48–50).

USING YOUR SKILLS

Is there a special day that you are looking forward to: a day off, a trip, a celebration? Tell about your plans for that day. Use the present progressive tense whenever possible to talk about this day in the future.

Using the Simple Present Tense to Talk about Future Time

The simple present tense is generally used to talk about future events only when those events are almost certain to take place at a scheduled time. It is common in talking about calendars, schedules, and timetables.

Examples

My birthday *falls* on a weekend next year.

Thanksgiving *is* next month.

The bus *leaves* at noon tomorrow and *arrives* in the city at 2:15 P.M.

The library *closes* at five on Saturday.

PRACTICING YOUR SKILLS

A. Look at a calendar for the coming year. On what day of the week do the following events (or other events of importance to you) take place: your next birthday, the next important legal holiday, a religious holiday, the last day of class, the beginning of the next term?

B. Report to the class on the opening and closing times next week of the following places (or other places of importance to you): public buildings, school offices, the library, your doctor's office, your workplace, your local grocery store, the closest drugstore, the movie theater you go to most often.

USING MODALS

Offers, Suggestions: *shall, should*

Both *shall* and *should* are used in questions to offer help or to suggest that something be done. When *shall* is used in questions, the subject of the sentence is almost always *I* or *we*.

Shall I open the window? (Do you want me to open the window?)

What *shall* we do tonight?

Should we go to a movie?

What *shall* we see?

PRACTICING YOUR SKILLS

A.   A friend of yours is in a bad mood and is complaining about everything. Offer your friend as much help as possible by asking questions beginning with *Shall I/Should I*.

Friend's Complaints	*Your Offers of Help*
1. I feel cold.	*Shall I close the window?*
	Should I get you some hot tea?

2.   I'm hungry.
3.   I'm thirsty, too.
4.   I don't have enough money for lunch.
5.   I don't understand the homework.
6.   I'm too tired to do the homework.
7.   I have a headache. Should I get some medecine for you
8.   It's too noisy in here. Should I stop playing

B.   Work with a partner. Make suggestions about how the two of you could work together to plan for each of the following events. Use questions beginning with *shall/should we*.

1.   Plan a one-day tour of the city you are now living in for two friends who have never visited before.

Shall we take them to the top of the Sears Tower?

Should we show them the university?

2.   Plan a large party with a great deal of food and professional entertainment. You can spend as much money as you like.

3.   Plan a visit by a head of state of one country to another country's capital. (Before you start the exercise, agree on the visiting official and the city he or she will visit.)

Necessity and Strong Advisability: *must, have to*

Affirmative Statements and Questions

Must and *have to* have similar meanings in affirmative statements and questions. Many English-speakers feel that *must* conveys a slightly greater sense of urgency than *have to.**

Examples

You *must* see a doctor right away. You look very sick.

He *has to* finish his work before he can leave. I'll make sure he does.

Does he *have to* see a specialist?

Do you *have to* call home right away or can you wait until evening when the long-distance rates are lower?

Comments

Must and *have/has to* in affirmative statements express the necessity to do something in present or future time.

Questions are generally asked with *do/does have to.*

Negative Statements: must not, don't/doesn't have to

Note the difference in meaning between *must not* and *don't/doesn't have to* in negative statements.

Example

You *must not* drive after you drink.

You *must not* forget to call home. Your parents will be worried.

I *don't have to* call my family tonight. I wrote them a few days ago.

He *doesn't have to* see the doctor again. He feels better now.

Comments

Must not means that it is very important not to do something. It may indicate that an action is forbidden or has undesirable consequences.

Don't/doesn't have to merely says that it is not necessary to do something.

---

*In informal speech *have/has got to* may be used.

He*'s got to* see a doctor soon.

I*'ve got to* call home now.

PRACTICING YOUR SKILLS

A. Fill in the blanks with the appropriate word(s): *must, has/have to, must not, don't/doesn't have to.*

1. You usually _____*don't have to*_____ pay to borrow books from the local public library.
2. However, at some libraries, patrons _____ pay a small fee to borrow new books or special materials such as records or videotapes.
3. To get a library card, you _____ show identification.
4. You _____ be a citizen to obtain a library card.
5. However, in many cases you _____ be a resident of the community that supports the public library.
6. The librarian will tell you that you _____ return books on time. If books are late, the borrower usually _____ pay a small fine for each late day. Therefore, if you don't want to pay a fine, you _____ keep books past their due date.
7. You _____ always _____ go inside the library to return books. Many libraries have a book deposit box near the front door.
8. You _____ take good care of the books you borrow. You _____ write in them or fold over the corners of pages. If you want to write notes in your book, you _____ buy your own copy.

B. What information can you share with your classmates about each of the following? Tell what you *must/have to* do to

1. get a driver's license
2. open a savings or checking account at the local bank
3. enroll children in elementary or high school
4. be admitted to a (specific) college or university
5. obtain financial aid or a loan for college expenses
6. obtain health insurance

C. On weekends and holidays, our daily routine is interrupted and we don't have some of the responsibilities or obligations that we usually have. Construct five sentences telling about some things you don't have to do at those times. Add comments if possible.

Example

On weekends, I don't always have to cook dinner. I usually eat at my cousin's house.

D. There are many situations in which people have to think and act fast. Do you or one of your classmates know what you *must/have to* do in any of the following situations? Is there anything you *must not* do?

1. Your car begins to slip on an icy road.
2. You burn yourself while cooking.
3. You smell gas in the kitchen.
4. You hear a tornado warning on the radio.
5. You see a small child swallow something from the medicine cabinet. You are not sure what it is.
6. You feel dizzy.
7. Someone faints.
8. A piece of food gets caught in someone's throat.

Advisability: *had better, should, ought to*

Had better

Examples

You*'d better* see a doctor about that cough. It sounds bad to me.

You*'d better* finish your work before you leave. If you don't, you'll never catch up.

Comments

Had *('d) better* is used to give forceful advice. Its use suggests that there may be negative consequences if that advice is not followed.

Note that *had better* is used to talk about present and future events.

Should, ought to

Should and *ought to* have similar meanings.

Examples

Everyone *should* see a doctor once in a while for a checkup.

You *ought to* finish your work before you leave. That's always a good idea.

Comments

Should or *ought to* is used to give friendly and (usually) not very forceful advice. There will be no serious consequences if the advice is not taken.

I think you *should* turn left here, but I'm not quite sure.	*Should* or *ought to* may be used when the speaker is not certain about the advice or thinks it is unlikely to be followed.
You *should* see the new Woody Allen movie. It's the best one in years. You *ought to* wear blue more often; it looks good on you.	*Should* or *ought to* may be used to give friendly suggestions or even to extend compliments.

PRACTICING YOUR SKILLS

Alone or in pairs, jot down 10–15 small tasks you plan to accomplish in the next few weeks. Decide which are very important, which are less important, and which you will do only if you have time. Tell your partner about your plans, indicating their importance by choice of a modal.

Examples

I *have to* pay my telephone bill.

I'*d better* shop for groceries before the stores get crowded.

I *should (ought to)* buy some new clothes.

USING YOUR SKILLS

A. Sometimes our knowledge or experience allows us to give advice to friends. Working in small groups each person should choose a topic on which he or she feels qualified to give advice to others. Other members of the group should ask questions about the advice that is given. Below are some suggested topics.

1. Tell a new driver about safe driving. Include information about traffic rules in your area.

2. Explain good health habits to a friend who you feel does not take good care of him- or herself.

3. Explain the rules of a game or sport to someone playing for the first time.

4. If you know how to use any special tools or equipment, explain their safe use to someone who has never used them before.

5. If you have had experience taking care of small children, explain procedures to a new baby-sitter. What must he or she do? Allow or not allow the child to do?

B.   *Must* and *should* are often used in job advertisements. *Must* is used for qualifications that are necessary. *Should* is often used to describe qualifications that are desirable but that may not be necessary.

Write an advertisement for a job that you know about. Make your description specific enough for readers to know if they have the necessary qualifications to apply.

Example

Wanted: Bilingual Secretary. Applicant *must* have a good knowledge of English and Spanish. *Must* be able to transcribe recorded dictation and to compose short business letters in both languages. *Should* have some knowledge of a third language (Portuguese or French preferred). *Must* be an accurate typist. *Should* type 40 words a minute or more. *Should* be familiar with at least one word-processing program and be prepared to learn others.

FINDING OUT ABOUT . . .

Imperatives

Examples	*Comments*
Listen. Relax.	Imperative sentences can consist of a single word — the base form of the verb. No subject is needed.*
Be careful. Turn left at the gas station. Help yourself to some coffee. Have a seat. Fold the paper in half lengthwise. Beat eggs and sugar until light. Call home right away.	Other words are often necessary to complete the thought or to give additional information.
Please listen carefully. Would you please listen carefully.	Softening words are often added to make the message more polite.
Listen! Be careful!	In written English, an exclamation point can be used to show urgency or strong emotion.

*The subject *you* is understood but not said or written.
   Listen. = You should listen.

■■■■■ *Using Imperative Sentences*

Imperatives have many uses. Not all imperatives are used as commands. They can be used for giving directions, instructions, or warnings. They can even be used to extend invitations.

Have another cup of coffee.

Stay and have dinner with us.

The politeness of an imperative sentence often depends on the situation, tone of voice, and added softening words.

PRACTICING YOUR SKILLS

Students should take turns using imperatives to get one or more of their classmates to perform simple actions. First, practice using a neutral tone of voice and no softeners. Next, try to be as polite as possible. (Use softening words and a polite tone of voice.) Finally, practice speaking in a rude or impatient tone of voice.

Here are some sample imperatives.

Open the door.

Put your book on my desk.

Write your name on the blackboard.

(Teacher's note: It is probably best if the teacher takes the first turn demonstrating the neutral, polite, and less polite variations.)

USING YOUR SKILLS

A.   Work in pairs. Each pair should be supplied with a sheet of white typing paper trimmed to a square shape.

One student should work with the book closed. The other student will explain how to fold the paper into a usable paper cup, based on a variation of the directions given below.

Sample directions for making a paper drinking cup

Take a square sheet of paper and fold on the diagonal to make a triangle.
Fold corner A to C.

Fold corner B to D.

Fold the two triangles at the top down on each side.

Squeeze the sides and the cup will open out. It may be used for drinking.

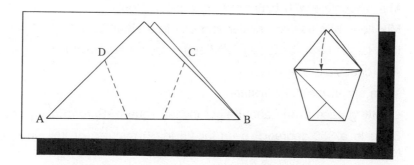

B. Working in pairs, students should take turns explaining a simple dance step to their partners, using words not actions.

Example

BASIC POLKA STEP

Hop quickly on right foot.

Step forward with left foot.

Bring right foot near left foot and step on it.

Step forward again with left foot.

Begin again, starting with a hop on the left foot.

C. Work in pairs. Each partner should choose two places within walking distance of the school or a well-known landmark. Partners should take turns explaining exactly how to get to each of the places chosen. Do not use maps, diagrams, or gestures to give directions.

D. The imperative form is often used for writing recipes. Here is a recipe for brownies, a popular American dessert.

Ingredients:

2 ounces unsweetened chocolate

½ cup (¼ pound) butter or margarine

¾ cup all-purpose flour

½ teaspoon baking powder

¼ teaspoon salt

1 cup sugar

2 eggs

1 teaspoon vanilla extract

Melt chocolate with butter over hot water. Cool.

Mix flour with baking powder and salt in a small bowl.

In a larger bowl, beat eggs and sugar for several minutes.

Add chocolate and butter.

Then stir in the flour mixture.

Lightly grease a pan about eight inches square. Spread dough evenly in pan.

Bake in a 350-degree F oven for 25 to 30 minutes or just until surface is firm to the touch.

Cool for 10 minutes and cut into 16 squares.

Write a recipe for something you know how to cook. Make your directions clear enough for anyone in the class to follow.

■■■■■■■ *Negative Imperatives*

Negative imperatives are formed by adding *do not (don't)* before the verb.

Don't worry.

Don't be late.

Don't drink before you drive.

The negative imperative usually has the same meaning as "You must not" or "You should not."

Don't worry. (You should not worry.)

Don't drink before you drive. (You must not drink before you drive.)

PRACTICING YOUR SKILLS

In the previous section (pages 101–105), you gave instructions and warnings using *must* and *should*. Rephrase some of your answers using imperatives.

USING YOUR SKILLS

A.   Often, pictures rather than verbal instructions will be used to explain how to take care of products to be sold in many different countries.

   Look at the following pictures showing the proper care of computer diskettes. With your classmates, try to explain what the pictures mean.

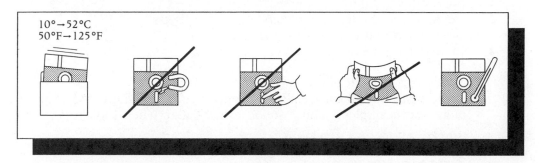

10°→52°C
50°F→125°F

B.   Look for examples of pictures used to give instructions or warnings: signs on highways and at airports, washing and ironing instructions on clothing labels. Bring to class simple drawings of the picture instructions you have found and, with your classmates, interpret the pictures in words.

Possessive Nouns

Examples	*Comments*
a dolphin's brain dolphins' brains the girls' dresses the women's dresses his mother's children (he and his brothers and sisters) his children's mother (his wife)	If two nouns are used together and the first noun refers to a human or animal, ' or 's may be added to express possession.
the legs of the table	*Of* is usually used to connect nouns referring to things.
the team's victory *or* the victory of the team	Either form may be used to talk about groups of people.
today's newspaper a week's vacation	The possessive ' or 's is also used in some expressions referring to time.

■■■■■■■■ *Adding ' or 's*

Note the addition of ' or 's in the following examples. Does example 1 refer to one or more than one mother? How about example 2? Does example 3 refer to one or more than one woman? How about 4?

1. the mother's children   mother + 's
2. the mothers' children   mothers + '
3. the woman's dresses   woman + 's
4. the women's dresses   women + 's

If the first noun does not end in -s, add 's.
If the first noun already ends in -s, only an ' is added.
Note that examples 1 and 2 sound exactly alike when spoken.

PRACTICING YOUR SKILLS

A. Note: Do this exercise orally first. Then write down the answers.
Rephrase the following sentences using ', 's, or *of* to show the relationship between the nouns. In some cases there is more than one possibility.

1. My mother has sisters. _____*my mother's sisters*_____
2. The room has windows. _____*the windows of the room*_____
3. My sister has friends.
4. My sisters have the same friend.
5. My sister has a friend.
6. The man has a cousin.
7. The men have cousins.
8. Both men have the same cousin.
9. The man has several cousins.
10. The country has a history.
11. The bicycle has wheels.
12. My friend has a sister.
13. My friends have sisters.

B. Do any of the phrases you wrote sound exactly alike? Do any of them look exactly alike? Check your answers on page 430.

USING YOUR SKILLS

A. Possessions are important to people. Some people will even say, "I can't live without my guitar" or "my collection of jazz records."

Think about a close friend or family member and the possessions that are most important to that person. What do his or her favorite objects tell you about the person? Write a paragraph using descriptions of someone's favorite possessions to explain what he or she is like.

B. Possessive nouns are often used to describe the way members of a family resemble one another in looks or personality. For example, people might say about a child, "She has her mother's determination, her grandmother's eyes, and her sister's smile." Do members of your family look alike or have similar personalities? Write a paragraph telling what you think are the most striking similiarities among members of your family.

LITTLE WORDS

Using *the* before Proper Nouns

Proper nouns include names of specific persons (Alfred Kazin), geographical place names (Belmont Avenue), brand names of products (Singer), languages and nationalities (English, Mexican), months (December), days of the week (Wednesday), holidays (Labor Day), and religions (Buddhism).

Proper nouns are easy to find in written English. They always begin with a capital letter.

In the majority of cases, no article or other determiner is needed before proper nouns. However, the definite article *the* is used before some geographical place names (the United States).

LOOKING AT FORMS

Read the following information about the land and people of Canada, adapted from *The Concise Columbia Encyclopedia*. Underline all proper nouns. List five proper nouns that are preceded by *the* and five that are not.

1   Canada is the second largest country in the world (3,831,012 square miles/9,922,330 square kilometers). It occupies all of North America east of Alaska stretching from the Atlantic to the Pacific and from its long boundary with the United States to the North Pole. Canada is divided into ten provinces which are, from east to west: Newfoundland,

5   Nova Scotia, Prince Edward Island, New Brunswick, Quebec, Ontario, Manitoba,

Saskatchewan, Alberta, and British Columbia. There are also two territories: the Northwest Territories and the Yukon Territory.

      The population of approximately 25,000,000 includes people of British origin (ap-
proximately 44%) and French origin (approximately 30%). There are about 300,000 indi-
10   genous Indian people. Vast areas of Canada are sparsely populated. Most Canadians
live within a hundred miles of the southern border of the nation, and most of the larger
cities, Toronto, Montreal, Quebec, and the capital, Ottawa, are located near the water-
ways of the Great Lakes and the Saint Lawrence Seaway. Both French and English are
official languages.

THE OR ∅ WITH GEOGRAPHICAL PLACE NAMES

Use the *before*	
rivers, oceans, seas, canals	the Saint Lawrence, the Pacific, the Black Sea, the Suez Canal
mountain ranges, groups of lakes or islands	the Rocky Mountains, the Great Lakes, the Hawaiian Islands (but Hawaii)
deserts	the Mohave, the Sahara
some large regions with indefinite boundaries	the Midwest, the East Coast, the Middle East
many place names that contain a noun modifying another noun or *of*	the French Riviera, the Gulf of Mexico

Do not use the *before*	
cities, states, provinces, continents	Toronto, California, Ontario, North America
most individual mountains and lakes	Mount Everest, Lake Superior, but the Matterhorn
most countries	Mexico, Poland, Greece, India, Korea but the United States (the USA), the Soviet Union (the USSR), the People's Republic of China (the PRC)

Note: Sometimes the use of the definite article helps us to distinguish between two place names.

Mississippi = one of the fifty states in the United States
the Mississippi = river in the United States

CHECK YOURSELF

Change lower-case letters to capitals and add *the* whenever necessary. Check your answers on page 430.

1. nile in Africa is the longest river in the world, more than a hundred miles longer than amazon in south america.
2. lake superior, between US and Canada, is the largest lake in north america. It is, however, much smaller than caspian sea, which borders on soviet union and iran.
3. sonoran and mohave are the two largest deserts in north america.
4. greenland, the largest island in the world, has the largest ice mass outside of antarctica.
5. new orleans is on mississippi river about one hundred miles north of gulf of mexico.

PRACTICING YOUR SKILLS

A.   Write ten place names you use often. Be sure to capitalize the first letter and to use *the* when necessary.

B.   After studying the previous page and looking at the map of the United States and Canada on page 115, write down as many sentences as you can describing the geographical features of the two countries: boundaries, lakes, rivers, mountain ranges, and deserts. Write for five minutes only without pausing. When you are finished, proofread your work carefully for use of capitals and *the*.

USING YOUR SKILLS

Taking as much time as you need, write a short but well-organized essay describing the land and people of a country you know well. Write for either a tourist or a businessperson visiting the country for the first time and planning to stay for several weeks. You may include a map if you wish.

THE OR ∅ BEFORE OTHER PROPER NOUNS

the *is usually used before*

nationalities	the Canadians, the Chinese, the French
names of most museums, monuments, hotels, theaters, famous buildings, bridges	the Art Institute, the Pyramids, the Hilton, the Goodman Theater, the Sears Tower, the Brooklyn Bridge

the *is usually not used before*

names of languages unless the word *language* is included	English, Chinese, French, but the English language
names of schools, colleges, or universities, unless they have the construction ——— of ———	Northwestern University, but the University of Chicago
months, days of the week, or specific years when they begin the phrase	September 11 Wednesday 1990
(However, *the* is used when the number is used alone or before the month, and with decades, centuries, and eras.)	the 11th the 11th of September the 1990s the 21st century the Middle Ages

LOOKING AT FORMS

Notice the use of capital letters and *the* in the following description telling tourists some of the important things to see in Chicago. Underline all proper nouns. How many did you find? Identify five proper nouns preceded by *the* and five proper nouns without *the*.

1   Many visitors to the United States believe that all the interesting places to see are either on the East Coast or the West Coast. However, Chicago, the nation's third largest city, has a great deal to offer any tourist.

Many of Chicago's attractions are located in the central shopping area, called the
5   Loop, and along a one-mile stretch of Michigan Avenue, north from the Chicago River
to the Gold Coast, called the Magnificent Mile. Many of these attractions are within
walking distance of one another. They include the Art Institute, famous for its collection
of 19th and 20th century European painting, the Goodman Theater, a repertory group,
Orchestra Hall, home of one of the world's major orchestras, the Chicago Symphony,
10   and the Lyric Opera. Three other museums, the Field Museum of Natural History, the
Shedd Aquarium, and the Adler Planetarium, are located just south of the Loop. They
can be reached on foot or by a short bus ride along the shores of Lake Michigan. The
same bus will take the tourist to the world-famous Museum of Science and Industry, a
few miles further south.

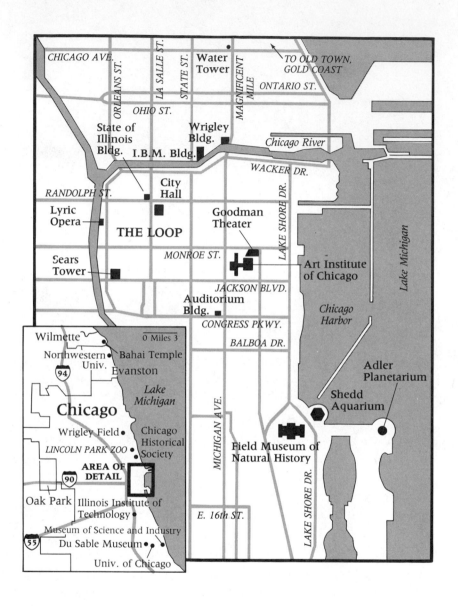

15   If you have the time to leave the central area, Chicago is a wonderful place to explore other cultures. In some parts of the northwest side, a few blocks' walk will reveal signs in Spanish, Korean, Chinese, Greek, Russian, Hindi, and Hebrew. There are hundreds of small restaurants offering food from all over the world. Even if you stay for only a short time, you can eat a different kind of food at every meal and still not have tasted **20**   many wonderful treats.

PRACTICING YOUR SKILLS

The following sentences are taken from the description of Chicago on pages 114–116 but have been printed with most capitals and definite articles missing. Correct them. Check your answers when you have finished.

1. Many of chicago's attractions are located in central shopping area, called loop, and along a one-mile stretch of michigan avenue, north from chicago river to gold coast.
2. Three other museums, field museum of natural history, shedd aquarium, and adler planetarium, are located just south of loop.
3. In some parts of the northwest side, a few blocks' walk will reveal signs in spanish, korean, chinese, greek, russian, hindi, and hebrew.

USING YOUR SKILLS

A. Write a few paragraphs for a brochure to be distributed to tourists visiting a city you know well. The visitor will be there for only a few days and wants to see the important monuments but also get a feel for life in the city. Emphasize the things that people normally come to see.
B. Sometimes tourists miss the most interesting things in a city. Write a paragraph about a place in your favorite city that you find especially interesting, beautiful, or meaningful but that most tourists seldom see. Try to convey your enthusiasm to the reader.

Accuracy Focus: Proofread your paragraphs for use of capital letters and *the*.

Personal Pronouns

Pronouns (*you, yourself, them*) are substitute words. They take the place of a word or a group of words that has been mentioned before or that is clear from the context.

You use body language to tell other people how *you* feel about *yourself* and *them*.

LOOKING AT FORMS

A.   There are only a limited number of personal pronouns. Study the forms in the chart below. What patterns of similarities and differences do you find? 1. Which pronoun is capitalized? 2. Which pronouns are the same in subject and object forms? 3. How do second-person singular pronouns compare with second-person plural pronouns? 4. Do any possessive determiners look the same as any possessive pronouns? 5. How are singular reflexive pronouns distinguished from plural ones?

Pronouns and Possessive Determiners

	Subject Pronouns	Object Pronouns	Possessive Pronouns	Possessive Determiners*	Reflexive Pronouns
First person singular	I	me	mine	my	myself
Second person singular	you	you	yours	your	yourself
Third person singular**	he	him	his	his	himself
	she	her	hers	her	herself
	it	it	—	its	itself
First person plural	we	our	ours	our	ourselves
Second person plural	you	you	yours	your	yourselves
Third person plural	they	them	theirs	their	themselves

CHECK YOURSELF

All of these sentences contain mistakes in the use of personal pronouns or possessive determiners. Find and correct each mistake. Check your answers on page 430.

1. The green one is my pen, and the blue one is your.
2. That watch is her.
3. They put on theirs coats and left.
4. What a pretty cat. What's it's name?

*Also called possessive adjectives. See also pages 77–78.

**The indefinite pronoun *one* is used in very formal style to talk about either a male or a female:

One has to make *one's* plans early if *one* wants to apply to graduate school.

In less formal styles, *you* is used:

You have to make *your* plans early if *you* . . .

5. He did the work hisself.
6. They walked there by themself.
7. She cut her when she was slicing the onions for a stew.
8. Babies talk and sing to oneself.
9. I said they could come with my friend and I.
10. Carlos and me are best friends.

Subject and Object Pronouns

Examples

She told him that she had begun
<u>s</u>   o   s
dressmaking in Poland.

People speak languages. They speak
s   o   s
them.
o

Comments

Subject pronouns substitute for subjects. Object pronouns substitute for objects.

Possessive Pronouns and Possessive Determiners

Examples

my mother

our kitchen

your gestures

His mother was a dressmaker.
Mine works in an office. (*mine* = my mother)

Our kitchen is old-fashioned.
Yours is very modern. (*yours* = your kitchen)

Comments

Possessive determiners (*my, our, your*) substitute for possessive nouns. Another noun always follows.

Possessive pronouns (*mine, ours, yours*) take the place of both the possessive determiner and the noun.

PRACTICING YOUR SKILLS

A. In the following story, adapted from a Spanish folktale, all pronouns and possessive determiners have been removed. Fill in the blanks with an appropriate word. Check your answers on page 430.

IT'S IMPOSSIBLE TO PLEASE EVERYONE

1   A farmer and _____*his*_____ son are going to the market.
_____*They*_____ have brought along _____ horse to help
_____ carry _____ purchases. Not wanting to tire
_____ animal on the way to the market, _____

5   decide to walk along beside _____ horse.

Along the way, _____ meet a man. The man laughs at
_____ and tells _____ that _____
are very foolish because _____ are walking while
_____ horse, a strong animal, goes on _____ way

10 without a load. Not wanting to be laughed at, the father orders _____
son to mount the horse.

Not long after, _____ meet a woman. _____
looks at the son on the horse and complains to _____. "How can
_____ ride and allow _____ father, an old man, to

15 walk?" The father and son decide that _____ is right. Both of
_____ climb up on the horse's back.

Burdened by _____ two passengers, the horse has begun to
slow down when the farmer and son meet a group of children on the road. The
children are shocked at the treatment of the horse. "How can two men allow

20 _____ beautiful horse to suffer?"

It seems that the farmer and _____ son cannot do anything
right. Whatever _____ do, someone will criticize
_____. After thinking for some time, the son has a plan. Both of
_____ should get off the horse and carry _____ the

25 rest of the way to the market. No one will be able to criticize _____
then. Or will _____?

B.   Construct several sentences telling about yourself, your family, and friends. Use possessive determiners, possessive nouns, and possessive pronouns whenever possible.

Examples

My friend's mother is a teacher. *Mine* is a _____.

Our next class is in the science building. Where is *yours*?

■■■■■■■■■ *Reflexive Pronouns*

Examples	*Comments*
I was surprised to hear *myself* say that.	Reflexive pronouns such as *myself, yourself* are used when the subject and object refer to the same person or thing.
You use nonverbal language every day to tell other people how *you* feel about *yourself* and them.	
I washed, dressed, and combed my hair.	When an action is one that people generally do by themselves, the reflexive pronoun is usually omitted.
but	
The baby is learning to dress *herself*.	
The president *himself* wrote the letter.	Reflexive pronouns are sometimes used for emphasis.
She learned to walk *by herself* when she was a year old.	*By* when used with a reflexive pronoun can mean either "without help" or "alone."
Sometimes I need to be *by myself* in a quiet place.	

Notice the difference between the following sentences.

They were laughing at *themselves*. (Each person was laughing at himself or herself.)

They were laughing at one another. (Each person was laughing at someone else in the group.)

PRACTICING YOUR SKILLS

Construct several sentences about the activities below. Which do you usually do yourself? Which do others do for you? Add other activities to the list.

personal: cut hair, curl hair, cook, shop for groceries, type letters, wash clothes, repair and alter clothing, make clothes

household: vacuum, make beds, wax furniture, wash walls, paint walls, repair plaster, repair electrical connections, do minor plumbing and heating repairs, do minor repairs to appliances, do minor carpentry, dig and weed garden

car: pump gas, check oil, change oil, check tires, change tires, tune up engine

SENTENCE SENSE

Headline English: Sentence Pattern 3

Sentence Pattern 3   Subject   + linking verb   + noun complement
                      BABIES   ARE   PEOPLE.

Sentence Pattern 3 has three essential parts: a subject, a verb, and a noun complement. The noun is necessary to complete the sentence.

S(ubject)	V(erb)	N(oun) C(omplement)
WOMAN	IS	CANDIDATE.
SHE	BECOMES	PRESIDENT.
HE	REMAINS	SENATOR.

Note the difference between this pattern and the other patterns we have studied. Unlike Pattern 1, Pattern 3 needs a noun to complete the meaning of the sentence. Unlike Pattern 2, the subject and the noun complement refer to the same person or thing.

Pattern 3 is used with only a few common verbs, in particular *be, become,* and *remain.* These linking verbs connect the subject and the noun complement. Pattern 3 is often used to talk about a person's nationality, identity, role in life, or profession. It is also used to give definitions of words or to explain ideas and processes.

Variation on Pattern 3

A similar pattern uses *appears to be, seems to be, seems like,* or *looks like.*

SHE   APPEARS TO BE   the WINNER.
  S   V   N C

HE   SEEMS TO BE   the LOSER.   or HE   SEEMS LIKE   the LOSER.
 S   V   N C   S   V   N C

IT   LOOKS LIKE   a VICTORY.
 S   V   N C

CHECK YOURSELF

Find the subject, verb, and noun complement in each of these sentences and write them in headline form. Check your answers on page 430.

1. My young, smart, ambitious cousin, just out of law school, is now a lawyer with a $35,000 salary in a big downtown law firm.

COUSIN	IS	LAWYER
S	V	NC

2. The young man with the tired look becomes a father for the first time.

Man	look	fathe
S	V	NC

3. After the re-counting of the ballots in the early hours of the morning, the incumbent seems to be the victor in the hotly contested mayoral election.

incumbent	seems	victor
S	V	NC

4. Despite his incompetence and his inability to get along with any of his employees, that man remains the manager of an important division of a very large company.

Man	remains	man
S	V	NC

5. For this important event, the press secretary is the spokesperson chosen by the president to give the news to the eager television reporters waiting in the conference room of the White House.

Secretary	is	spokesperson
S	V	NC

6. A square is a rectangle with four equal sides.

Square	is	rectangle
S	V	NC

7. Success is a word that has different meanings for different people.

Success	is	word
S	V	NC

8. Diabetes is a disease that most frequently attacks people more than 15 percent overweight, who are past middle age, and who have a history of the disease in their families.

S	V	NC

USING YOUR SKILLS

A.   Expand each of the following headlines into the longest good sentence you can make by adding modifiers. You may change the tense of the verb.

1.   WOMAN IS PRESIDENT.
2.   PLAYERS ARE WINNERS.
3.   INCUMBENT REMAINS GOVERNOR.
4.   ELECTION IS LANDSLIDE.
5.   CANDIDATE IS LIAR.
6.   DANCER BECOMES CITIZEN.
7.   MOVIE LOOKS LIKE HIT.
8.   STAR BECOMES DIRECTOR.
9.   EMPLOYEE IS THIEF.

B.   In pairs and with the help of a dictionary, one student will write definitions of geometric terms in Group A; the other will write definitions for Group B. After definitions have been completed, students will exchange papers and attempt to draw the shape from their partner's definition. (Check your answers on page 431.)
    Note that definitions are often written in the following form.

Example

A quadrilateral is a figure   that has four sides.
  S   V   NC   *or*
                    with four sides.

GROUP A: Write definitions for the following geometric terms.

1.   rectangle
2.   square
3.   right angle
4.   triangle
5.   isosceles triangle
6.   pentagon
7.   hexagon
8.   octagon

Are all rectangles squares? Are all squares rectangles?

GROUP B: Write definitions for the following.

1.   radius (of a circle)
2.   diameter (of a circle)

3. circumference (of a circle)
4. semicircle
5. parallel lines
6. perpendicular lines
7. a horizontal line
8. a vertical line

Do parallel lines ever meet? Do perpendicular lines meet?

C. *Medical specialties*: There are many different kinds of doctors and other health-care providers. Do you know what these health-care workers do? Do you know which have medical degrees and which have other specialized training? Use your dictionary and other sources of information to find out. Then give a one-sentence definition.

Example

A pediatrician is a doctor who takes care of children.

1. pediatrician
2. ophthalmologist
3. optician
4. dermatologist
5. obstetrician
6. nurse-midwife
7. cardiologist
8. orthodontist

D. *Specialized vocabulary*: Many fields use special words or special meanings of common words that the average English speaker may not know. For example, someone who knows about computer programming would probably understand *byte*, *debugging*, *software*, *hardware*, *random access memory (RAM)*, *binary code*, and *ASCII numbers*. Any architect would know the meaning of *elevation*, *façade*, *barrel vault*, *arcade*, *lintel*, *cornice*, *flying buttress*. A student of music would know the musical meaning of *vibrato*, *common time*, *dotted note*, *flat*, *sharp*, *natural*, *accidental*, *octave*, *minor key*, *modulation*. A baseball fan would know *home run*, *double play*, *walk*, *strike out*, *fly ball*, *fast curve*. People who work in offices or in factories, medical professionals, automobile mechanics, and people with other jobs or interests know words that some of their friends do not know.

You have probably learned, through study, your job, or a hobby, some specialized words in English. Write them down along with a short English definition.

CHECKING IT OVER

Some Additional Proofreading Symbols

Symbol	Meaning	Example	
C ∉	add or delete capital	He speaks ~~f~~french and ~~s~~spanish.	c
		I'm studying ~~H~~istory.	∉
pro	incorrect pronoun	My landlady is a good friend of my. *mine.*	*pro*
poss	error in the use of possessive noun	*woman's* The womans' friend helped her.	*poss*

USING YOUR SKILLS

Look over several pieces of writing you have done for class. Look at some writing that you did at the beginning of class and some you have done more recently. Are there mistakes you made earlier that you no longer make? What mistakes do you still have to watch out for?

Nouns, Pronouns, and Their Modifiers: A Review

PRACTICING YOUR SKILLS

The following is the opening paragraph in an article by two social scientists, Mihaly Csikszentmihalyi and Eugene Rochberg-Halton, describing a study they made of the significance of people's personal possessions.

1   A lawyer who had accumulated many valuable things in his home over a lifetime spoke of most of them with indifference. When asked what his most prized possession was, however, he paused, and then invited the interviewer into the basement family room. There, from an old chest, he carefully unpacked a trombone. It turned out that he
5   had played the instrument in college; for a middle-aged lawyer, it epitomized a life of freedom and spontaneity that he looked back on with nostalgia. Even now, when depressed or overwhelmed by responsibilities, he retires to the basement and blows on the old trombone.

VOCABULARY

indifference: lack of interest
family room: informal living room
epitomized: was typical of
spontaneity: the ability to act freely, without planning
nostalgia: feeling for something in the past

1. Identify all the nouns in the paragraph. Note the adjectives and determiners that often precede them.

2. Identify five singular countable nouns, two plural countable nouns, and three mass nouns. *things, responsibilities*   *indifference, freedom, nostalgia*

3. Which nouns are preceded by descriptive adjectives? Identify three noun-adjective combinations. Check your answers to 1–3 on page 432.

4. Without looking at the paragraph, fill in the blanks with missing articles *a/an* or *the*. If no article is necessary, write ∅.

1   _____ *A* _____ lawyer who had accumulated many valuable things in

his home over _____ *a* _____ lifetime spoke of most of them with

_____ *∅* _____ indifference. When asked what his most prized possession

was, however, he paused, and then invited _____ *the* _____ interviewer into

5   _____ *the* _____ basement family room. There, from _____ *an* _____

old chest, he carefully unpacked _____ *a* _____ trombone. It turned out that

he had played _____ *the* _____ instrument in _____ *∅* _____ college;

for _____ *a* _____ middle-aged lawyer, it epitomized _____ *a* _____

life of _____ *∅* _____ freedom and _____ *∅* _____ spontaneity that he

10   looked back on with _____ *∅* _____ nostalgia. Even now, when depressed or

overwhelmed by _____ *∅* _____ responsibilities, he retires to _____ *the* _____

basement and blows on _____ *the* _____ old trombone.

Check your answers with the original. Note: In a few cases an answer different from the one used in the original may also be correct. Check with your teacher.

5. This time, fill in the blanks with the missing possessive determiners and pronouns. Do not look at the previous exercise.

1   A lawyer who had accumulated many valuable things in _____ *his* _____

his home over a lifetime spoke of most of _____ *them* _____ with indifference.

When asked what _____ *his* _____ most prized possession was, however,

_____ *he* _____ paused, and then invited the interviewer into the basement

5   family room. There, from an old chest, _____ *he* _____ carefully unpacked a

trombone. It turned out that _____ *he* _____ had played the instrument in

college; for a middle-aged lawyer, _____ χ _____ epitomized a life of freedom
and spontaneity that _____ looked back on with nostalgia. Even now,
when depressed or overwhelmed by responsibilities, _____ retires to
10   the basement and blows on the old trombone.

Check your answers with the original.

Question Formation: A Review

Read John Joyce's short essay in *The Observor* column of the *Chicago Tribune*
and note the number of questions the author asks.

WHAT IS THE ORDER OF THINGS?

1   Sculptor Louise Nevelson once was asked how she decided in what order she
heaped and gathered her beams and blocks and blobs. "Well, darling," she said, "how
do you eat a pear?"
       Good question. In what order do *you* eat the various parts of a pear? Do you first
5   bite off the little narrow end? Do you leave the stem in and eat the pear apple-style?
       Try watching yourself do things that require deciding on the order in which you
carry out various parts of the action. What is the order, and is it always the same?
       Where do you begin to eat a piece of pie? Do you always do it the same way?
Do you know that if you eat the crust arc first you—as the psychologists would say—are
10   "postponing gratification?"
       How about a sandwich? If it comes in two cute triangles, where do you start? Do
you ever eat all the crust first? I once saw a kid start on a hot dog right in the middle
as if he were playing a harmonica.
       Do you see to it that the meat, potatoes, and peas all come out even by the end
15   of the meal? I can't recall ever seeing anybody eat all of one thing and then go on to the
next. How about corn on the cob? Do you eat all the way around, or all the way along?
       And there are many orders of things beside eating. When you put on a shirt or
coat, which sleeve goes first? How about shoes? Which first? Always the same?
       Men, when you shave, do you always take on the various parts of the face in the
20   same order? Women, do you put on lipstick from right to left? Anybody, in what order
do you take off your clothes?
       In what order do you dry the various parts of your body after a shower? Watch
yourself. Is it always the same? Watch yourself washing a car, the windows, the dishes.
How about when clearing away the dishes?
25   Are you one of those people who thumbs through a magazine from the back?
       Beware: The centipede was asked, "Just exactly in what order do you move your
hundred legs?" The poor thing stood frozen in indecision and starved to death.

Sculptor Louise Nevelson

1. Working in small groups, practice asking one another some of the questions in the essay. Add questions of your own, asking about the order in which people do things.
2. Practice asking questions about the future. Use *will* or *be going to*.

    Examples

    The next time you eat a pear, how *are* you *going to eat* it?

    Will you *eat* it the same way you eat an apple?

CHAPTER 4

TIME AND TENSE

The Simple Past Tense

Forming the Simple Past Tense: The Verb be

Subject	Verb	
I	was	late for work yesterday.
My sister	was	late also.
He	was	in a hurry this morning.
It	was	difficult to get ready on time.

Was is used with first- and third-person singular subjects.

	Subject	Verb
	We	were both late.
	You	were late also.
Unfortunately, our bosses		were on time.

Were is used with all other subjects.

Forming the Simple Past Tense: Other Verbs

The same form is used for all subjects.

REGULAR VERBS		
Subject	Verb	
I	worked	in a restaurant last year.
My friend	worked	with me.
We	worked	there for six months.

The simple past tense for most verbs is formed by adding *-ed* to the base.

+---+
| **IRREGULAR VERBS** |
+---+

Subject	Verb	
We	*left*	our jobs when school started.
The boss	*wrote*	us letters of recommendation.

Many common verbs have irregular forms which must be learned. (See pages 416–419 for a list of common irregular verbs.)

HOW IT SOUNDS

The -*ed* ending of regular verbs is actually pronounced three different ways:/əd/ (added syllable), /t/, and /d/.

A. Listen as your teacher reads aloud the base form and then the past-tense form of 15 regular verbs. As you listen, try to decide whether the final sound you hear is /t/, /d/, or /əd/ (extra syllable). The second time you hear them, write each verb in the appropriate column.

1. recommend-recommended (ded)
2. pass-passed (t)
3. achieve-achieved (d)
4. exceed-exceeded (ed)
5. transfer-transferred (d)
6. complete-completed (ed)
7. ask-asked (t)
8. look-looked (t)
9. prefer-preferred (d)
10. plan-planned (d)
11. accumulate-accumulated (ed)
12. finish-finished (t)
13. study-studied (d)
14. discuss-discussed (t)
15. admit-admitted (ed)

/əd/(extra syllable)　　　*/t/*　　　*/d/*

_____　　_____　　_____

_____　　_____　　_____

_____　　_____　　_____

_____　　_____　　_____

_____　　_____　　_____

Check your answers on page 432.

B. You may have realized that the last sound in the base form of the verb determines how the *-ed* ending will be pronounced. Say the base and the past-tense forms aloud. Which final base sounds make *-ed* sound like /əd/ (extra syllable)? Which make it sound like /t/? Which make it sound like /d/? Check your answers on page 432.

Using the Simple Past Tense

1. The simple past tense is used to indicate an action, series of actions, or a situation that began and ended in the past.

I *completed* high school in my country.

I *started* college last semester. (Even though you may be still attending college you are no longer starting.)

We *tried* to call you several times.

He *lived* with his cousins when he first came to the city.

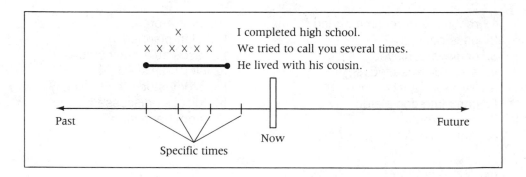

2. The simple past is usually used to talk aout specific events in the past. Words and phrases showing specific times—*ago* (*a week ago, a month ago, a year ago*), *the day before yesterday, last year, on November 7, 1965*—are often used with this tense.

I *was* born on May 3, 1962.

My family *moved* into a larger apartment *a month ago.*

PRACTICING YOUR SKILLS

Respond in complete sentences. Add details when possible.

1.   Tell three things you did (didn't do) last week.
2.   Tell three things a friend or relative did (didn't do) last week.
3.   Tell three things you and some friends did together last week.
4.   Tell three things your friends did but you didn't.

ASK AND ANSWER

A.   With a partner, take turns asking and answering questions about past activities. Respond in full sentences in order to practice the use of the simple past tense. Add details to explain your answers when possible.

Examples

When did you last . . . stay up all night studying?

read a book you couldn't put down?

meet someone you knew could be a good friend?

B.   What were the eight most important events in your life? Begin with your birthdate and fill in the chart with information about yourself, arranged in chronological order.

19_____   _____*I was born.*_____

19_____   _____

19_____   _____

19_____   _____

19_____   _____

19_____   _____

19_____   _____

19_____   _____

Then, working with a partner or in a small group, take turns asking and answering questions about important events in your partner's life.

■■■■■■ *Spelling Regular Verbs*

Sometimes small spelling changes must be made when adding *-ed* to regular verbs.

1. Base ends in *e*. Add *-d* only.

   change — changed
   use — used

2. Base ends in *y* preceded by a consonant. Change *y* to *i* before adding *-ed*.

   study — studied
   apply — applied

   but
   enjoy — enjoyed (*y* preceded by a vowel)

3. Base ends in *one* vowel and *one* consonant. Double the final consonant* (one-syllable words and longer words with stress on final syllable).

   stop — stopped
   preFER — preferred

   but
   LISten — listened (first syllable stressed)

CHECK YOURSELF

Write down the past-tense form of the following regular verbs. Check your answers on page 432.

1. save *saved*   6. hop *hopped*   11. dry *dried*
2. hope *hoped*   7. carry *carried*   12. refer *referred*
3. help *helpt*   8. start *ed*   13. succeed *succeeded*
4. try *tried*   9. worry *ied*   14. love *d*
5. control *controlled* 10. plan *ned*   15. visit *ed*

*Do not double *x* or *w* — snow — snowed, mix — mixed.

■■■■■■■■ *Irregular Past-Tense Verbs*

There are thousands of verbs in English. Most of them are regular (past tense ends in *-ed*). There are about 250 irregular verbs. However, only about 100 of them are used often. It is more important for you to know these common forms well than to worry about the others.

CHECK YOURSELF

As an advanced student of English, you probably already know many of the common irregular past-tense forms. Check your knowledge by writing the correct past-tense forms of these irregular verbs without looking in a dictionary.

1. become *became*	6. feed *fed*	11. light *lit*	16. sit *sat*
2. bite *bit*	7. fly *flew*	12. put *put*	17. spring *sprang*
3. build *built*	8. give *gave*	13. rise *ris*	18. swear *swore*
4. come *came*	9. hit *hit*	14. sell *sold*	19. teach *taught*
5. draw *drew*	10. lay *laid*	15. shoot *shot*	20. throw *threw*

Check your own answers, using the list on pages 416–419. If you made three mistakes or fewer, go on to the next exercise and review the rest of the verbs later. If you made four mistakes or more, it may be useful to review irregular past-tense forms before going on.

PRACTICING YOUR SKILLS

Maxine Hong Kingston is a Chinese-American writer. Although she was born in the United States, she grew up speaking her parents' language—Chinese—and did not use English until she went to kindergarten. This passage is from her autobiography, *The Woman Warrior*. It describes her first years at school, years in which she did not speak at all.

All the past-tense verbs have been removed from the passage. Fill in the blanks with an appropriate verb in the past tense. The base form of the words Kingston uses is given in the margin, but the exercise is more challenging if at first you cover up the words and try to guess the ones Kingston might have chosen. Check your answers on page 432.

SILENCE

1   My silence was thickest—total—during the three years
that I _____*covered*_____ my school paintings with black   cover
paint. I _____ layers of black over houses and   paint
flowers and suns, and when I _____ on the   draw
5 blackboard, I _____ a layer of chalk on top. I   put
was making a stage curtain, and it _____ the   be
moment before the curtain _____ or   part
_____ . The teachers _____   rise/call
my parents to school, and I _____ they had   see
10 been saving my pictures, curling and cracking, all alike and
black. The teachers _____ to the pictures   point
and _____ serious, _____   look/talk
seriously too, but my parents _____   understand (neg.)
_____ English.
15   During the first silent year I _____ to no   speak
one at school, _____   ask/(neg)
before going to the lavatory, and _____   flunk
kindergarten. My sister also _____ nothing for   say
three years, silent in the playground and silent at lunch. There
20 _____ other quiet Chinese girls not of our   be
family, but most of them _____ over it sooner   get
than we _____ . I _____ the   do/enjoy
silence. At first it _____   occur (neg)
to me that I _____ supposed to talk or to   be
25 pass kindergarten. I _____ at home and to   talk
one or two of the Chinese kids in class. I _____   make
motions and even _____ some jokes.   make

USING YOUR SKILLS

Maxine Hong Kingston tells a story about something that happened to her when she was a young child. (Kingston was probably between five and eight years old when the story she tells took place.) Tell or write a story about an event in your own childhood that took place when you were quite young (four to eight years old).

PRACTICING YOUR SKILLS

After coming home from the American public school each day, Maxine Hong Kingston attended a Chinese school in the afternoons. Here she describes that school and the breaking of her silence.

Fill in the blanks with the appropriate form of the past tense. Check your answers on page 432, 433.

FINDING A VOICE

1 Not all of the children who were silent at American	
school _____ [a] voice at Chinese school.	find
One new teacher _____ each of us	say
had to get up and recite in front of the class, who	
5 _____ to listen. My sister and I had	be
memorized the lesson perfectly. We _____ it	say
to each other at home, one chanting, one listening. The teacher	
_____ on my sister to recite first. It	call
_____ the first time a teacher had called on	be
10 the second-born to go first. My sister _____	be
scared. She _____ at me and	glance
_____ away; I _____ down	look/look
at my desk. I _____ that she could do it	hope
because if she could, then I would have to. She	
15 _____ her mouth and a voice came out that	open
_____ a whisper, but _____	be (neg) be (neg)
a proper voice either. I _____ that she would	hope
not cry, fear breaking up her voice like twigs underfoot. She	
_____ as if she were trying to sing through	sound
20 weeping and strangling. She _____ or	pause (neg)
_____ to end the embarrassment. She	stop
_____ going until she _____	keep on/say
the last word, and then she _____ down.	sit
When it _____ my turn, the same voice	be
25 _____ out, a crippled animal running on	come
broken legs. You could hear splinters in my voice, bones	
rubbing jagged against one another. I _____	be
loud, though. I _____ glad I	be
_____. There	whisper (neg)
30 _____ one little girl who _____.	be/whisper

USING YOUR SKILLS

Write about an event in your own life when—like Maxine Hong Kingston—you were worried or frightened before you did something, but after you tried, you managed to do it well. Describe your feelings before the event and after.

USING MODALS

Expressing Ability in the Past

Could

Examples

Her child *could* read before he started school.

Comments

Could is used to express the ability to do something in the past. When used with this meaning, *could* is the past tense of *can*.

Was/were able to

Examples

In high school my sister *could* swim fast. She *was able to* break the school record for the 100-meter backstroke.

Comments

Was/were able to has approximately the same meaning as *could,* but is more likely to be used when discussing specific abilities.

ASK AND ANSWER

A.   In the following list, check the things you can (are able to) do now. Could you (were you able to) do them two years ago? When you were a child?

	Can do now	Could do two years ago	Could do as a child
light a fire without matches	_____	_____	_____
swim freestyle (crawl)	_____	_____	_____
make spaghetti sauce	_____	_____	_____
write a computer program	_____	_____	_____
draw a recognizable portrait	_____	_____	_____
touch-type	_____	_____	_____
type 40 words a minute (any way)	_____	_____	_____
run a mile	_____	_____	_____
run 10 kilometers (6.2 miles)	_____	_____	_____
change a tire	_____	_____	_____
ice-skate	_____	_____	_____
recite a poem by heart (in any language)	_____	_____	_____
say a sentence in English	_____	_____	_____
read an English newspaper	_____	_____	_____
write an essay in English	_____	_____	_____

B.   Work with a partner. Ask your partner about what he or she can (can't) do now; could (couldn't) do two years ago; could (couldn't) do as a child.

USING YOUR SKILLS

A.   Look at some of your old homework and tests for this class. What are some things you have learned to do (or learned to do better) in English that you weren't able to do before you took this class?

B.   Think of a skill you have learned recently that you are proud of. Write a paragraph explaining how you learned to do it step by step. Explain what you were able to do at each stage of learning.

C.   Young children learn many things before they go to school. If possible, find out at what age a child you know learned how to do various things. Ask friends or classmates who are parents, or — if this is possible — ask your own parents about the age at which you were able to do the following things:

sit	say first sentence
crawl	brush teeth
stand	tie shoes
walk	button clothes
say first word	count to five

Report to the class or write a paragraph explaining the development of skills during the first five years of life of the child you found out about.

FINDING OUT ABOUT . . .

Making Suggestions with *let's*

Examples

Let's have lunch together.
(I suggest that we have lunch together.)*

Let's not eat in the cafeteria today.

Comments

Let's (let us) + base is used to make suggestions that include the speaker and at least one other person.

Negative suggestions are made with *let's not*.

PRACTICING YOUR SKILLS

A.   Working with a classmate, practice making suggestions about sharing activities together. Use *let's* or *let's not*.

1.   where the two of you should eat a meal
2.   what you should eat together
3.   what you should do together
4.   what to do the next time you both have some spare time

B.   Sometimes while working with others we think about a better or more efficient way of doing the work. Practice making suggestions to some person or people

*Another, more informal way of making a suggestion is to use *Why don't we?* (Why don't we have lunch together?)

with whom you are working. Use *let's* or *let's not* to make your suggestions. Then add a few sentences explaining the advantages of following each of your suggestions.*

Adjectives as Complements

Examples

The *tall* boy
　ADJ　N

The boy is *tall*.
S　V ADJ

She seems *confident*.

The table looks *old*.

The food tastes *spicy*.

Comments

In Chapter 2 we observed that adjectives usually come before the noun they describe.

Adjectives like *tall* can also come after the subject and verb. The adjective in this position is called a complement. It completes the idea expressed by the subject and verb.

Adjectives as complements often appear after verbs like *be, become, remain, seem,* and with some meanings of *appear, look, feel,* and *taste*. These verbs are called linking verbs. The verbs link the adjective to the noun or pronoun it describes.

PRACTICING YOUR SKILLS

A. Use adjectives as complements to describe the color, texture, or shape of rooms and objects in them. Find as many appropriate adjectives as possible.

Examples

The floor in the classroom is *brown/waxed/polished*.

It feels *smooth/slippery*.

It looks *worn/used*.

---

*Teachers and other people in positions of leadership will sometimes use *let's* to suggest actions they really want others to do.

Let's turn to page 110.

Let's do the first four exercises.

B. Use adjectives as complements to describe the color, texture, and other qualities of a piece of clothing you own.

Example

My favorite sweater is *blue* and feels *soft*. It looks *new*.

C. Use adjectives as complements to describe the taste of several foods you like or dislike.

Example

The coffee in the cafeteria tastes *bitter*.

D. Use adjectives as complements to describe how you feel at this moment.

Example

I feel *calm*.

LITTLE WORDS

Prepositions: An Introduction

Prepositions are words like *at, by, for, from, in, of, on, to,* and *with*.

Note the use of prepositions in the following paragraphs about how different cultures write numbers.

1 Several different numbering systems have been used *through* the ages. One *of* the earliest systems, devised *by* the Egyptians, used a simple pen stroke or a mark *in* clay to represent one. Other numbers *up to* nine were formed *by* repeating the symbol *for* one. The Romans and the Mayas had an additional symbol *for* five. *On* the other
5 hand, Arabic and Chinese had different symbols *for* each number *through* nine, and the Arabs and the Mayas also had a symbol *for* zero.

The system used *in* Europe, the Americas, and many other parts *of* the world today was adapted *from* the Arabic numbering system. *In* this system the position *of* a digit is significant. Using the basic digits 0 and 1 *through* 9 it is possible to con-

Egyptian						
	1	10	100	1,000	10,000	100,000

Roman										
	I	II	III	IIII	V	VI	VII	VIII	IX	X
	1	2	3	4	5	6	7	8	9	10

Mayan										
	1	2	3	4	5	6	7	8	9	10

Modern Arabic										
	1	2	3	4	5	6	7	8	9	0

Chinese									
	1	2	3	4	5	6	7	8	9

10 struct any number. This base-10, or decimal, system was introduced *into* Europe *by* Adelard *of* Bath *about* 1100 and *by* 1600 was *in* almost universal use. One historian *of* science, Otto Neugebauer, considers positional, or place-value, numeration *as* "one *of* the most important inventions *of* humanity, *in* a way comparable *to* the invention *of* the alphabet."

Learning to Use Prepositions

It is often difficult even for advanced learners of English to know which preposition to use. Most prepositions have several different meanings, depending on context. Often, more than one preposition can be used in a phrase.

In addition, many idiomatic expressions, such as *in a way* and *comparable to,* contain prepositions. There is usually no way of predicting which preposition will be used in these expressions. Learn the whole expression, including the preposition that is a part of it.

The next several chapters focus on groups of prepositions that cause problems for many students. However, no book can cover each student's individual problems or questions. In addition to doing the exercises, you need to pay attention to your own use of prepositions and develop strategies for correcting the mistakes you make frequently. Your teacher can help you find patterns of preposition use in your own writing.

Prepositions Showing Place

Many prepositions, such as *in, inside, on, at, over, above, under, underneath, below, near, by, next to, between, behind, in back of, in front of,* and *beside,* can be used to express place or position in space.

■ *Trouble Spots:* in, on, at

in — enclosed in a three-dimensional space	*in* my pocket *in* the drawer *in* the library	
on — contact with a vertical or horizontal surface	*on* the desk *on* the wall	
at — near or in contact with a point in space or a place whose size and shape is not relevant	*at* the top of the stairs *at* the library*	

■ *Other Points to Remember*

1. *In front of* is the opposite of *behind*.

    Don't put the lamp *in front of* the picture.
    Don't put the picture *behind* the lamp.

2. Use *opposite* or *facing* for things on the other side of a room or street.

    There is a mirror *opposite/facing* the door.

---

*Both *in* and *at* can be used with buildings, sometimes with little difference in meaning. However, *in* the library always means inside the actual building, while, *at* the library may mean on the outside or near the building.

My car is parked *at* the library.

PRACTICING YOUR SKILLS

With a classmate, practice asking each other to put small objects (pens, pencils, notebooks) in different positions.

Example

Put the green pen *on* the floor/*under* the chair/*next to* the red pen/*between* our chairs/*in* your hand/*on* your shoe/etc.

■■■■■■■ **In, on, at** *with Addresses, Geographical Locations*

in — before continents, countries, states, cities, neighborhoods	in Europe in Poland in Illinois in Chicago in Brownsville
on — before streets	on Michigan Avenue *also* on the first floor on the corner on the north (south) side on the East (West) coast
at — before street numbers	at 111 Michigan Avenue

PRACTICING YOUR SKILLS

Indicate in several different ways the locations or addresses of several places you know — your house, school, place of work — using the prepositions *in, on,* and *at.*

CHECK YOURSELF

Fill in the blanks with the most appropriate preposition, *in, on,* or *at.* Check your answers on page 433.

1. That's my friend standing _____ the window.
2. I think I have some change _____ my pocket.

3. You should put the ice cream _____ the freezer before it melts.
4. I think I have a cavity _____ the last molar _____ the right side.
5. My dentist is downtown _on_ Washington Avenue, _on_ the north side of the street.
6. Did you say you lived _at_ 3014 North Kimbell or _at_ 3040?
7. Please write your address _on_ this sheet of paper.
8. Is your apartment _on_ the second floor or_on_ the third?
9. You have a small stain _on_ your shirt.
10. How long are you going to be staying _on_ the West Coast? _in_ San Francisco?

USING YOUR SKILLS

Imagine you are moving to a new apartment. The main room is twice as large as the one you have now and is shaped very differently. You must rearrange all your furniture, pictures, and possessions. Draw plans of your new room and describe how you will arrange your things in it.

■■■■■ *Prepositions of Movement*

1. Some prepositions are frequently used to talk about movement to or from a place: *to, from, toward, into, out of, around, across, by way of, through,* and *along.*

in(to)  *out of* (three dimensions)

She jumped *into* the pool. She climbed *out of* the pool.

on(to)  *off* (surface)

The ball rolled *off* the table and *onto* the floor.

to  *from* (point)

The plane goes *to* Kennedy Airport. You must take a bus *from* the airport *to* the hotel.

2. *From* is also used for a place of origin.

    He's *from* Colombia.
    The coffee comes *from* Brazil.

3. *Toward* and *away from* show movement in a particular direction without reaching the destination.

    toward ———————►|————————► *away from*

    Walk *away from* the river, *toward* the center of town.

4. *By* can be used to talk about going past a place or point without stopping.

    You will go *by* the fountain on your way to my house.

5. *Go by* or *stop by* can also mean a short stop.

    Please *stop by/go by* the grocery store and pick up a carton of milk on your way home.

6. *By way of* means with a stop on the way.

    You can fly to Philadelphia *by way of* New York City.

7. *Up* a street and *down* a street can mean the same thing. Go in the direction a person is facing or pointing to, or ask.

8. *Around* can mean in a circular direction or in many different directions.

    Walk *around* that puddle.
    Let's walk *around* campus to get an idea of where most of the buildings are.

9. *Across* emphasizes movements from one side to another on a two-dimensional surface or over a long, narrow shape. *Through* suggests the same movement in three-dimensional space. *Along* suggests movement on or near a line or long, narrow shape such as a river, a road, or the side of a building.

    The explorers went *through* the jungle, swam *across* the river, and then walked *along* the river bank until they reached an ancient pile of stones that was once a pyramid.

CHECK YOURSELF

Cross out the preposition that should *not* be used in each sentence. Check your answers on page 433. *circle wrong one*

1. The plane circled (around/over/~~through~~) the city before landing.
2. Please stop (~~on~~/at/by) my office for a minute after class.
3. Go (up/down/~~through~~) the street and then take the turn (in/on/to) your left just before you get to the bridge. There is a gas station (at/~~in~~/on) the next corner, and my apartment is across the street (facing/opposite/~~in front of~~) the station.
4. There is a nice path (along/~~facing~~/beside) the river that you can take.
5. If we have some time after we arrive, let's walk (around/~~over~~/through) the neighborhood to see what it looks like.
6. My bed is near the wall (in front of/facing/~~opposite~~) the door.
7. If you hang the picture (over/above/~~behind~~) the radiator, we can all see it.
8. Drive (toward/~~at~~/in the direction of) the center of town but turn right (~~into~~/at/by) the river.
9. If you want to park your car in the parking lot, go (through/~~by~~/in) the entrance on your left and back (in/into/~~on~~) the nearest empty space.
10. If you have some time, please stop (by/~~through~~/at) my office. There is something I want to show you.
11. I just saw your friends go (into/~~onto~~/in) the store a minute ago.
12. Please take the dirty dishes (off/~~out from~~/away from) the table.

USING YOUR SKILLS

Choose three places in your area that you think any new classmate should know how to find. These can be everyday places, like your own house, good places to shop, or some of the sights of the city. Explain to a classmate exactly how to get to each place from where you are now. If possible, students should pair up with classmates who are not familiar with their selections.

SENTENCE SENSE

Headline English: Sentence Pattern 4

Sentence Pattern 4   Subject   + linking   + adjective
                                 verb   complement

                    BABIES   ARE   CUTE.

Sentence Pattern 4 is similar to Pattern 3, except that an adjective is used to complete the sentence. The adjective and the subject both refer to the same person or thing. The verb links the subject to its complement.

Many of the verbs used in Sentence Pattern 3 — *be, become, remain* — can also be used in Pattern 4. The single-word verbs — *seem, appear,* and *look* (meaning "appear") — can be used in Pattern 4.

WITNESS REMAINS SILENT.

ASTRONAUT LOOKS TIRED.

Some verbs that are not used in Pattern 3 are used in Pattern 4.

THE FOOD TASTES DELICIOUS

THE MUSIC SOUNDS WONDERFUL.

CHECK YOURSELF

Find the subject, verb, and adjective complement in each of these sentences. Write them in headline form, labeling the parts. Check your answers on page 433.

1. Several of the reviews of the long-awaited controversial new movie, which is based on a Pulitzer prize-winning novel, are bad.

REVIEWS	_ARE_	_BAD_
S	V	ADJ C

2. Reviewers from some of the major daily newspapers and a few of the most popular weekly magazines are disappointed.

3. Some reviewers who consider film to be a serious art form are disturbed about the movie's distortion and oversimplification of the book.
4. Some audiences in various parts of the country seem hostile to the theme of the film and to the portrayal of some of the characters.
5. Other audiences appear enthusiastic about the movie's dramatic story and the quality of the actors' performances.
6. Despite all the controversy about the film, the failure of the well-known director to be nominated for an important award is surprising.

USING YOUR SKILLS

Expand each of the following headlines by adding modifiers. You may change the tense of the verb.

1. PRICES BECOME INFLATED. *The prices, with the inflation always there hav...*
2. WEATHER TURNS STORMY. *The wonderful weather we had Saturday turned in the*
3. BUDGET APPEARS VULNERABLE. *early terno...*
4. CONFERENCE APPEARS SUCCESSFUL. *After the comments heard in the office*
5. KILLER ACTS CRAZY. *today, the conference*
6. PRISONER IS TERRIFIED. *gave by the president*
7. WITNESS REMAINS SILENT. *appears ...*
8. DEFENDANT SEEMS WORRIED.

CHECKING IT OVER

Reviewing Tenses

PRACTICING YOUR SKILLS

A. The past tense is used along with other tenses in the following passage telling about people who lived between 35,000 and 10,000 years ago. Note the verbs in tenses other than the past tense. Then, fill in the blanks with the missing past-tense forms. Check your answers on page 433.

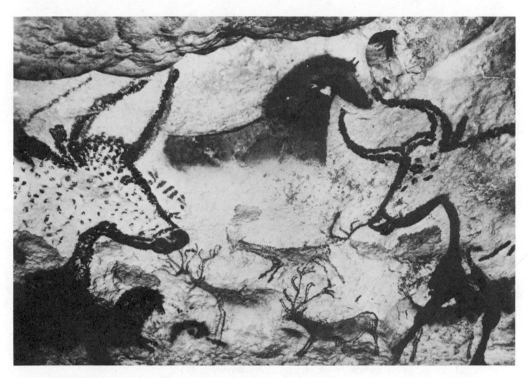

Prehistoric wall paintings from the Lascaux Caves in France.

A NEW UNDERSTANDING OF THE PAST

1   Recently, anthropologists have changed their minds
about the people who _____*lived*_____ from 35,000 to   live
10,000 years ago. They once _____*considered*_____ these   consider
250 centuries to be a period of time in which the ancestors of
5   modern man _____*made*_____ little progress. However,   make
the the past decade, researchers *have begun* to conclude that,
on the contrary, this period, the late ice age,
_____*was*_____ a time that _____*witnessed*_____ a   be/witness
great explosion of civilization. In fact, the people of this time
10   *are* probably the inventors of language, music, art, and the
foundations of trade.
       Around 35,000 years ago, a new group of people called
Cro-Magnons _____*began*_____ to dominate or replace   begin
the more primitive Neanderthal man. The Cro-Magnons

15 _____ less muscular and thinner boned than   be

the Neanderthals. Although their total brain size

_____ no bigger than that of their more   be

primitive predecessors, the frontal lobes of the Cro-Magnon

brain—the seat of reasoning— _____ larger   be

20 and more developed. This no doubt _____ the   give

Cro-Magnons a greater capacity for symbolic thought and

invention. Furthermore, while Neanderthals _____   die

before their mid-40s, there *is* evidence that some Cro-

Magnons _____ into their 60s, long enough to   live

25 pass on accumulated knowledge to several generations.

Cro-Magnons _____ not "cave men" as   be

many people *believe.* They _____ in natural   live

rock shelters or dwellings built of wood, stone, bone, or skin.

However, they _____ caves for special   use

30 purposes, as evidenced by the wonderful cave paintings found

in many places.

Henri Delporte, general inspector at the Museum of

National Antiquities outside Paris, *thinks* that the famous cave

paintings, such as the ones at Lascaux, *may represent*

35 milestones in a clan's history, a brush with death by a former

leader, or a lucky hunt that _____ families   save

from winter starvation. He *speculates* that ancient people

_____ the caves to initiate the young into the   use

tribal tradition. Viewed in the flickering light of a sandstone

40 lamp, the animals on the walls *might seem* to come to life.

The discovery of dozens of youthful footprints in close

patterns in some caves *suggests* that the Cro-Magnons

_____ caves for dancing, perhaps as a   use

religious rite or as part of an initiation of the young.

VOCABULARY

predecessors: people who lived at an earlier time
frontal lobes: large sections in the front part of the brain
accumulated knowledge: knowledge built up over time
dwellings: houses
milestones: important events
clan: a group of families with common traditions

VOCABULARY (CONT.)

brush with death: coming close to dying
initiate: introduce
religious rite: religious ceremony

B. Even though the rate of population growth has declined recently, the world's population continues to grow. Experts predict that it will reach 6 billion by the year 2000. The charts below show population figures for the major areas of the world in 1950 and 1985 and projections for the year 2000.

Summarize the information in paragraph form, using appropriate tenses—past, present, and future. Note: Use 1985 figures for present or, if possible, update the information by finding more recent figures in the library.

C. It is predicted that the number of cities with more than 2 million people will double in the years 1985–2000. According to the United States Census Bureau, more than half the world's population will live in urban areas by the turn of the century.

Use the charts below and any other information you can find in the library to write paragraphs about urban population growth in the past, present, and future.

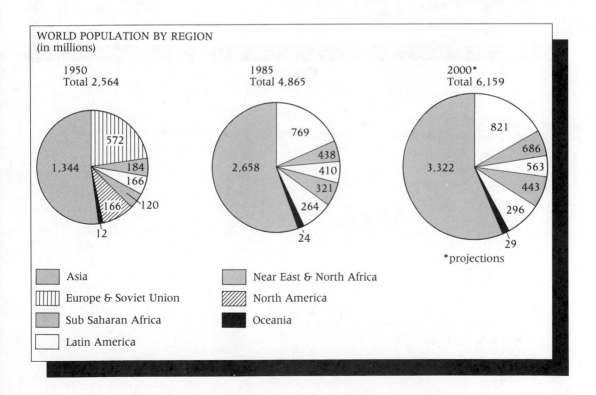

WORLD POPULATION BY REGION
(in millions)

1950
Total 2,564

1985
Total 4,865

2000*
Total 6,159

*projections

Asia

Europe & Soviet Union

Sub Saharan Africa

Latin America

Near East & North Africa

North America

Oceania

THE FUTURE: MASSIVE TRAFFIC JAMS

Urbanization is expected to continue on a massive scale into the next century. But in the U.S., only New York will make the Top 10 in 2000.

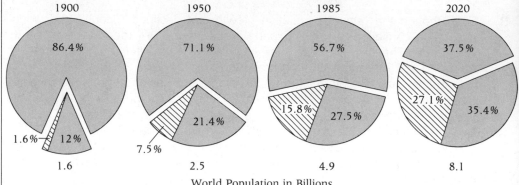

| 1900 | 1950 | 1985 | 2020 |

86.4%   71.1%   56.7%   37.5%

1.6% 12%   7.5%   21.4%   15.8% 27.5%   27.1% 35.4%

1.6   2.5   4.9   8.1

World Population in Billions

Rural   Cities fewer than 1 million   Cities more than 1 million

THE TOP 10 IN 2000
(Population in Millions)
1. Mexico City   27.6
2. Shanghai   25.9

3. Tokyo/Yokohama   23.8
4. Peking   22.8
5. Sao Paulo   21.5
6. New York/N.E. New Jersey   19.5

7. Greater Bombay   16.3
8. Calcutta   15.9
9. Jakarta   14.3
10. Rio de Janeiro   14.2

CHAPTER 5

The Present Perfect Tense

Forming the Present Perfect Tense

The present perfect tense is formed with the auxiliary verb *have ('ve)* or *has ('s)* and the past participle of the main verb.

Subject	Verb	
He She My sister	*has written*	several letters.

Has ('s) is used with third-person singular subjects.

Subject	Verb	
I You We They My sisters	*have written*	most of the essay.

Have ('ve) is used with all other subjects.

Past Participles: Regular

Most past participles—*talked, walked, tried*—are regular. They end in the spelling *-ed*. They look and sound the same as the past-tense form.

ASK AND ANSWER

Working with a partner, take turns asking and answering questions about language and language-learning, using the present perfect tense. Use the following regular verbs.

ask	finish	search	talk
change	help	start	try
correct	learn	study	work

Example

Have you *studied* any other language besides English?

Yes I *have*. I've *studied* a little French.

No I *haven't*, but I'd like to study Russian.

▬▬▬ *Past Participles: Irregular*

About 100 common past participles are irregular. For some irregular verbs (*thought*) the past participle is the same as the irregular past-tense form. A few past tense participles are the same as the base form (*run*). Several other irregular past participles end in *-en* (*written, driven*). Other past participles have completely unpredictable forms (*gone*).

CHECK YOURSELF

As an advanced student of English, you probably already know many of the common irregular past participle forms. Check your knowledge by writing the correct past participle form of these 20 irregular verbs.

1. beat *beat*   6. feel *felt*   11. make   16. sleep *slept*
2. bleed *bled*   7. forget *ot -* 12. quit *quit*   17. stand *stood*
3. burst *burst* 8. go *went*   13. run *ran*   18. sweep *swept*
4. cost *cost*   9. hold *hold*   14. send *sent*   19. tear *tore*
5. drink *dronk* 10. lead *led*   15. show *ed*   20. understand *ood*

Check your answers on pages 416–419. If you made only a few mistakes, go on to the next exercise and review the rest of the verbs later. If you made several mistakes, you should review the irregular past participle forms before continuing.

▬▬▬ *Using the Present Perfect Tense*

Examples

1. I've already *seen* that movie.
   She's *thought* about it.

Comments

The present perfect is used to express states and actions that took place at an indefinite time in the past.

He*'s gone* home to visit his family several times. He must miss them a lot.

It may be used to express a series of repeated actions that took place some time in the past, especially when they are important for understanding the present or are expected to happen again.

I *haven't talked* to her yet.

The present perfect can also be used to talk about things that have *not* happened until now.

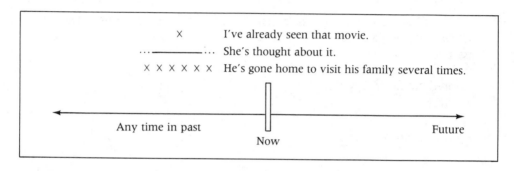

He*'s just left* the office. You may be able to catch her before she leaves the building.

We're not hungry. We*'ve just eaten* lunch.

The present perfect may be used to talk about the very recent past. The word *just* is often used between the auxiliary and the verb.*

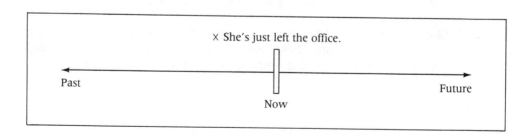

---

*In informal English, especially in the United States, the simple past is also used for recent actions. "We just ate lunch."

3. He's *been* in love with her since the moment he first saw her. (He still loves her now.)

   Their families *have known* each other for 30 years. (They still know each other.)

The present perfect is used, particularly with nonaction verbs, to talk about conditions that begin in the past and continue to the present.*

PRACTICING YOUR SKILLS

A. Use the present perfect tense to construct five sentences about places you have been to or interesting things you have done in the area in which you are now living. Talk about things that you have done anytime since you moved here. Do not mention an exact time.

Examples

I've *been* to the museum once.

I've *eaten* at several interesting restaurants.

B. Use the present perfect tense and *just* to construct five sentences about things that have happened very recently in class.

Example

The teacher *has just erased* the board.

---

*The present perfect progressive tense (see Chapter 6) is also used for this purpose, particularly with action verbs.

Using ever *and* never

Notice the use of *ever* with the present perfect tense in the questions, which ask about events that took place at any time up until the present moment.

> *Have* you *ever played* baseball?
>
> Yes, I *have*. An American friend taught me how last summer.

The word *never* may be used in a negative response.

> No, I *never* have. But I've *watched* the World Series on TV.

ASK AND ANSWER

A.   Work with a partner asking and answering questions. Add one or more additional comments to the answers if possible.

Have you ever . . .

1.   get up / before dawn?
  Have you ever gotten up before dawn?

2.   see / a cowboy movie?
3.   meet / a cowboy?
4.   enjoy / taking a test?

5.   eat / Korean food?
6.   cook / Korean food?
7.   hike / 10,000 feet above sea level?
8.   swim / in salt water?
9.   go / deep sea diving?
10.   fly / in an airplane?

B.   What has your partner done that you would like to try? What wouldn't you like to try? What have you done that your partner has never done? Talk about your plans with your partner or with the class.

Yet *and* already

The words *yet* and *already* are often used in asking and answering questions about events that took place some time before the present moment.

> Have you seen the new Stephen Spielberg movie *yet*?
>
> Yes, I've *already* seen it twice.* I really liked it.
>
> No, I *haven't seen* it *yet*, but I'd like to. Do you know where it's playing?

*Some English-speakers put *already* at the end of sentences. "I've seen it twice *already*."

ASK AND ANSWER

Think of the names of five movies you have seen recently. (You may substitute books you have read and enjoyed, or music you like to listen to.)

Then, with one or more of your classmates, ask and answer questions about things you have enjoyed. Use the present perfect and the words *yet* and *already* in your questions and answers. Add additional comments to help your classmates find out about things you have enjoyed and think they might like too.

The Present Perfect Tense vs. the Simple Past Tense

PRESENT PERFECT TENSE	SIMPLE PAST TENSE
Focus on an indefinite time in past.	Focus on a definite time in the past.
Focus on continuation into present or relevance for present.	Focus on completion of action or situation in the past.
Examples	*Examples*
He *has thought* about the problem and has come up with a good solution.	He *thought* about the problem last week before he *made* his decision to quit.
Have you *met* my friend? No, I *have*n't, but I'd like to.	*Did* you *meet* my friend at the reception last week? No, I *did*n't *meet* her.
I *have seen* several Mayan archaeological sites in Central America. I'll visit Palenque next year.	I *visited* Uxmal in Mexico five years ago and Copán in Honduras last year.
She *has* always *loved* music.	She *loved* music when she was a child.
My father *has worked* hard all his life. He gets up at six each morning.	My father *worked* hard until he *retired* a year ago.

USING YOUR SKILLS

Every once in a while most of us look back at our lives and think about the changes that have taken place over a long period of time. Sometimes these are changes in the way we act; sometimes they are changes in the way we think or feel. Most changes are gradual. It may be hard to identify exactly when we began to feel a certain way or look at the world differently.

Write a short essay about one or two important changes in your life that have developed over a period of time. You probably will want to use the present perfect tense to talk about these changes. You may use the past tense to talk about events that had a definite beginning or end.

> ## Using the Present Perfect Tense and the Simple Present Tense

---

PRACTICING YOUR SKILLS

Andy Rooney is a humorous writer whose columns appear in many American newspapers. He also appears on the television show "60 Minutes."

In this selection, Rooney tells about his frustration with dictionaries. They never help him when he needs them most. Perhaps you feel the same way.

Most of the verbs have been removed. Most missing verbs are in the simple present tense, but one is in the present perfect tense. The base form of the verbs Rooney used is in the right-hand margin, but the exercise is more challenging if you cover the margin. Check your answers on page 433.

DICTIONARIES

1   When I look up something in the dictionary, it is never where I look for it first.

    The dictionary _____*has been*_____ a particular   be

disappointment to me as a basic reference work, and the fact

5   that it _____*is*_____ usually more my fault than the   be

dictionary's does not _____*make*_____ it any easier on   make

me. Sometimes I cannot _____*come*_____ close enough   come to knowing how to spell a word to find it; other times the word

just does not ____seem____ to be anywhere in the   seem

10   dictionary. I cannot for the life of me ____find____   find

out where they ____put____ some of the words I   put

____want____ to look up. They must   want

____be____ in there someplace.   be

Other times I ____want____ more information   want

15   about a word than the dictionary is prepared to give me. I

don't _____ to know how to spell a word or   want

what it _____. I _____ to   means / want

know how to use it. I _____ to know how to   want

make it possessive and whether I _____ the   double

20   final consonant when I _____ -ing to it. And   add

as often as I ____had written____ it, I always   write

_____ what you _____ to   forget / do

make a word that _____ in s possessive. "The   end

Detroit News' editor"? "The *Detroit New'es* editor"? I

25   _____ the *Detroit News*'s editors   suppose

_____, but I never _____   know / remember

and the dictionary _____ no help.   be

USING YOUR SKILLS

A.   What is your own experience with dictionaries? Have you found them to be as frustrating as Andy Rooney says, or have you found a dictionary (or a few dictionaries) that serve you well? Examine the dictionary (dictionaries) that you use most of the time and be prepared to report on its advantages and drawbacks. What features does it have? Would your dictionary be useful to others in the class?

B.   Many English learners like to have more than one kind of dictionary available. Are you aware of different types of dictionaries that might be useful to you: (a) English and your language; (b) English-only dictionaries prepared for native English speakers; and (c) English dictionaries prepared especially for learners of English?

Go either to a bookstore that has a large selection of dictionaries that you can browse through or to the library. Examine several of the dictionaries available. Write a short report (150–200 words) on your dictionary and the dictionaries you find, stating the advantages of each.

PRACTICING YOUR SKILLS

Continue to fill in the blanks in Andy Rooney's essay. Most of the time Rooney uses the simple present tense. In a few cases he uses the present perfect tense. Check your answers on page 433.

SPELLING

1   I _____ *have* _____ at least twenty words that I   have

_____ have looked _____ up ten times a year. I did not know   look

how to spell them in high school and I still do not.

    I _____ am _____ even nervous about some words   be

5 I should have mastered in grade school. I

_____ when to use "compliment" instead of   know

"complement," when to use "stationery" and not "stationary" and

"principle" not "principal," but I always _____   pause

just an instant to make sure.

10   You would _____ someone who   think

_____ a living all his life writing words on   make

paper would _____ how to spell everything. I   know

_____ not a bad enough speller to be   be

interesting, but there _____ still some words   be

15 I _____ up in the dictionary because I   look

_____ too embarrassed to ask anyone how   be

they _____ spelled. Probably, I   be

_____ up "embarrassed" nine times within the   look

last few years, and I often _____ to make   check

20 sure there _____ not two s's in "occasion."   be

"Occassion" _____ me as a more natural way   strike

to spell the word.

    Sometimes people _____ words that are   use

wrong because they _____ better than the   sound

25 right ones. I often _____ that. I would not   do

_____ of using the word "data" as a plural   think

word, which it _____. You would not   be

_____ me saying, "All the data are in" even   catch

though it _____ proper. I often   be

30 _____ myself using the word "hard" when I   find

should _____ writing "difficult." It   be

_____ hard to stick to the rules when the   be

rules _____ you sound more formal than you   make

_____ to be.   want

LOOKING AT SOUND AND SPELLING

A.   Look up the words *compliment* and *complement*, *stationery* and *stationary*, *principle* and *principal* in your dictionary and write their meanings. These pairs of words, called homophones, sound exactly the same but are spelled differently and have different meanings.

B.   In every language there are words that are pronounced the same but have different meanings and often different spellings. These words can be confusing to learners. Make your own list of words that sound the same but have different meanings. Look up each word in a dictionary and write a definition and any other information that will help you remember the differences in spelling and meaning.

C.   Learners may also be confused by words that sound almost the same like *fall* and *feel*, *live* and *leave*. Write down pairs of words that are difficult for you to distinguish. Check the pronunciation key in your dictionary for differences in pronunciation and/or have your teacher pronounce them for you.

USING MODALS

Expressing Possibility and Probability

Expressing Possibility: may, might, could, should

Examples	*Comments*
The phone is ringing. It *might be* my sister, or it *may be* a friend, or it *could* even *be* the woman I met last week.	*May*, *might*, and *could* + base are used to talk about possibilities in present or future time.

I'm not sure what I'm going to do this weekend. I *might go* to a movie, or I *might not*. I *may not have* the time.

The negative: *may not/might not* is used to express uncertainty.

It *couldn't* be my sister at the door. She's out of town.

The negative of *could*, however, expresses impossibility.*

It *may be* a friend.
Maybe it is a friend.

Maybe (one word) can be used to express the same meaning as *may* + base. Notice the difference in sentence construction.

PRACTICING YOUR SKILLS

A.   Make at least two guesses about each of the following situations. You are not certain about the truth, only expressing one of several possibilities. Use *may, might,* or *could, may not* or *might not* + the base form of the verb.

1.   One student is not in class yet.

She *might be* sick.

She *may come* to class later.

She *could be* on her way.

She *might not get* here on time.

She *may not come* at all.

2.   Someone in the class looks nervous.
3.   Someone in the class looks happy.
4.   Someone in the class looks tired.
5.   Someone in the class always wears blue.
6.   There is someone waiting at the door of the classroom.
7.   There is a long line at the cafeteria.
8.   There are a lot of people studying in the library this week.
9.   There is a lot of noise in the hallway.

B.   Use the situations from the previous exercise to talk about impossibility. Use *couldn't* + base.

She *couldn't be* very sick. I talked to her this morning.

Can't is also used to talk about impossibility.
   The car *can't* be out of gas. I just filled it.

▰▰▰▰▰▰ *Expressing Possibility in the Past:* may have, might have, could have

Examples	*Comments*
I can't find my keys. I *may have left* them in my coat pocket this morning.	*May have*, *might have*, and *could have* + past participle are used to talk about possibilities in the past.
My friend didn't call me. She *might have forgotten.*	
I don't know why I feel so bad. I *could have eaten* something for dinner last night that disagreed with me.	
That *might have been* the reason I am sick, or it *may not have been*. It's hard to know.	*May not have* and *might not have* express uncertainty.
They *couldn't have known* I was coming. I didn't tell anyone.	*Couldn't have* expresses impossibility.

PRACTICING YOUR SKILLS

Make two or more different guesses about what happened in the past to cause each of the following situations. Use *might have, may have, might not have, may not have*, or *could have* + past participle.

1. I haven't gotten a letter from my friend in a long time.

    She *may have been* too busy to write.
    She *might not have had* the time.
    The letter *could have been lost* in the mail.

2. Several people were late for class yesterday.
3. There was more traffic than usual on the expressway this morning.
4. The bookstore doesn't have enough copies of the textbook.
5. My watch is sometimes slow.
6. I didn't do as well as I thought I would on the test.

■■■■■■■ *Expressing Probability in the Present:* must + *base**

There are times when we are almost sure that something is true. We are not 100 percent certain, but all evidence points to a particular conclusion.

Examples	*Comments*
My car won't start. I left the lights on. The battery *must be* dead.	*Must* + base is used to make logical deductions about events in present time.
Dinner *must be* ready. I can smell the food.	
I *must have* the wrong number.	

PRACTICING YOUR SKILLS

A. Working with a partner, construct sentences stating a probable reason for each of these difficulties. Use *must* + base. Add additional sentences explaining your reasoning.

1. There is no sound on my portable radio.

The batteries *must be* dead. I haven't changed them in a long time.

2. The picture on my TV set is not good.
3. The ice cream in the freezer is melting.
4. My house plants are turning brown.
5. I can't open the door with this key.
6. It is hard to read anything typed on my typewriter. *when worn out*
7. My clothes don't look clean after I have washed them in the washing machine.

B. When something goes wrong with a machine or appliance, we usually look for the most probable cause of the difficulty. Often it is something very simple like a loose plug connection or batteries that need to be recharged.

To save people from bringing in products for unnecessary repairs, many products come with instructions about "troubleshooting." These instructions list the most probable cause of trouble first and then continue to list other causes.

Read the following instructions about what to do when a stereo receiver is not operating properly.

*Should or ought to is usually used to express a deduction or expectation about a future event. (See Chapter 6, page 206.)

In Case of Difficulty

If your unit should not perform as expected, consult the table below to see if the problem can be corrected before you ask your dealer or service representative for help.

Problem	Probable Causes	Advice
Power switch on but no sound	1. Cord not plugged in	1. Check plug contact.
	2. Poor connection at wall outlet or power outlet inactive	2. Check outlet using lamp or other appliance.
	3. Volume control set at lowest point	3. Adjust volume.
No sound from left or right	1. Speaker cords disconnected	1. Check speaker connections.
	2. Speakers switched off	2. Check speaker switch.
Sound from either left or right but not both	1. Poor speaker connections	1. Check connections at both ends of speaker cord.
	2. Defective speaker	2. Reverse speakers. If problem stays with same speaker, have speaker checked.
		3. Check setting of control.

Working with a partner, rephrase these directions using *must* + base to talk about probable causes in sequence. After you have eliminated the first possibility go on to the second. Use *couldn't* to talk about each possibility you have eliminated.

Example

The power switch is on but there is no sound. The power cord *must not be* plugged in.

It *couldn't be* the plug. I've just checked it. It *must be* the outlet.

■ *Expressing Probability in the Past:* must have

Sometimes we are almost sure that something has happened in the past. Although we are not 100 percent sure we are right, all the evidence seems to indicate a certain conclusion.

Examples	*Comment*
You wrote a really good essay. You *must have worked* hard on it.	*Must* + *have* + past participle is used to express probability in the past.
There is no gas in the car. My husband *must have forgotten* to fill the tank yesterday.	

PRACTICING YOUR SKILLS

Construct sentences about what probably happened in the past to cause each of the following events. Use *must* + *have* + past participle. If necessary, add information to explain your deduction.

1.   The ground is wet.

It *must have rained* last night.

2.   The couch is full of dog hair.
3.   The store on the corner has a new name.
4.   The kitchen is a mess.
5.   The book that I need is not in the library.
6.   My rear fender has a dent in it. It was OK this morning.

USING YOUR SKILLS

A.   People-watching: some people like to make a game out of watching strangers and making guesses about their lives. Imagine you are sitting in a restaurant with nothing much to do. Try to tell about the people at all the other tables. Give as many sentences as possible about each table. Use appropriate modals and other structures and explain your reasoning when necessary.

Table 1. Two women are sitting together. It's dinner time but one woman is eating only a small salad and drinking a diet soft drink.

She *must be* hungry. I would be.

She *might have had* a large lunch.

She *may be* on a diet, although she looks very thin.

She *may be* going to someone's house for dinner later.

She *may not have* enough money for a full dinner, but I don't think so because she is wearing nice clothes.

Table 2. The man is eating very quickly. He keeps looking at his watch. His companion seems irritated.

Table 3. A woman is sitting alone at a table, but the table is set for two. She has been sitting there for ten minutes, but she has not ordered yet. Every once in a while she looks toward the door. She seems anxious.

Table 4. A man and woman are sitting very close to each other. They are talking quietly. They don't seem to notice that the waiter standing near their table is ready to take their order.

Table 5. An older woman and a child are eating ice cream. The child is dressed in her best clothes. The woman is smiling. On the chair next to them is a package wrapped in silver paper with a ribbon.

B.   Look at the pictures of people talking on page 173. Who do you think they are? What is their relationship to one another? What do you think they are saying?

FINDING OUT ABOUT . . .

It as Subject: Time, Weather, Distance*

It is often used in sentences that tell about time, weather, or distance. In these sentences *it* has no meaning but exists to provide a subject for the sentence.**

Time

Examples	Comments
It's 12:30.	*It* is often used as a subject when talking about times, days, and dates.
It's half past twelve.	
It's Friday, the 13th of June.	
It's time for lunch.	

*Some other kinds of sentences that use *it* as a subject are explained in Chapter 7.

**Generally, all English sentences must have subjects. You cannot say, "Is cold and rainy."

■ *Weather, Climate, Temperature*

Examples

It's cold and rainy outside.
It's not usually this cold in April.
It's only a few degrees above freezing.

Comments

It is frequently used in sentences describing weather conditions.

■ *Distances*

Examples

It's about a mile.
It's not too far.
It's a 20-minute walk.

It takes just a few minutes to get there by car.

Comments

It is often used to talk about distances.

The expression *it takes* may be used to talk about the time needed to travel from one place to another.

PRACTICING YOUR SKILLS

A. Construct several sentences beginning with *it* that describe the present time, day, or date.

B. Construct several sentences describing the present time in your home town; in other places you know about.

C. Describe the current weather in several different ways. Is it typical of weather for this time of the year?

D. Describe typical weather conditions for several different times of the year in your home country.

E. Construct several sentences about distances between places you go to frequently—home, school, place of work. Tell how long it usually takes to get to each place.

F. Use the map on page 176 to construct several sentences about distances between major cities in the United States and Canada.

G. It takes between 2½ and 3 hours to fly nonstop from Chicago to Miami. A bus trip along major highways takes approximately 30 hours. Estimate how long it would take to travel between several of the major cities in North America by plane and by bus. If possible, obtain actual timetables and compare the times given with your estimates.

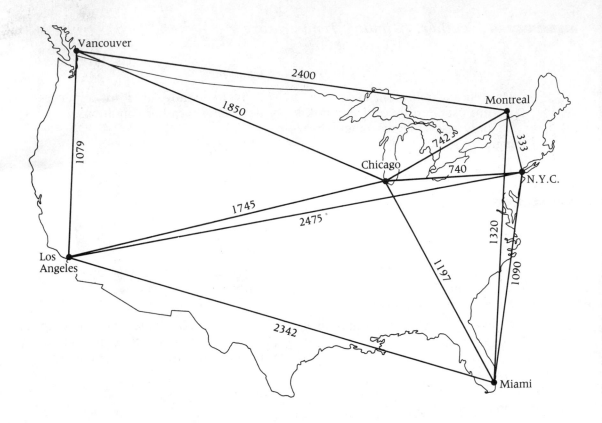

H. Imagine you are talking to someone who plans to visit your home country for the first time. Give as much information as you can about distances and travel times between major points of interest.

Frequency Words

A group of adverbs and other time expressions are used to tell how often something happens. Frequency words are often used with the simple present tense and other tenses that stress repeated action. They are not often used with progressive tenses.

It *usually* rains in the afternoon.

It rains in the afternoon *most of the time*.

COMMON FREQUENCY WORDS		
	Adverbs of Frequency	*Other Frequency Expressions*
100 percent	always	every time every day (week, etc.)
	almost always usually normally generally typically frequently	as a rule by and large most of the time in general
	sometimes occasionally	from time to time every so often (every) now and then once in a while
		once (twice, three times) a day (week, month, year)
	seldom* rarely* hardly ever* almost never*	
0 percent	never*	

■■■■■■ *Usual Position of Frequency Words in a Sentence*

Many frequency words and expressions can appear in more than one place in a sentence. However, some positions are more common than others. The guidelines below indicate the most common placements.

1. Adverbs of frequency with the simple present and simple past tenses.
    After *be*: It's *often* cold in the evening.

    Before other verbs: It *usually* rains in April.

Seldom, rarely, hardly ever, and *(almost) never* are already negative. Do not add another negative.
  It *seldom* snows in April. *Not*: It doesn't seldom snow.

2. Adverbs of frequency in sentences with auxiliary verbs.
After the first auxiliary:

It has *often* snowed in March.

3. Other frequency expressions are usually placed at the beginning or at the end of the sentence.

It's very cold in winter *most of the time.*
Most of the time it's very cold in winter.

Note: One position to avoid is between verb and object.

Not: ~~The TV tells us frequently the weather forecast.~~

DECEMBER 1987

	Average High	Low	Forecasted High	Low	Average Precipitation	Forecasted Precipitation
Atlanta	53	34	51	31	4.24	4.00
Boston	39	27	38	26	4.24	4.50
Chicago	35	20	38	24	2.10	2.00
Cincinnati	42	27	40	29	2.87	2.75
Dallas	59	37	59	37	1.82	1.75
Denver	46	19	48	21	0.43	1.20
Detroit	35	23	38	26	2.52	2.00
Honolulu	80	57	82	68	3.69	4.50
Las Vegas	57	34	58	33	0.39	1.50
Los Angeles	67	47	67	50	1.75	1.75
Miami	77	60	77	60	1.64	1.75
Minneapolis	27	12	29	15	0.87	0.75
Nashville	50	31	51	32	4.45	4.00
New Orleans	64	45	66	46	5.13	5.50
New York	41	28	40	26	3.60	3.60
Orlando	72	52	73	53	1.90	2.00
Phoenix	66	39	66	41	0.82	1.20
San Francisco	57	43	59	45	3.98	4.10
St. Louis	43	27	45	29	2.04	2.00
Washington, D.C.	45	30	43	30	3.04	3.30

ASK AND ANSWER

With a partner, look at the chart on page 178 and take turns asking and answering questions about typical weather conditions in American cities during the month of December. If you and your partner are from different parts of the world, continue asking and answering questions about the weather in your home countries.

USING YOUR SKILLS

In recent years North Americans have become more aware of the relationship between good nutrition and good health. Studies of American eating habits seemed to indicate that most Americans eat more fatty foods (butter, whole milk, red meat) than people in many other parts of the world. Many researchers are convinced that a high-fat diet puts people at a greater risk for heart disease and possibly for cancer.

The following is similar to a survey that thousands of people in the United States completed. Fill out the survey yourself and then, with your classmates, use it to talk and write about eating habits and health.

SURVEY OF EATING HABITS

In the average week, how often do you eat the following foods (every day, once, twice, three, four, five times a week, seldom, never)?

Beef _____once a week_____

Pork _____''_____

Chicken _____once a week_____

Ham _____once a month_____

Fish _____once two week_____

Frankfurters/sausage _____seldom_____

Spaghetti/macaroni/white rice _____once a week_____

Brown rice/whole wheat/barley, other unprocessed grains _____every day_____

Raw vegetables _____twice a week_____

Cooked vegetables _____every day_____

Fresh fruits/juices _____four times a week_____

Butter _____every day_____

Cheese _____5_____

Eggs _____once a week_____

How often do you eat fried foods? _____*seldom*_____

Fried eggs ___*once a week*___   Hamburgers ___*once a month*___

Fried chicken/fish ___*seldom*___   French fries ___*__ ___

Other fried foods ___*seldom*___

How many cups or glasses of the following beverages do you usually drink a day?

Whole milk ___*seldom*___   Skim milk ___*every day*___

Regular coffee ___*twice a month*___   Decaffeinated coffee ___*seldom*___

Regular tea ___*twice a month*___   Herbal or decaffeinated tea ___*seldom*___

Regular soft drinks ___*once a week*___   Diet soft drinks ___*seldom*___

Are there other foods that you eat often? _____

1.   How would you describe your own eating habits? Do you choose what you eat carefully, or do you eat whatever is put in front of you, or whatever is easiest or cheapest to prepare?
2.   Have you changed your eating habits in the last several years? If yes, when and for what reason?
3.   If you know about eating habits in two different countries, tell about each. Which is healthier? Which offers more choices? Which kind of food, in your opinion, tastes better?

Adverbs of Manner

Examples

She spoke *loudly*. (The adverb *loudly* tells how she spoke.)

She was *extremely* nervous when she had to speak in front of the class. (The adverb *extremely* tells how nervous she was.)

Comments

Many adverbs tell how an action is done. They modify the verb.

Adverbs can also modify adjectives like *nervous*.

■■■■■ *Position of Adverbs in a Sentence*

Although English sentences usually have a fairly fixed word order, adverbs are one part of speech that can be placed in many different parts of a sentence. However, there are some positions that are more common than others and other positions that are never used.

1. When there is no object, the adverb that tells how something is done often comes directly after the verb.

    She looked *nervously* around the room.
      S   V   ADV

    When there is an object, the adverb frequently comes after the object. It cannot come between the verb and its object.

    She memorized the lesson *perfectly*.
      S   V   O   ADV
    Not: ~~She memorized *perfectly* the lesson.~~

2. Other adverb positions tend to emphasize the adverb.

    End of sentence: She looked around the room *nervously*.

    Beginning of sentence: *Nervously*, she looked around the room.*

    After auxiliary: She is *nervously* looking at her notes.

    Before verb: She *nervously* tapped her feet.

CHECK YOURSELF

In all but one of the following sentences, the adverb is placed in an unnatural position—between the verb and its object. When necessary, correct the sentence by moving the adverb. Check your answers on page 433.

1. After each class, she did thoroughly each assignment.
2. The week before the test, she reviewed carefully all previous assignments.
3. The evening before the test, she studied briefly her notes.
4. She slept soundly the night before the exam.
5. She ate calmly a good breakfast.
6. She entered confidently the room.
7. Because she was so well prepared, she was able to answer rapidly most of the questions.

*Adverbs at the beginning of a sentence are more common in written than in spoken English.

USING YOUR SKILLS

Experiment with adding adverbs to each of the following sentences in positions marked by ˆ. All positions are possible, but some are used more frequently than others. With your class, take turns reading the different versions aloud. Discuss any variations in emphasis with your classmates and teacher.

1. ˆ She ˆ ran her fingers ˆ through her hair ˆ .   quickly
2. ˆ She ˆ tapped her foot ˆ .   nervously
3. ˆ She ˆ shifted her weight ˆ from one foot
to the other ˆ .   rapidly
4. ˆ She looked ˆ around the room ˆ .   shyly
5. ˆ She ˆ looked up ˆ and ˆ saw several of her friends
in the front row.   suddenly
6. ˆ She ˆ gained confidence ˆ in her ability to speak
to the crowd.   slowly
7. ˆ She ˆ looked ˆ out at her audience ˆ .   boldly
8. ˆ She ˆ delivered her speech ˆ .   confidently

▬▬▬▬ *Forming Adverbs*

1. Many adverbs can be formed simply by adding *-ly* to adjectives.

> *perfect* + *-ly* — perfectly
> *real* + *-ly* — really
> *complete* + *-ly* — completely
> *beautiful* + *-ly* — beautifully

2. Sometimes small spelling changes must be made before adding *-ly*. Drop the final *e* only for adjectives ending in *-able* or *-ible*.

> comfortable — comfortably
> responsible — responsibly
> also: true — truly, due — duly

y after a consonant is usually changed to *i*.

> happy — happily
> easy — easily
> but: shy — shyly

CHECK YOURSELF

Form adverbs by adding *-ly* to the following adjectives, making all necessary spelling changes. Check your answers on page 432.

Look in a dictionary or check with your teacher or classmates for the meanings of any unfamiliar words.

1.	aggressive	**8.**	courageous	**15.**	patient
2.	angry	**9.**	cynical	**16.**	sensitive
3.	arrogant	**10.**	generous	**17.**	shy
4.	audacious	**11.**	lazy	**18.**	sincere
5.	boastful	**12.**	mischievous	**19.**	skeptical
6.	capable	**13.**	naive	**20.**	thoughtful
7.	casual	**14.**	normal	**21.**	timid

PRACTICING YOUR SKILLS

Construct ten sentences using the adverbs from the previous exercise.

Distinguishing between Adverbs and Adjectives

Both adverbs and adjectives give additional information about other words in a sentence. Remember that adjectives tell about nouns or pronouns; adverbs usually tell about the verb or about another adjective. Adjectives, not adverbs, are used after linking verbs like *look*.

Adjective	*Adverb*
It was a *perfect* lesson. The lesson was *perfect*. (*Perfect* describes the lesson.)	I had memorized the lessons *perfectly*. (*Perfectly* describes how the lessons were memorized.)
The teachers looked *serious*. (*Serious* describes the teachers.)	The teachers talked *seriously*. (*Seriously* describes how they talked.)

CHECK YOURSELF

Choose the correct form—adjective or adverb. Check your answers on page 434.

1. She covered the paper (complete, completely) with black paint.
2. She was (complete, completely) silent during the first year of school.
3. Her (complete, completely) silence worried her teachers.
4. The teachers looked at her paintings (solemn, solemnly).
5. They looked (solemn, solemnly) when they discussed the problem with her parents.
6. Her parents listened to the teachers (careful, carefully).
7. They made a (serious, seriously) effort to understand but could not (complete, completely) understand what the teachers were saying.
8. When she finally spoke, she spoke in a (loud, loudly) voice.
9. She recited the lesson (loud, loudly).

■■■■■■■■ *More about Adjectives and Adverbs*

1. A few common words that end in *-ly* are adjectives, not adverbs: *friendly, lovely, lonely, deadly, cowardly, lively.*

   a *friendly* teacher   a *lovely* place   a *deadly* poison
      ADJ   ADJ   ADJ

2. A few common adverbs that do not end in *-ly* have the same form as their corresponding adjective.

Adjectives	*Adverbs*
a *fast* runner	He runs *fast*.
a *hard* worker	She worked *long* and *hard*.*
a *long* time	

3. *Well* can be either an adjective or an adverb. As an adverb, *well* corresponds in meaning with the adjective *good*.

   You are making *good* progress in English. You are working *well*.

   When *well* is used as an adjective, it means healthy.

   You look much better than you did last week. Are you completely *well* now?

*The adverb *hardly* means *almost not*.
  It was so noisy that I could hardly get to sleep.

CHECK YOURSELF

Choose the correct form. Check your answers on page 434.

1.   The (live, lively) child joked with her classmates.
2.   Some of the children were not (friend, friendly).
3.   She worked (hard, hardly) to memorize the lesson.
4.   (Surprising, Surprisingly) the teacher called on her younger sister first.
5.   After she recited the lesson (successful, successfully), she felt (good, well) about her achievement.
6.   When some people are (nervous, nervously), they are (silent, silently). Others speak very (quick, quickly) when they are (anxious, anxiously).

USING YOUR SKILLS

A.   Write or tell about yourself as a child. What were you like? What did you do? Use adverbs and adjectives to make your descriptions exact.
B.   What kind of person do you admire? What kind of person do you like to be with? Write or tell about the kind of person you would like to have as a friend. Explain as precisely as possible the personality and the behavior of this ideal friend.
C.   What kind of person do you disapprove of or dislike? Write or tell about the kind of person you would never choose as a friend.
D.   Describe yourself as a friend. What are your own best qualities? How does your behavior show those qualities?
E.   Write a short essay about an actual person you admire greatly. You may write about a political leader, artist, scientist, or other famous person, or about a friend or relative who is not well known. In your essay, describe as clearly as possible the qualities and actions that make this person admirable.

LITTLE WORDS

Prepositions of Time

In, on, at

in — before centuries, decades, years, seasons	in the twelfth century in 1126 in the 1990s in 1995 in the fall *also* in a day (week, month, etc.) in the past (present, future) in the morning (evening, afternoon) *but* at night
on — before days of the week and dates with numbers, holidays	on Friday on the 13th of May on May 13 on New Year's Day *also* on weekends, on vacation
at — before exact times	at 11:45 at noon (midnight, dawn, sunrise, sunset) *also* at present

CHECK YOURSELF

Fill in the blanks with the appropriate prepositions — *in*, *on*, or *at*. Check your answers on page 434.

1. _____ vacation, I like to play _____ the morning, sleep _____ the afternoon, and watch TV _____ night.
2. _____ weekdays I get up _____ 7:00, leave my house _____ 8:00, and break for lunch _____ noon. _____ Sundays and _____ the summer I sleep a little later.
3. According to my mother I was born _____ a Sunday _____ 3:20 _____ the morning _____ the 3rd of May.
4. My great-grandmother was born either _____ 1887 or 1888. I know she was born _____ the 1880s. My grandmother was born early _____ the 20th century, _____ November 7th, 1906.

USING YOUR SKILLS

1. Tell about your schedule on weekdays. On weekends and holidays. Pay attention to the use of *on*, *in*, and *at* and other prepositions.
2. Tell as much as you know about the day, date, and time you were born. Tell the exact or approximate day, date, and year and time some of your relatives were born.

▰▰▰▰ *Points to Remember: Prepositions of Time*

1. *Around* or *about* means "approximately" when used before time expressions.

    Europeans first began to use the decimal system *around (about)* 1100.

2. *By* means at or before a particular time.

    By 1600 almost everyone in Europe used the new system.

3. *Through* means for the entire duration of a time.

    She slept *through* the second act of the play and only woke up at intermission.

    Through includes the last time mentioned. *Up to*, *until*, and *till* do not.

    I was in my office *through* the lunch hour. (including the lunch hour.)
    I was in my office *until*, *up to* the lunch hour. (I left before lunch time.)

4.   *For* in a time expression usually means the entire period of time. *During* usually means part of a time.

I was on vacation *for* two weeks *during* the summer.

5.   *In time* means at or before the required time. *On time* means the exact time.

You should get to the airport *in time* to check your baggage. Do you expect the plane to arrive *on time*?

6.   Other time expressions using prepositions are listed below.

in a (little) while = soon

in no time = very soon

once *in* a while = intermittently

at once = immediately

for the time being = temporarily

from time to time = intermittently

from now *on* = beginning now and continuing

CHECK YOURSELF

A.   Select the correct preposition. Answers are found on page 434.

1.   If I finish my work _____by_____ (by, for) seven, I can meet you _____in time_____ (in time, on time) for the concert. It's scheduled (for, during) _____for_____ eight and it always starts _____on_____ (on time, in time).

2.   I slept _____through_____ (through, over) the alarm and didn't wake up _____to_____ (until, to) 10:00 A.M.

3.   I'll call you some time tonight. Will you be home _____around_____ (around, during) eight?

4.   My appointment is _____at_____ (at, on) 3:00, but I'll be a half hour late. I can't get there _____till_____ (till, at) 3:30.

5.   The office will be open _____for_____ (for, during) two hours in the evening _____during_____ (during, at) September.

6.   The doctor is not in his office now. Can you call back _____in a little while_____ (in a little while, at once)?

7.   We don't have enough room for everyone right now, but we will have more space next month. _____For the time being_____ (For the time being, From now on) the two of you will have to share a desk.

8.   I can't leave _____ *at once* _____ (at once, by now). Can you wait for a minute or two? I'll be finished with my work _____ *in no time* _____ (in no time, in time).

SENTENCE SENSE

Headline English: Sentence Pattern 5

Sentence Pattern 5   subject   + verb   + object   + object
                     Parents   give   babies   love.

Sentence Pattern 5 has two objects: a direct object (DO) like the one in Sentence Pattern 2 and an indirect object (IO).*
The indirect object can go first.

S(ubject)   V(erb)   IO   DO
OFFICE   FINDS   STUDENTS   JOBS.

Or the direct object can go first. In this case, the indirect object is preceded by either *to* or *for*.

S(ubject)   V(erb)   DO   IO
OFFICE   FINDS   JOBS   FOR   STUDENTS.

CHECK YOURSELF

A.   Listed below are several sentences that follow Pattern 5. Write each sentence in headline form and label parts. Check your answers on page 434.

1.   The placement office at the university gives the students a booklet about finding jobs in the computer industry.

OFFICE	GIVES	STUDENTS	BOOKLET
S	V	IO	DO

*The following verbs often have two objects: *bring, buy, cost, give, lend, make, offer, owe, pay, promise, send, show, tell, write.*

2.   A counselor in the placement office shows them several books about employment opportunities for computer science majors.

_____   _____   _____   _____

3.   A workshop teaches them several techniques useful in writing good résumés.

_____   _____   _____   _____

4.   The students write several large software companies on the West Coast a short letter asking for information about job opportunities.

_____   _____   _____   _____

5.   The student's friend lends her a magazine with several ads for computer programming jobs in California.

_____   _____   _____   _____

6.   At the beginning of their senior year, the students send software companies their résumés.

_____   _____   _____   _____

B.   Rewrite the sentences, reversing the order of the direct and indirect objects.

USING YOUR SKILLS

Expand the following headline sentences into the longest good sentence you can make by adding modifiers. You may change the tense of the verb.

1.   CANDIDATE PROMISES PEOPLE PROSPERITY.
2.   AGENCY FINDS JOBS FOR WORKERS.
3.   MILLIONAIRE GIVES MUSEUM PAINTING.
4.   GORBACHEV WRITES LETTER TO BUSH.
5.   OWNER BUYS PLAYER FOR TEAM.
6.   BANK LENDS CORPORATION MONEY.
7.   SENATE SENDS BILL TO HOUSE.
8.   DIRECTOR SHOWS FILM TO PUBLIC.

EXPANDING THE NOUN PHRASE

Phrases and Clauses That Modify Nouns

When groups of words (phrases or clauses) describe nouns, they are placed directly after the noun they modify. Single word modifiers almost always precede the nouns they modify. (See Chapter 2, page 86.)

| a | large | intelligent | sea | *mammal* | *with a reputation for friendliness* (prepositional phrase) |
| a | large | intelligent | sea | *mammal* | *that scientists study* (relative clause) |

Using Prepositional Phrases to Modify Nouns

Groups of words beginning with prepositions like *with*, *by*, *on*, *at*, and *about* are called prepositional phrases. They are often used to give further information about the person, place, thing, or idea represented by the noun.

	Noun	*Prepositional Phrase*
a	*mammal*	*with a large brain*
our	*table*	*in the center of the kitchen*
the	*student*	*from Korea*

PRACTICING YOUR SKILLS

In the following exercise, the modifiers for each noun have been scrambled. Put them in correct order. Then add a verb and any other words that are necessary to complete the sentence.

Example

table   / polished / with four slender legs / our / wooden /

Our polished wooden table with four slender legs is my mother's favorite piece of furniture.

Noun *Modifiers*

1. man / with a red beard / blue-eyed / thin / tall / Canadian / the /

The tall thin blue - eyed Canadian with a red beard

2. flowers / yellow / those / faded / in the vase / large /

those large yellow faded flower in the vase

3. jacket / velvet / blue / comfortable / with the tiny collar /

the Comfortable blue velvet jacket with the tiny collar

4. magazines / travel / glossy / new / with beautiful pictures / four /

Four glossy travel new magazines with ...

5. cousin / female / attractive / his / on his father's side of the family /

6. information / new / surprising / some / about the government's foreign policy /

USING YOUR SKILLS

Describe the following topics using both single-word modifiers and prepositional phrases.

1. a unique or unusual object you know
2. a fashionable piece of clothing (your own or one you have seen)
3. your favorite flower
4. someone with an unusual personality
5. a gesture
6. a favorite piece of music
7. a food you hate
8. your most unconventional idea

Using Relative Clauses to Modify Nouns

Relative clauses usually begin with a relative pronoun like *which, who,* or *that. Who* (and sometimes *that*) is used for humans; *which* and *that* are used for things.

	Noun	Relative Clause
a	*mammal*	*that has a reputation for friendliness*
the	*table*	*which stands in the middle of the room*
the	*student*	*who is wearing a red scarf*

PRACTICING YOUR SKILLS

In the following exercise, modifiers (including relative clauses) for each noun have been scrambled. Put them in correct order. Then add a verb and any other necessary words to form a complete sentence.

Example

table   / old / the / oak / that belongs to her mother / kitchen

The old oak kitchen table that belongs to her mother is the most interesting piece of furniture in the house.

Noun   *Modifiers*

1. woman   / who is wearing blue jeans / slender / dark / small / the /

_____

2. tree   / oak / gnarled / a / which stands in the middle of the garden / old /

_____

3. couple   / helpful / the / who live in the house next door / young /

_____

4. sister   / intelligent / his / young / who just graduated from medical school /

_____

5. lake   / blue / clear / that is near my childhood home / the /

_____

6. personality   / wonderful / her / optimistic / which encourages everyone /

_____

7. government   / popular / that was elected recently / the /

_____

USING YOUR SKILLS

Construct sentences describing several of the following, using single-word modifiers and relative clauses beginning with *who*, *which*, or *that*.

1.   an object that you usually have with you in your purse or pocket
2.   something that you are wearing today
3.   something that you usually see on your way to class
4.   the kind of person that you do not like to be with
5.   your favorite meal
6.   a personal quality you admire (intelligence, kindness . . .)

SUMMARY EXERCISES

A.   Write a paragraph giving as complete a description as possible of an object that you can see as you are writing. Fill your description with as many details as possible, even details most people would not notice. Imagine you are writing for someone who cannot see the size, shape, color, and texture or location of the object. Use words to try to make that person see what you can see. Use many different kinds of modifiers (single words, phrases, and clauses) in your paragraph.

B.   Write a paragraph giving as complete a description as possible of a person's face. Write about someone you can see, or have a photograph of, or know so well that you can picture his or her face in your mind. Write for someone who does not know the person. Think of painting a portrait in words. Make your reader see the person as you do.

CHECKING IT OVER

Reviewing Articles, Pronouns, and Capitalization

PRACTICING YOUR SKILLS

A.   In the first four paragraphs of Carol Levin's review of *Books that Made the Difference* by Gordon and Patricia Sabine that follows, the articles *a/an* and *the* have been replaced by blanks. Fill in the blanks with the appropriate article.

Check your answers on page 434. (In a few cases, your answer, though different from that of the author, may also be appropriate. Discuss these differences with your teacher and classmates.)

WHAT A DIFFERENCE A BOOK MAKES

1   "What book made _____*the*_____ greatest difference in your life?
What was that difference?"

Gordon Sabine, _____ journalism professor at Virginia
Polytechnic Institute, and his wife, Patricia, _____ English instructor
5   at _____ same college, spent _____ year traveling
around _____ country and asking some 1,400 famous and not-so-
famous Americans these questions. They found that _____ printed
word, far from being obsolete, can have _____ profound impact on
people's personal lives. Books can mark milestones of change and learning. They can
10   help people overcome obstacles, accept tragedy, and understand themselves.

In *Books that Made* _____ *Difference* (Shoe String Press),
_____ Sabines present excerpts from 200 of their interviews, which
were part of _____ project sponsored by _____
Center for _____ Book, part of _____ Library of
15   Congress.

B.   In the following paragraph, there are 27 missing capital letters. Supply them.
Check your answers on page 434. Note: If they are not the first word in a title,
articles and prepositions are not usually capitalized.

1   Of the 165 books cited, the *bible* got the most votes: 15. no other book came
close. Among the few books mentioned more than once were *the white company* by
arthur conan doyle, *markings* by dag hammarskjold, *the power of positive thinking* by
norman vincent peale, and *walden* by henry david thoreau. a few authors—among them
5   homer, aristotle, erich fromm—were named for more than one book.

C.   In the last two paragraphs there are 14 missing capital letters, 7 missing articles, and 3 missing personal pronouns or possessive determiners. Supply them.
Check your answers on page 434. In a few cases an answer that is different
from the one given may also be correct. Discuss these differences with your
teacher and classmates.

1   Other authors ranged from shakespeare to lawrence ferlinghetti, from dale
carnegie to virginia woolf, from benjamin spock to mark twain. almost no one in
_____ survey cited _____ current best-seller.

the sabines concluded that there was no way to predict which book would
5   make _____ difference to whom, at what ages, or in what kinds of
life situations. In fact, _____ say: "the reading experience is so
personal _____ borders on _____ intimate. And
in _____ time when identity increasingly is lost, _____
reading of books may remain as one of _____ few truly personal acts
10   left to _____."

USING YOUR SKILLS

Is there a book that has made a difference in your life? Write a short composition telling about the book and explaining why it is important to you. Or write a short review of a book you have read recently. Show why someone else should or should not read it.

Accuracy focus: Proofread your composition, paying special attention to capitalization, and the use of articles, pronouns, and possessive determiners.

CHAPTER 6

The Present Perfect Progressive Tense

Forming the Present Perfect Progressive Tense

The present perfect progressive tense is formed with the present tense of *have*, the past particle of *be* (been), and the present participle of the main verb (verb + *ing)*

Subject	have	been	Verb + -ing	Contracted Forms
She	has	been	writing.	She's been writing.
I	have	been	resting.	I've been resting.

Using the Present Perfect Progressive Tense

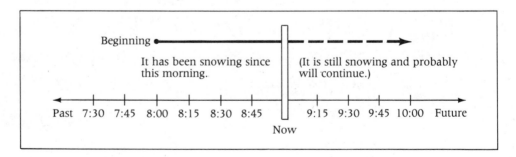

1. With action verbs, the present perfect progressive is the tense that is most often used to talk about activities that began at a particular time in the past and are still in progress. A time expression, usually beginning with *for* or *since*, is used to tell how long the activities have been in progress.

It *has been snowing* since this morning. (It is still snowing.)

We *have been driving* for several hours. (We are still in the car.)

With nonaction verbs such as *be* or *know*, the present perfect tense expresses the same idea. (See Chapter 5 and see also Chapter 2, pages 48–50, for a list of common nonaction — stative — verbs.)

He*'s been* my best friend since high school. (He still is.)

I *have known* about the problem for a long time. (I knew about it a long time ago, and I know about it now.)

2.   Two kinds of time expressions are used with the present perfect progressive or the present perfect to indicate how long the activity has lasted. *For* and *all* are used before expressions that describe the length of time. *Since* is used before time expressions that tell when the action began.

	Length of Time	*Beginning of Action*
I have been working	for five minutes	since 3:15
	for a couple of hours	since 12:00
	for a day	since yesterday
	for a week	since last Monday
	for two years	since I started college
	for several years	since 1985
	for a long time	since I was young
	all morning, all day	
	all week, all year	

PRACTICING YOUR SKILLS

A.   Complete the following sentences using time expressions beginning with *for*, *all*, or *since*. When you have finished, repeat the exercise using another time expression.
     While doing the exercise, note the use of the present perfect progressive with action verbs and the present perfect with nonaction verbs.

Example

They've been listening to the news since 6:00.
or
They've been listening to the news for twenty-five minutes.

	Starting Time	*Present Time*
1. They've been listening to the news	6:00	6:25
2. I've been going to the same dentist	last May	this May
3. He's been studying English	1987	19____

4. I've been trying to reach you on the phone 9:00 A.M. noon
5. I've been keeping a record of my expenses *for* January December
6. She's been waiting in line 3:00 3:44
7. It's been raining morning evening
8. The baby has been sleeping 4:00 5:30
9. I've been wearing the same clothes 8:00 A.M. midnight
10. I've been working on this project last year this year
11. I've been saving money for a car spring fall
12. I've known his family 1975 this year

B. Use the present perfect progressive (action verbs) or the present perfect (nonaction verbs) and either *for, all,* or *since* + time expression to talk about yourself or someone you know. You may change the times slightly.

Examples

I've been working part time for several months.

My brother has been in this country since January.

1. several months
2. January
3. I was a child
4. several days
5. yesterday

6. early this morning
7. a couple of hours
8. the class started
9. a long time
10. the summer before I moved

ASK AND ANSWER

With a partner, ask and answer the questions on the following topics. In your answers, use time expressions beginning with *for, all*, or *since.* If some of the questions do not apply to you or your partner, substitute others that do.

Example

Student A: How long have you been living in this country?

Student B: I've been living here for six months.
    or
    I've been living here since May.

How long have you been

1. live / in this country?
2. live / at your present address?
3. study / at this school?
4. major / in (field of study)
5. take / (name of a course)
6. work / as a (name of job)
7. work / at (place of employment)
8. drive / a car
9. play / (a sport)
10. play / (a musical instrument)
11. talk / with me

How long have you

12. know / (a person)
13. know / (how to do something)
14. like / (someone or something)
15. be / a student here

The Present Perfect Progressive Tense vs. The Present Perfect Tense

1. With action verbs, either tense can be used to express an action that began in the past and is in progress at the moment of speaking. The progressive form is more common.

   She*'s been teaching* for five years. (present perfect progressive)

   She *has taught* for five years. (present perfect)

   The meanings are similar, although the progressive tense emphasizes the fact that she will continue to teach in the future.

2. Do not use the progressive form with nonaction verbs.

   I *have known* how to drive since I was 16. (present perfect)

3. Use the present perfect progressive to ask and answer questions about the duration of an activity that is still in progress. (How long?) Use the present perfect to talk about quantities. (How many?)

How long *has* she *been teaching*? (present perfect progressive)
She*'s been teaching* for over ten years.

How many classes *has* she *taught*? (present perfect)
She*'s taught* at least 60 classes.

ASK AND ANSWER

With a partner, ask and answer questions beginning with How long? (present perfect progressive) and How many? (present perfect) for each of the activities listed.

Example

A: How long *have* you *been* reading?   A: How many pages *have* you *read*?

B: I*'ve been reading* for two hours /   B: I*'ve read* 80 pages.
     since 7:30 P.M.

	Activity	Quantity	Starting Time	Present Time
1.	reading	80 pages	7:30 P.M.	9:30 P.M.
2.	drive	150 miles	10:45 A.M.	1:50 P.M.
3.	bake	1 cake	3:15 P.M.	4:30 P.M.
4.	watch TV	3 programs	7:30 P.M.	9:30 P.M.
5.	play tennis	2 games	9:00 A.M.	9:20 A.M.
6.	type	6 pages	11:00 A.M.	noon
7.	do homework	3 exercises	6:15 P.M.	7:00 P.M.
8.	talk on the phone	3 phone calls	4:30 P.M.	5:30 P.M.

▬▬▬▬▬ *Using the Present Perfect Progressive without* for *or* since

The present perfect progressive is sometimes used with no time expression or with the words *recently* or *lately*. When used this way, it refers to activities that began in the recent past and are still in progress or will be repeated in the near future.

My husband *has been complaining* about his back. He should see a doctor.

Friends who have not seen one another for a while often begin a conversation with the expression, "What *have* you *been doing* lately?"

ASK AND ANSWER

1. Note the use of the present perfect and present perfect progressive tenses in the following dialogue.

    A: I *haven't seen* you in a while. What *have you been doing* lately?
    B: I*'ve been working* hard. I*'ve been studying* for my exams next month, and I*'ve been trying* to decide if I should apply to graduate school. How about you?
    A: Not much. I*'ve been doing* the same things I usually do. I*'ve been working* and *spending* a lot of time with my family, and I*'ve been playing* the guitar whenever I get a chance.

    With a partner, practice short conversations between two friends who have not seen each other for a while.

    A: What have you been doing?
    B: I _____ and _____. How about you?
    A: I _____ and _____.

Choosing the Present Perfect Progressive or the Present Perfect in Sentences *without* for or since

1. The present perfect progressive when used without *for* or *since* refers to an action that began recently and is still in progress or will resume in the near future.

    I*'ve been traveling* a lot recently. (present perfect progressive)

2.   The present perfect tense used without *for* or *since* usually refers to a completed activity (or series of activities) that happened any time before the present moment.

    Have you ever *traveled* in South America? (present perfect)

    Yes, I*'ve visited* Colombia, Argentina, and Brazil.

3.   When the present perfect is used with *just,* it refers to an activity completed in the very recent past.

    You*'ve* just *missed* the professor. (present perfect)

    She left a few minutes ago.

PRACTICING YOUR SKILLS

Fill in the blanks with either the present perfect or the present perfect progressive form of the verb given. In some cases, either choice is possible.

1.   Since I *(live)* _____ in this country, I *(have)* _____ many experiences, some good and some bad. One good thing is that I *(learn)* _____ to do many new things.

2.   This is the first time I _____ ever *(live)* _____ so far away from my parents.

3.   It is also the first time that I *(manage)* _____ all my own money. My parents *(send)* _____ me a small check every month, but I *(earn)* _____ most of my money myself.

4.   At first, I didn't know how to manage money, but for the past six months I *(keep)* _____ a record of all my expenses and *(pay)* _____ all my own bills. So far, I *(manage)* _____ to pay all my bills on time, and for the last three months I *(put)* _____ a few extra dollars into a savings account.

5.   When I first came, I lived with my aunt and uncle in order to save money, but I _____ just *(move)* _____ into a tiny apartment, which I share with a roommate. We *(work)* _____ hard to make our new place as attractive as possible. We *(clean)* _____ everything, and my roommate *(wax)* _____ the floors.

6. We *(buy neg.)* _____ much furniture yet. My aunt
    (lend) _____ us a few chairs, a small desk, and a kitchen
    table. We *(buy)* _____ a few pots and pans and shades for some
    of the windows that need them. A few of our friends *(give)* _____
    us small housewarming gifts like plants, posters, and coffee cups.

7. The hardest thing will be learning to cook our own food. Neither my
    roommate nor I *(do)* _____ much cooking in our lives. My aunt
    (offer) _____ to teach us to cook some foods from home. I
    (learn) _____ how to make some simple foods from an American
    cookbook a friend gave me. We *(make)* _____ a few simple
    meals for ourselves, although we *(have neg.)* _____ any
    guests for dinner yet.

CHECK YOURSELF

The following sentences adapted from student essays contain errors in the use
of the present perfect and present perfect progressive tenses. Correct each error
and, if possible, explain your correction. Check your answers on page 435.

1. What you have been doing lately?
2. When you try to open a bank account, they will ask you how long you are living
    at your present address.
3. My daughter has been watched soap operas for three hours.
4. I been trying to get a driver's license for a year.
5. Our family has been living in the same town since a hundred years.
6. I have been knowing my husband's parents since I was a child.
7. My mother have worked in my family's business since my youngest brother
    started school.
8. She has just been leaving.
9. Recently I be trying to speak English with my friends.
10. Have you ever been seeing the beautiful mountains in my country?

USING YOUR SKILLS

Write a letter to a good friend (or to yourself) in which you review what you
have been doing and thinking about for the past year. Emphasize your accomplishments, but also tell what you haven't achieved yet.

Accuracy focus: You should use a variety of tenses in your letter, but you will
probably use the present perfect and present perfect progressive several times.
Check all verb forms, especially those covered in Chapters 5 and 6.

USING MODALS

Expressing Expectation and Obligation: *should, ought to, be supposed to*

Expectation in Present or Future Time: should / ought to + base

Examples	*Comments*
She *should be* at home now. She usually doesn't leave for work until later. (meaning: She is probably home now.)	In these sentences, *should* or *ought to* expresses the expectation that something is true or will be true in the future.*
He *should be* here soon. He's not often late. (meaning: He will probably be here soon.)	
The incumbent *ought to* win the election. She's ahead in all the polls. (meaning: She is probably going to win.)	

PRACTICING YOUR SKILLS

Use *should* or *ought to* + base in the following sentences to talk about what will probably happen in the future.

1. My parents always call me on Sundays. They *(call)* _____ this evening.

---

*If you are certain something is going to happen in the future, use *will*. If you are not sure at all, use *might, may,* or *could.*

I *will graduate* this June. (I'm certain.)

I *should/ought to graduate* this June. (I'm 90% certain.)

I *may/might/could graduate* this June. (It's only a possibility.)

2. I've been doing well on all my math tests. I *(get)* _____ a good grade in the course.

3. The mail usually arrives before noon. It *(be)* _____ here soon.

4. The plane *(arrive)* _____ on time. It took off on schedule.

5. The movie *(start)* _____ soon. The newspaper said the next show was at 8:00.

6. The professor is in class now, but she *(return)* _____ to the office before her next class.

7. I *(get)* _____ a raise soon. I've been working in the office for six months now and have been doing good work.

8. My brother *(visit)* _____ me sometime next summer. He's made plans, and I think he has been saving money for his ticket.

9. I *(graduate)* _____ in two more years if I go to school in the summer.

Expectation in the Present or Future Time: be supposed to

Example	*Comment*
It's supposed to rain this afternoon.	*Be supposed to* has a meaning similar to *should* or *ought to*.

Be supposed to is often used when people talk about the weather forecast. Notice how *be supposed to* is used in the following dialogue.

A: Have you been listening to the weather forecast? What*'s it supposed to be* like later on today?

B: It*'s supposed to be* hot with a high temperature in the mid-80s. Then tonight *it's supposed to turn* cloudy, and it may rain. The weekend *is supposed to be* nice, though.

TOMORROW'S WEATHER

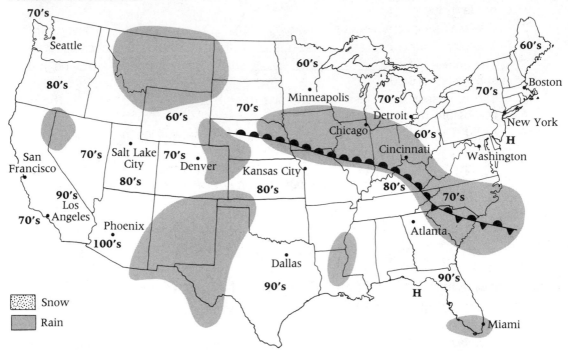

Snow

Rain

PRACTICING YOUR SKILLS

According to the map above,

1. Which cities are supposed to have weather in the 80s tomorrow? in the 70s? in the 60s?
2. Which city is supposed to be hotter tomorrow, Boston, or Minneapolis?
3. Is it supposed to rain in Chicago? How about San Francisco?
4. Is it supposed to snow anywhere?

ASK AND ANSWER

With a partner, ask and answer questions about the weather shown on the map. Note: If a local weather map is available, it may be substituted.

Should, ought to, be supposed to: *Advisability, Rules, and Customs**

Examples	*Comments*
Should I shake hands when I am introduced to someone?	*Should/ought to* and *be supposed to* are often used to talk about
You ought to call her Ms. Peters, not "Teacher."	rules and customs that can be interpreted in various ways. *Be supposed to* often suggests that
Children are supposed to be seen and not heard.	the "rules" are not always followed.

PRACTICING YOUR SKILLS

Construct several sentences explaining what people in your country *should*, *ought to*, *are supposed to* do when they greet a friend.

USING YOUR SKILLS

Miss Manners is the name used by Judith Martin, who writes a column on etiquette (polite behavior) that appears in many newspapers. In her column, Miss Manners answers letters from readers. Note: Miss Manners tries to be humorous as well as informative. She often writes tongue in cheek.

DEAR MISS MANNERS:

1   My parents did their best to impress good table manners upon me, but I refused to listen to their advice. Consequently, while I have pleased my parents in every other respect, my table manners are atrocious, slightly below the level of barbarian. I have just graduated from law school and I am terrified of going out to eat with associates and
5   clients.
    A list of my table etiquette faults could cover several pages, but I have questions about two situations that have occurred more than once.

   1.   Eating fish or chicken, small bones are found. Do I:
        a. chew them until they are ground fine, then swallow them?
10   b. hold a napkin to my mouth and spit them out?
        c. pick the bones out with my fingers?
        d. order steak and avoid the problem altogether?

*See also pages 103–105 for *should/ought to* to express advisability.

2. Cutting something, it will skitter off my plate and onto the floor. Do I:
a. pick the food off the floor and place it back on my plate?
15
b. pick the food off the floor and place it somewhere other than my plate, like an ashtray?
c. kick the food under the table leg so that nobody will notice it?
d. ignore it.

MISS MANNERS' ANSWERS

20 How often does food leap off your plate? Never mind. Miss Manners will endeavor to ignore it.

Question 1. It depends on the identity of the victim. Solution (a) applies to very small game birds and pickled herring; (b) applies to nothing; (c) applies to fish; (d) depends on who's paying.

25 Question 2. This depends on the scene of the crime and the likelihood of your being caught. Solution (a) is for dining in a private home, where you can contrive to make others believe that the only thing you dropped was your napkin; (b) depends on the size of the evidence (a grape could be placed in the ashtray but a corncob could not); (c) applies only to open-air eating; and (d) is passable in restaurants, although it would be

30 kinder to call the waiter's attention to the fact that there is a fish on the floor before he discovers this with the sole of his foot.

VOCABULARY

(to write or say something) tongue in cheek: not seriously
atrocious: very bad
skitter: move quickly

1. What do you think of Miss Manners' advice? Is it realistic? helpful? What advice would you give?

2. Rules about polite behavior at mealtime vary from country to country. For example: in some places it is good manners to accept food the first time it is offered; in other places a polite guest is supposed to refuse food the first time and wait until it is offered again.

Imagine a friend from another country has been invited to a rather formal dinner party in your country and has asked for your advice as an expert on etiquette. Your friend wants to be polite but does not know exactly what to do.
Your friend asks you,

Am I supposed to arrive exactly on time? A little late?

Am I supposed to bring a gift? What kind?

Is there any gift that is inappropriate?

Should I accept food the first time it is offered?

How should I refuse food I don't want without insulting my host?

Should I ask for a second helping?

What am I supposed to say when I leave?

Am I supposed to compliment the host on the food?

Give your best advice on these questions and add other information your friend needs to know. Remember, your friend is counting on you to help him or her to make a good impression.

Unfulfilled Expectation Referring to Past Events: should have, ought to have, was / were supposed to have

Examples	*Comments*
She *should have finished* her paper before she left, but she didn't have enough time.	*Should have, ought to have* are used with a past participle. They usually refer to events that were expected to happen in the past but *probably did not happen.*
The incumbent *ought to have won* the election. (The incumbent did not win.)	
The plane *was supposed to arrive* an hour ago, and it's still not here.	*Was / were supposed to* is followed by the base form. It indicates that the event *did not happen.*

PRACTICING YOUR SKILLS

Fill in the blanks with *should / ought to* + *have* + past participle or with *was/ were supposed to* + base. Remember that the event you are talking about probably did not happen.

1. The mail *(arrive)* _should have arrive_ by now; it's almost 2:00 P.M.
2. I haven't gotten a check from my parents yet. They *(send)* _should_ _____ it two weeks ago.
3. She didn't come for her appointment. She *(call)* _suppose_ _____ to cancel it.
4. We're almost out of gas. You *(fill)* _supposed_ _____ up the tank before we got on the highway.
5. My report is late. I *(start)* _suppo_ _____ it sooner.
6. Many classes are full by now. You *(wait neg.)* _shouldn't have to_ so long to register.

USING YOUR SKILLS

Most of us think that there are things we should have done but did not do. Tell about three or four unrealized expectations or obligations in your own life. If possible, tell why you didn't do what you expected to do.

FINDING OUT ABOUT . . .

The Passive Voice

Most sentences with objects can be written in either the active or the passive voice.

ACTIVE

Example

Many modern inventions *make* our lives more convenient.

Comments

The active and passive versions of a sentence usually have similar meanings but a different emphasis.

The active voice is more frequently used than the passive. It emphasizes the subject of the sentence and what that subject does.

PASSIVE

Example

Our lives *are made* more convenient by many modern inventions.

Comments

The passive voice emphasizes other parts of the sentence. It is likely to be used when an action is more important than who does it.

The passive voice is used frequently in academic and technical writing.

Looking at Active and Passive Sentences

Compare the active and passive sentences in the following example. The verb phrase in a passive sentence contains one more word than its active counterpart. A passive verb phrase always includes a past participle and some form of the verb *be*. The object of the active sentence becomes the subject of the passive sentence.

> *Active*
>
> She *answers* letters from readers.
>   s   v   o
>
> *Passive*
>
> Letters from readers *are answered*.
>   s   v
>
> When you want to say who did or caused the action use a "by phrase."
>
> Letters from readers are answered *by Miss Manners*.

PRACTICING YOUR SKILLS

First, identify each of the following sentences as active (A) or passive (P). Then change active sentences to passive and passive sentences to active. Include a "by phrase" in the passive sentence only if it contains new or important information. Do not change the tense of the sentence. (Teachers' note: since students have many things to remember in using the passive voice, it may be useful to do the exercise in both oral and written form.)

1. People use dictionaries to check spelling. *A*

   Dictionaries are used to check spelling.

2. Similar sounds are made by tiny babies all over the world. *P*

   Tiny babies all over the world make similar sounds.

3. Later, they learn the sounds and rhythms of their own language.
4. The sounds that are not part of their language are discarded.
5. People speak French and English in Canada.
6. The government prints all official documents in both languages.
7. In 1968 someone discovered large oil and gas reserves in Alaska.
8. People needed a way to transport the oil and gas to more populous areas of the United States.
9. People built a pipe line to transport the oil and gas.
10. People completed the 800-mile-long pipe line in 1977.

■■■■■■■■ *Using the Passive Voice*

The passive voice is often used in talking about writers, artists, performers, and the works they create or perform.

Examples

"Blowing in the Wind" was composed by Bob Dylan. It has been recorded by several well-known singers.

"Jewels" was choreographed by George Balanchine and was performed by the New York City Ballet. In the performance I saw, the principal role was danced by Suzanne Farrell.

For Whom the Bell Tolls was written by Ernest Hemingway in 1940. The paperback edition is published by Charles Scribner's Sons.

PRACTICING YOUR SKILLS

Try to match these famous 20th-century works and their creators. (Check your answers on page 435). Then use the information to construct full sentences using the passive voice.*

Example

"Mood Indigo" was composed and performed by Duke Ellington.

The Color Purple	composer and performer Duke Ellington
Robie House	painter Edward Hopper
"Appalachian Spring"	director Orson Welles
A Farewell to Arms	choreographer Jerome Robbins
Nighthawks	writer James Joyce
"Let It Be"	designer (architect) Frank Lloyd Wright
Citizen Kane	composer Aaron Copland
Ulysses	director Alfred Hitchcock
"Mood Indigo"	writer Alice Walker
"Fancy Free"	composers John Lennon and Paul McCartney
The 39 Steps	writer Ernest Hemingway

*Titles of books, plays, and films and paintings appear in italics in print: *A Farewell to Arms*. They should be underlined when handwritten or typed.

  A Farewell to Arms   *a Farewell to arms*

Names of shorter written works and musical and dance pieces are usually enclosed in quotations when they appear within a sentence.

  "Mood Indigo" is one of Ellington's most famous works.

USING YOUR SKILLS

A.   What are your favorite contemporary books, films, musical works, etc. ? Which works do you think will have lasting value? Construct several sentences about creative works using the names of their creators or performers. Use the passive voice.

B.   Chose one writer, artist, or performer that you admire and that you would like others in the class to know about. Write a paragraph or give a very short talk introducing that person's work to someone who is unfamiliar with it. Take care to explain why you think this work is important or enjoyable. Use both the active and passive voice.

PRACTICING YOUR SKILLS

The passive voice is often used to talk about scientific investigations, discoveries, and inventions.

Since 1901 the Nobel Foundation in Stockholm, Sweden, has awarded a yearly prize for outstanding achievement in physics, chemistry, and physiology or medicine. The following are among the scientists who have won the award.

Using the information from the list below, construct sentences in the passive voice about Nobel Prize winners and their achievements. If possible, add sentences about other scientists.

Examples

The X ray *was discovered* by William Roentgen.

Roentgen *was awarded* the first Nobel Prize in physics in 1901.

1901	(physics) William Roentgen	discovered the X ray
1903	(physics) Marie Curie	discovered the elements radium and polonium
1918	(physics) Max Planck	discovered the quantum theory
1921	(physics) Albert Einstein	originated the theory of relativity*
1922	(physics) Niels Bohr	investigated the structure of atoms
1932	(physics) Werner Heisenberg	created quantum mechanics
1945	(medicine) Alexander Fleming, Howard Florey, Ernest Chain	discovered penicillin
1962	(physiology) James D. Watson, Francis Crick	determined the structure of DNA
1971	(physics) Dennis Gabor	invented holography (a method of taking three-dimensional photographs using laser beams)

*Einstein actually received his award for another, less important discovery.

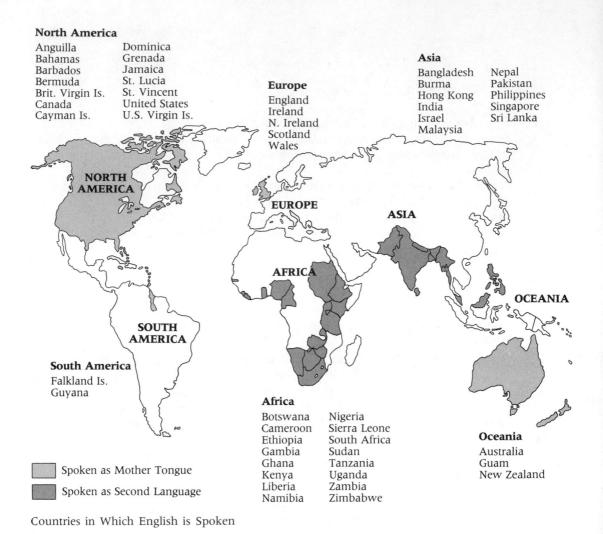

North America

Anguilla
Bahamas
Barbados
Bermuda
Brit. Virgin Is.
Canada
Cayman Is.

Dominica
Grenada
Jamaica
St. Lucia
St. Vincent
United States
U.S. Virgin Is.

Europe

England
Ireland
N. Ireland
Scotland
Wales

Asia

Bangladesh
Burma
Hong Kong
India
Israel
Malaysia

Nepal
Pakistan
Philippines
Singapore
Sri Lanka

South America

Falkland Is.
Guyana

Africa

Botswana
Cameroon
Ethiopia
Gambia
Ghana
Kenya
Liberia
Namibia

Nigeria
Sierra Leone
South Africa
Sudan
Tanzania
Uganda
Zambia
Zimbabwe

Oceania

Australia
Guam
New Zealand

Spoken as Mother Tongue

Spoken as Second Language

Countries in Which English is Spoken

USING YOUR SKILLS

Look in a reference work for information about someone who you believe has made an important contribution to science. Summarize your information in a paragraph or brief talk. Use both the active and passive voices.

ADDITIONAL PRACTICE: PASSIVE VOICE

A. Use the information given in the map above to construct sentences about where English is spoken as a first or second language.

Example

English is spoken in Australia.

B. Construct sentences naming some of the countries in which the following languages are spoken. Add languages you and your classmates speak. See page 435 for additional information.

Languages Spoken by over 100 Million People

Arabic	Japanese	Hindi	Russian
Bengali	Mandarin Chinese	German	Spanish
English	Portuguese		

Forming Passive Sentences with Auxiliaries

Look carefully at the active and passive versions of sentences with auxiliaries. Remember that the passive verb phrase always contains a form of the verb *be* and a past participle. Notice that *be* in the passive sentence is in the same tense as the verb of the active sentence.

Present Progressive

Active: The company *is making* a new product

Passive: A new product *is being made.* (by the company)

Future Time

Active: The company *will make* a new product.

Passive: A new product *will be made.*

Active: The company *is going to make* a new product.

Passive: A new product *is going to be made.*

Modal Auxiliaries

Active: The company *can make* a new product.

Passive: A new product *can be made.*

Active: The company *must make* a new product.

Passive: A new product *must be made.*

Modals with have

Active: The company *could have made* a new product.

Passive: A new product *could have been made.*

Present Perfect Tense

Active: The company   *had made*   a new product.

Passive: A new product   *has been made.*

The passive voice is not used with the present perfect progressive tense, the past perfect progressive tense (Chapter 8), or the future perfect progressive tense (Chapter 9).

PRACTICING YOUR SKILLS

Change most of the sentences in the following exercise to the passive voice. (Not every sentence can be changed.) Include a *"by* phrase" only when the subject of the active sentence is a proper noun or contains new or important information.

1.   Alfred Nobel invented the explosive, dynamite.

     The explosive, dynamite, was invented by Alfred Nobel.

2.   He became one of the richest men in the world. (Sentence has no object and cannot be made passive.)
3.   Two weeks before his death in 1896, he made his will.
4.   He wrote the will on a torn half sheet of paper.
5.   He could have left his money to relatives.
6.   However, he did not believe in inherited wealth.
7.   He wanted to use his fortune to reward persons whose work had contributed to the benefit of mankind.
8.   He may have wanted to ease his conscience about developing the deadly explosive.
9.   Nobel's will established the Nobel Foundation.
10. Since 1901, the foundation has awarded prizes to individual writers, scientists, and other persons who it believes have contributed to human welfare.
11. Since its inception, the foundation has awarded prizes in five fields: literature, physics, chemistry, medicine, and peace.
12. In 1968 it added a prize for economics.
13. Some years it cannot find a suitable person for each award.
14. In that case they do not give the award in that field.
15. Some of the Nobel Committee's awards have been controversial.
16. People have questioned the Nobel Committee's judgment.
17. Most people believe that they should have given Albert Einstein the award in 1914 for his work on the theory of relativity.
18. However, the committee ignored Einstein's contribution at that time.
19. Instead, they gave Einstein the award seven years later for a minor discovery.

20. The committee has nominated most of the best writers of the twentieth century for the literature award.

21. In some cases, the judges may not have selected the best nominee.*

22. In many cases, they have chosen a minor writer.

23. They have ignored a major one.

USING YOUR SKILLS

Practice writing out some active and some passive sentences from the preceding exercise to form paragraphs. Start the second paragraph with sentence 9, the third with 15. Compare your version with that of other students in the class. Decide which combination of active and passive sentences you like best.

■ *The Passive Voice in Sentences with Two Objects*

ACTIVE

Examples

The employment office *gives*
                       s   v
information to students about jobs.
    DO   IO

Comments

PASSIVE

Examples

Information about jobs *is given* to students by the employment office.

or

Students *are given* information about jobs by the employment office.

Comments

When the active sentence has both a direct and an indirect object (Pattern 5, page 189), the passive sentence can be formed in two different ways. Either object can become the subject of the passive sentence.

---

*Among the twentieth-century writers nominated but not selected for the Nobel Prize in literature are Leo Tolstoy, Anton Chekhov, Henrik Ibsen, Joseph Conrad, Mark Twain, Rainer Maria Rilke, Henry James, Bertolt Brecht, Marcel Proust, and Virginia Woolf.

PRACTICING YOUR SKILLS

The following sentences describe the standard procedure followed by the student placement office at a North American university. Almost all American universities maintain offices to help students find jobs after graduation.

Change the active sentences to passive ones. If the active sentence has both a direct and an indirect object, give both passive versions. Include the "*by* phrase" only when it contains new or important information.

1. The university employment office follows a standard procedure.

    A standard procedure is followed by the university's placement office.

2. Someone gives students an appointment with a counselor.

    Students are given an appointment with a counselor.

    An appointment with a counselor is given to students.

3. The counselor asks students about their interests and abilities.
4. The counselor shows them a list of job offerings.
5. The counselor gives the students details about the jobs that interest them.
6. They can ask additional questions about the salary and working conditions of each job.
7. The counselor will usually give students a brochure about preparing their resumé.
8. They should show a sample resumé to the counselor.
9. The counselor gives students advice about how to present themselves at the interview.
10. Someone in the office shows students a videotape about a typical job interview.
11. Prospective employers interview students.
12. Students complete job interviews.
13. Students should tell the placement office the results of their interviews.

USING YOUR SKILLS

A.   The passive voice is common when we talk about standard procedures in schools, offices, factories, and other institutions. For example, the passive voice might be used to explain registration to new students, or office routines or manufacturing processes to new employees. Since these procedures are similar no matter who performs them, the passive voice is appropriate.

Write a paragraph explaining a fixed procedure that you know well. Since the procedure will be similar no matter who performs the action, use the passive voice in many of your sentences.

B.   Look over some of the written work you have done for this class or other classes. When have you used the passive voice? Experiment with changing active sentences to passive sentences and passive sentences to active ones. What is the effect?

LITTLE WORDS

Prepositions of Manner, Agent, Instrument, and Purpose

Using by

1.   *By* can show ways of traveling: *by* car, *by* bus, *by* subway, *by* train, *by* plane (*by* air), *by* boat (but *on* foot).

The museum is a few miles away. You could get there *by* car, or I can give you directions on how to go *by* subway.

2.   *By* can be used to show ways of sending a message: *by* mail, *by* airmail (*by* air), *by* telegram, *by* telephone.

If you want to send a letter to another country, you had better send it *by* air. If you send it *by* surface mail, it will take several weeks.

3.   *By* can be used to show how something is made: *by* hand, *by* machine (also handmade, machine made).

Clothing, originally made *by* hand in the small villages in my country, is now made *by* machine.

4.   *By* can show the person who performs an action.

The song "This Land Is Your Land," written *by* Woody Guthrie and recorded *by* many folk singers, is one of my favorites.

PRACTICING YOUR SKILLS

A.   Name several places you have visited that you think other classmates would be interested in seeing. Include places that are nearby and places that are far away. Explain how to get to each of the places most quickly (most economically, most comfortably).

B.   What's the fastest (most economical, most convenient) way to send a message (a package) to someone in a nearby city? In a distant city? In another country? Discuss some alternatives.

C.   Do you own objects or clothes that are made *by* hand? Do you know anything about how they are made? If possible, bring a handmade object to class and talk about it.

D.   In your country, what products are made by hand? By machine?

████████████ *Using* with

1.   *With* can show the instrument or tool used to perform an action.

The early settlers made most of their furniture *by* hand, *with* simple tools. You can't open the front door *with* the back door key.

2.   *With* can show things that go together. *Without* has the opposite meaning.

Do you take coffee *with* cream or *without? With* your meal or after?

PRACTICING YOUR SKILLS

A.   Name several small tools that most people have in their house or car (a hammer, screwdriver, pair of pliers, an automobile jack) and tell what you can do with them.

B.   How many things can you think of to do with a brick? Of course you can build a wall. But you can also use it to hold down a stack of papers or to keep a door from closing. Can you think of some other common uses?

C.   How do you take your coffee? tea? salad? (with/without cream, sugar, dressing)?

 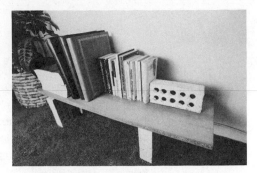

Using in, as, *and* for

1. *In* can show a technique or a material used to produce something.

    writing: *in* ink, *in* pencil, *in* capital letters, *in* italics
    painting: *in* oil, *in* watercolor
    sculpture: *in* clay, *in* wood, *in* bronze, *in* stone
    movies: *in* black and white, *in* color

    You can write the first draft of your essay *in* pencil, but the second must be written *in* ink.

2. *As* can show the job someone has, or the role an actor plays.

    During college I have worked *as* a waitress and *as* a clerk in a store.
    The film stars Laurence Olivier *as* Hamlet.

3. *For* can show the purpose of something or tell who benefits.

    My parents saved money *for* their children's education.
    They didn't buy many things *for* themselves.

CHECK YOURSELF

Fill in the blanks with an appropriate preposition. Check your answers on page 435.

1. Picasso, an extremely versatile and prolific artist, painted both _____ oil and _____ watercolor, and sculpted _____ clay and _____ plaster. Some of his sculpture was also cast _____ metal.

2. Of course, it's faster to travel from Chicago to the West Coast _____ air, but you see much more of the country _____ train or _____ bus.

3. The beautiful sweater I saw is made entirely _____ hand, but it costs much more than I can afford. Because most clothes are made _____ machine these days, handmade clothes are becoming more and more expensive.

4. Shall I order pizza _____ sausage, _____ mushrooms and green peppers, or _____ any extra ingredients?

5. I need to buy a present _____ my cousin's wedding, and a small gift _____ my nephew's birthday. If I have any money left, I'll buy something new _____ myself.

6. If your package has to get there fast, you'd better send it _____ air, or even _____ express mail. If you send it _____ surface mail, it might take a week.

7. My brother worked part-time _____ a stock clerk and _____ a night watchman to help pay for his education.

8. Most of the Beatles' songs have been recorded _____ other artists, but I still like the originals, sung _____ Lennon and McCartney.

9. It's faster to make a bookcase _____ power tools, but it can be more satisfying to work _____ an ordinary saw, hammer, and nails.

10. Although many people remember Sean Connery _____ James Bond, the role has been played _____ several different actors.

SENTENCE SENSE

Headline English: Sentence Pattern 6

Sentence Pattern 6

Subject	+ verb	+ object	+ complement (noun or adjective)
PARENTS	CONSIDER	BABIES	GENIUSES.
PARENTS	CONSIDER	BABIES	WONDERFUL.

Pattern 6 has a subject, a verb, and an object, like sentence Pattern 2. However, Pattern 6 needs either a noun or an adjective to complete the sentence.

Below are some examples of Pattern 6 with noun complements.

S(ubject)	V(erb)	O(bject)	N(oun) C(omplement)
PARENTS	CALL	DAUGHTER	ELIZABETH.
FRIENDS	CALL	HER	LIZ.
PEOPLE	ELECT	HIM	PRESIDENT.

Below are examples of Pattern 6 with adjective complements.

S(ubject)	V(erb)	O(bject)	A(djective) C(omplement)
THEY	CONSIDER	HIM	FOOLISH.
IT	MAKES	HER	SAD.
SHE	FINDS	HIM	INTERESTING.

CHECK YOURSELF

Find the subject, verb, object, and complement (noun or adjective) in each of the following sentences. Write in headline form, labeling the parts. Note: In the United States, the president appoints ambassadors but the Senate must approve them. Check your answers on page 435.

1. The president considers several people qualified for the position of ambassador to an important South American country.

PRESIDENT	CONSIDERS	PEOPLE	QUALIFIED.
S	V	O	ADJ. C

2. After a long deliberation, he appoints the former governor of a large western state ambassador.

   _____   _____   _____   _____

3. Several senators call the appointment of a man without experience in foreign affairs unwise.

   _____   _____   _____   _____

4. Some people from the opposition party call the president's selection a mistake.

   _____   _____   _____   _____

5. On the other hand, several important leaders from the president's own party consider the choice excellent.

   _____   _____   _____   _____

USING YOUR SKILLS

Expand the following headlines. You may change the tense of the verb.

1. PEOPLE ELECT HIM GOVERNOR.
2. CRITICS CONSIDER MOVIE SUCCESS.
3. JUDGE BELIEVES DEFENDANT HONEST.
4. JURY FINDS DEFENDANT GUILTY.
5. POLLS CALL INCUMBENT WINNER.
6. REPORTER CALLS MAYOR THIEF.
7. MAYOR CALLS REPORTER LIAR.
8. LOTTERY MAKES MAN RICH.

CHECKING IT OVER

Reviewing Sentence Patterns

CHECK YOURSELF

Identify the pattern to which each of the following sentences belongs. Write in headline form and identify each part. Check your answers on pages 435, 436.

1. S(ubject)	+ V(erb)		BABIES CRY.
2. S(ubject)	+ V(erb)	+ O(bject)	BABIES MAKE SOUNDS.
3. S(ubject)	+ V(erb)	+ N(oun) C(omplement)	BABIES ARE PEOPLE.
4. S(ubject)	+ V(erb)	+ Adj. (C)omplement	BABIES ARE CUTE.
5. S(ubject)	+ V(erb)	+ O(bject) + O(bject)	PARENTS GIVE BABIES LOVE.
6. S(ubject)	+ V(erb)	+ O(bject) C(omplement)	PARENTS CONSIDER BABIES GENIUSES.

or

PARENTS CONSIDER BABIES WONDERFUL.

1. In the first six months of life, the average healthy baby grows very rapidly both physically and mentally.

    <u>*BABY*</u>   <u>*GROWS*</u>   Pattern   <u>   1   </u>

        S   V

2. A huge fire of unknown origin destroys several historic government buildings.

    _____   _____   _____ Pattern _____

3. Every year thousands of people from all over the world arrive at the world's busiest airport on the northwest side of Chicago.

    _____   _____ Pattern _____

4. A cardiologist is a doctor who specializes in treating diseases of the heart.

    _____   _____   _____ Pattern _____

5. The university gives all students entering their sophomore year a ten-page booklet explaining the requirements for declaring a major.

    _____ _____ _____ _____ Pattern _____

6. In many parts of the world, people speak more than one language in their daily lives.

    _____   _____   _____ Pattern _____

7. The girl standing in the corner with her friend seems unhappy about something.

    _____   _____   _____ Pattern _____

8. Her uncle, who has always been one of her favorite relatives, lends her some money for tuition every fall.

    _____ _____ _____ _____ Pattern _____

9. The jury, after long deliberation, finds the defendant guilty of most of the charges against her.

    _____ _____ _____ _____ Pattern _____

10. Despite injuries to three players, several changes of management, and lukewarm support from previously loyal fans, the home team remains the winner in the final contest.

    _____   _____   _____ Pattern _____

11. With 90 percent of the votes counted, the major networks declare the incumbent the loser.

    _____ _____ _____ _____ Pattern _____

12. On today's episode of one of the most popular soap operas of the season, the angry young woman, with clenched teeth and a determined look in her eyes, tears the mysterious letter into tiny pieces.

    _____   _____   _____ Pattern _____

13. The ability of the average baby to understand a large number of words and sentences increases a great deal during the second year of life.

    _____   _____ Pattern _____

Reviewing Tenses

PRACTICING YOUR SKILLS

In the following paragraph from an article "Fear of Dearth" in the *Saturday Review* written in the simple present tense, the author Carll Tucker talks about something he does every day but hates to do.

1   I hate jogging. Every dawn as I thud around New York City's Central Park reservoir, I am reminded of how much I hate it. It's so tedious. Some claim jogging is thought conducive; others insist the scenery relieves the monotony. For me, the pace is wrong for contemplation of either ideas or vistas. While jogging, all I can think about is jog-
5   ging — or nothing. One advantage of jogging around a reservoir is that there's no dry shortcut home.

A.   Imagine the author's doctor has just told him to begin jogging every morning. He has never gotten much exercise before and is sure that he will hate jogging. Change the paragraph to talk about the future. Begin, "I know that I *will hate* jogging. Every dawn I *will thud* around New York City's Central Park reservoir . . ."

B.   Now imagine that the author has tried jogging for three weeks. From that time until the present his attitude has not changed. He has hated every moment. Change the paragraph to focus on the time between when the author begins to jog and the moment of writing. Use the present perfect for nonaction verbs and the present perfect progressive for action verbs. Begin, "I *have hated* jogging for three weeks. Every dawn as I *have been thudding* around New York City's Central Park reservoir . . ."

C.   Now imagine that after several months the author has given up jogging and is now getting his exercise by bicycling. He is writing about his past experience. Change the paragraph one more time, this time using the simple past tense. Begin, "For six months I *jogged* every morning and hated it. Every dawn as I *thudded* around New York City's Central Park reservoir . . ."

Check your answers for A., B., and C. on page 436.

VOCABULARY

jogging: running slowly
thud: make a heavy sound
thought conducive: encouraging thoughts
reservoir: man-made lake used to maintain the water supply for a community

USING YOUR SKILLS

Write or talk about an activity you hated at first but later came to enjoy. What brought about the change? Did the activity change, or your attitude, or both? Explain, being careful to make time relationships clear through your use of tenses.

Reviewing Articles and Prepositions

A. In the following paragraph by Robert Capon, from *Capon on Cooking*, the articles *a/an* and *the* have been removed. Supply them. If no article is necessary, write ∅. Check your answers on page 436. Note: In some cases an answer that is not the same as the original may still be correct. Discuss any differences with your teacher or classmates.

1 It is _____ ultimate kitchen gadget. It serves as _____ juicer for lemons, oranges, and and _____ grapefruit, and as _____ combination seed remover and pulp crusher for _____ tomatoes. It functions as _____ bowl scraper, _____ egg separator, and _____ remover of unwelcome particles— _____ stray bit of eggshell, _____ odd

5 grain of black rice—from _____ mixing bowl or saucepan. It is _____ thermometer capable of gauging temperatures up to 500 degrees Fahrenheit and, in addition, is _____ measuring device for _____ dry ingredients in amounts from 1 tablespoon down to ⅛ teaspoon or less, and for whatever liquids may be called for in _____ cooking of grains and stocks. It can be used as tongs for removing hot cup

10 custards from _____ oven, as _____ mixer of _____ water into pastry dough, and as _____ kneader of bread. Best of all, it cleans up in a trice, presents no storage problems, will not chip, rust, or tarnish, and, if it cannot be said to be unlosable or indestructible, it nevertheless comes with _____ lifetime guarantee to remain _____ one household convenience you will have the least desire either to lose or to destroy. It is,

15 of course, _____ human hand.

B. This time several of the prepositions in the paragraph have been omitted. Supply them. Check your answers against the original. Note: In a few cases a preposition other than the one used by the author could be used without changing the meaning. Discuss any substitutions with your teacher and classmates.

1 It is the ultimate kitchen gadget. It serves _____ a juicer _____ lemons, oranges, and grapefruit, and _____ a combination seed remover and pulp crusher _____

tomatoes. It functions _____ a bowl scraper, an egg separator, and a remover
_____ unwelcome particles—the stray bit of eggshell, the odd grain of black
5 rice—from mixing bowl or saucepan. It is a thermometer capable of gauging
temperatures _____ _____ 500 degrees Fahrenheit and, in addition, is a measuring
device _____ dry ingredients in amounts _____ 1 tablespoon _____ _____ ⅛ teaspoon
or less, and _____ whatever liquids may be called for _____ the cooking of grains
and stocks. It can be used _____ tongs _____ removing hot cup custards _____
10 the oven, _____ a mixer _____ water _____ pastry dough, and _____ a kneader
_____ bread. Best of all, it cleans up in a trice, presents no storage problems, will not
chip, rust, or tarnish, and, if it cannot be said to be unlosable or indestructible, it
nevertheless comes with a lifetime guarantee to remain the one household
convenience you will have the least desire either to lose or to destroy. It is, of course,
15 the human hand.

VOCABULARY

gadget: a small tool or machine useful for some relatively unimportant task
gauging: estimating
in a trice: instantly

CHAPTER 7

The Past Progressive Tense

Forming the Past Progressive Tense

The past progressive tense is formed with the past tense of *be* (*was/were*) + verb + *-ing*.

Subject	was/were	*Verb* + -ing	
She	was	writing	when the phone rang.
They	were	watching	TV.

Using the Past Progressive Tense

1. The past progressive tense without a reference to another time or action is sometimes used to set the scene or show the mood in a descriptive or narrative paragraph.

   It *was raining.* The wind *was blowing* hard. The trees *were shaking,* and the leaves *were falling* to the ground.

2. The past progressive expresses an action in progress at a particular time in the past or in progress when another shorter action took place. The simple past tense is used for the shorter action. The time expression *when* (meaning "at that time") or *while* (meaning "during that time") helps show the relationship between the two events.*

Action in Progress (Past Progressive)	*Particular Time or Action*
(7:15–9:05)	(9:00)
She was writing	at nine o'clock.
While she was writing	she heard us shout.

*When can also be used before the shorter action.
   She was writing *when* she heard us shout.

While is generally only used before the part of the sentence expressing the longer action or one of two simultaneous actions.
   not: She was writing while she heard us shout.

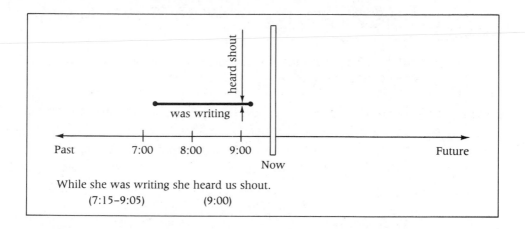

While she was writing she heard us shout.
    (7:15–9:05)   (9:00)

3. The past progressive can be used in both parts of a sentence to show two actions in progress at the same time or overlapping times. The time expression *while* (meaning "during that time") is generally used to show the relationship between simultaneous or overlapping actions.

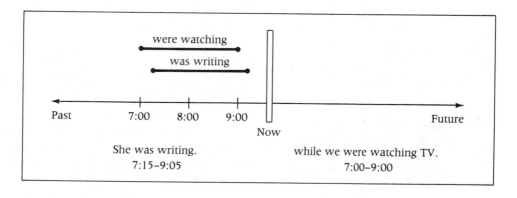

She was writing.   while we were watching TV.
7:15–9:05   7:00–9:00

4. Remember that nonaction verbs such as *be, seem,* and *know* are not generally used with progressive tenses. Use the simple past instead.

correct: She seemed tired.
not: ~~She was seeming tired.~~

PRACTICING YOUR SKILLS

A.   Fill in the blanks using the past progressive wherever possible. If the past progressive cannot be used, use the simple past.

Last night I *(have)* _____ an unusual experience. I had a date with a friend who lives near my office. I *(work)* _____ late, and it *(be)* _____ almost dark when I *(leave)* _____ my office. The wind *(blow)* _____ hard. In the twilight, every-

5   thing *(seem)* _____ strange and beautiful. The streets *(glisten)* _____ in the rain.

While I *(walk)* _____ down the street, I *(think)* _____ about how beautiful everything *(look)* _____. I *(notice neg.)* _____ where I *(go)*_____. Al-

10   though I couldn't have been far from my friend's house, I *(realize)* _____ that I *(be)* _____ on an unfamiliar street. My friend *(wait)* _____ for me, but I couldn't find a phone to call her and ask directions. While I *(think)* _____ about what to do next, I *(hear)* _____ a strange noise.

B.   What do you think happened next? Complete the story in your own words. Be careful to use appropriate verb tenses.

C.   Using the information given in the chart on page 235, construct sentences using the past progressive and simple past tenses to tell what happened.

Example

Last night my sister and I *were watching* TV while one of my roommates *was typing* her term paper in the other room. While *we were watching* the end of our favorite sitcom, my sister *smelled smoke.*

D.   Use the sentences you have constructed to write a narrative telling about the fire. Add whatever details you need to make the story clearer and more interesting. Add your own ending to the story.

Accuracy focus: Check verb forms, especially the use of the simple past and past progressive tenses.

Time	Subject	Action
7:00–9:00	my sister and I *were*	watch / TV
7:15–9:08	one roommate	type / a term paper
6:00–10:00	other roommate	study / in library
8:59	sister	smell / smoke
9:00	I *smelled*	check / our kitchen
9:03	both of us	smell / smoke again
9:05	my sister	look / in the hall
9:05	my sister and I	see / smoke coming from the upstairs hall
9:06	I *shouted*	shout / fire
9:10	we *left*	leave / our apartment
9:10–9:15	my roommate and I *were*	try / to alert the neighbors
9:10–9:12	*from* my sister *called*	call / the fire department
9:15–9:25	all of us *were waiting*	wait / for the fire department
9:24	we *heard*	hear the / fire siren
9:30–9:40	the firemen *was trying*	try / to put out fire
9:30–9:45	we *were watching*	watch / from a safe distance

USING YOUR SKILLS

Most of us have been witness to sudden or unusual events such as fires, storms, or minor accidents. Tell or write your own story about such an event. What were you and others doing when the event took place? The incident you describe does not have to be an important one. Minor events can make good stories when they are told in an interesting way.

The Habitual Past Tense: *used to, would*

Used to and *would* both express repeated actions in the past.

Forming the Habitual Past Tense: used to

Subject	used to	*Base*	
She	used to	write	with a pen or pencil.
I	used to	smoke,	but I've managed to quit.
They	used to	be	my friends. (We're not friends now.)

Using the Habitual Past Tense

Used to + base expresses repeated actions, continuous states, or situations that existed in the past but are different now.

I used to smoke. (I don't smoke now.)

I used to live with my parents. (I don't live with them now.)

I never used to have many American friends. (I have several American friends now.)

Do not confuse the habitual past (*used to* + base) with *be used to* + (verb +*-ing*) (see page 382).

Examples	*Comments*
I *used to write* all my papers in long-hand.	Meaning: That is what I did in the past, but I do not do it now.
I *am used to writing* all my papers in longhand.	Meaning: That is what I do now, and I am accustomed to it.

PRACTICING YOUR SKILLS

Six years ago, Young He left the small town in Korea where she was born in order to study in a large American university. Although many of her values are the same now as they were before, other parts of her life have changed a great deal. Below is a list of some of the differences.

In My Home Town	*In Boston*
lived with my parents	live with my husband and baby
never cooked meals	my husband and I cook
wore uniform in school	like to buy clothes
never had a job	have a part-time job
walked or rode bicycle	drive or take bus
saw my cousins frequently	write to my cousins once a month
was shy with strangers	am less shy
ate only Korean food	eat Korean and other foods
never ate spaghetti or pizza	love spaghetti and pizza
didn't drink coffee	drink two cups of coffee at breakfast
parents gave me allowance	have my own checking account
didn't believe women should work after marriage	like working as an accountant
spoke English only in class	speak English most of the time
walked for exercise	jog and lift weights for exercise

Construct sentences telling what Young He used to do and what she does now.

Example

She *used to live* with her parents; now she lives with her husband and baby.

USING YOUR SKILLS

A. Alone or with a partner ask, How has your own life changed? Are there many things you used to do but do not do now? Are there things you never used to do in the past but do now? Tell the class or your partner about some things you used to do when you were younger; when you were living somewhere else; when you had different habits, beliefs, or values. Add details to explain the change.

B. Write about something you used to believe and no longer believe. Tell when and why your ideas have changed.

▬▬▬▬ *Forming the Habitual Past:* would

Subject	would	Base	
She	would	write	letters every day.
My parents	would	tell	me about our family's traditions all the time.

▬▬▬▬ *Using the Habitual Past:* would

1. *Would* + base can be used to talk about repeated actions in the past. When used this way, *would* has the same meaning as *used to* + base.

    When she was younger she *would write* in her diary each night.

Or

    When she was younger she *used to write* in her diary each night.

2. *Would* + base cannot be used to talk about continuous states or situations in the past. Use *used to.*

    Salaries *used to be* lower when my father was young.
    Not: ~~Salaries *would be* lower when my father was young.~~
    We used to live in the country when I was a child.
    Not: ~~We would live in the country when I was a child.~~

PRACTICING YOUR SKILLS

Use *would* + base whenever possible to fill in the blanks. Otherwise use *used to.*

1. When I was a child we *(live)* ____used to live____ on a farm. My parents *(work)* ____would work____ hard all summer and all the children *(help)* _____. There was much less to do in the winter, so during the long winter evenings we *(sit)* _____ around the fire, and my father *(read)* _____ to us.

2. I *(live)* _____ with my grandparents. My grandmother *(tell)* _____ me stories about ghosts that lived in the mountains. I *(believe)* _____ her. Every time I *(go)* _____

near the mountains I *(be)* _____ afraid that a ghost *(catch)* _____ me.

3. I *(love)* _____ butterflies. Whenever I could, I *(chase)* _____ after them. Sometimes I *(follow)* _____ them so far that I *(get)* _____ lost.

4. In my grandmother's time, all the women in my village *(wash)* _____ clothes in the river. They *(meet)* _____ and gossip. Now everyone has a washing machine.

5. When my daughter was young, she *(want)* _____ me to read her the same stories over and over again. Then she *(pretend)* _____ to read them herself, but she _____ really *(read neg.)* _____ them. She knew them by heart.

6. When I was a child, I *(sit)* _____ for hours staring at the clouds. My parents *(ask)* _____ me to stop. They _____ often *(say)* _____, "He's a dreamer. He'll never amount to anything."

7. When I was small, I _____ always *(put)* _____ large amounts of food on my plate and *(finish neg.)* _____ it. My father _____ always *(say)* _____, "Your eyes are bigger than your stomach." He *(force)* _____ me to finish everything on my plate before I got any dessert.

USING YOUR SKILLS

A. Do you have a story to tell about your childhood? Tell or write it. Use the habitual past — *would* or *used to* — when appropriate.

B. What did your parents say to you when you were young? When did they say it? Do you think it helped you or not?

Past Intentions: *was/were going to*

Subject	was/were	going to	Base	
She	was	going to	clean	her room before she left.
I	was	going to	call	you earlier.
We	were	going to	take	a vacation last month.

■■■■■■■■ *Using* was/were going to

Was/were going to + base is used to talk about intentions or plans made in the past. Statements with *was/were going to* usually imply that plans were never carried out.

For example, when a student tells a teacher, "I *was going to hand in* my work this morning," the student usually means that the work was not done, only planned.

PRACTICING YOUR SKILLS

In each of the following situations, an event was planned but the plans were never carried through. Repeat the cue and add a plausible reason why the event never took place.

Example

I was going to call you earlier, but I was so busy at work this morning I couldn't find the time.

1. I was going to get you a present for your birthday, but . . .
2. My friend and I were going to study harder this term, but . . .
3. My family was going to visit me this summer, but . . .
4. I was going to proofread my essay before I handed it in, but . . .
5. We were going to clean the refrigerator yesterday afternoon, but . . .
6. My roommate and I weren't going to stop studying so soon, but . . .
7. I was going to do my laundry this morning, but . . .
8. I wasn't going to buy any new clothes until I had saved some more money, but . . .
9. I was going to apologize to my sister when I saw her, but . . .
10. My husband and I weren't going to buy a new car until next year, but . . .

USING YOUR SKILLS

Construct several sentences about what you were going to do but didn't do. Give additional details and tell why you didn't carry out your plans.

Past Necessity: *had to*

Examples	Comments
My grandmother *had to make* all the family's clothes by hand. (It was necessary for her to make them.)	*Had to* expresses necessity in past time.
Did you *have to get* a passport before you could travel abroad? (Was it necessary for you to get a passport?)	
I *didn't have to have* a visa. (It wasn't necessary to get a visa.)	*Didn't have to* expresses lack of necessity.

PRACTICING YOUR SKILLS

A student wrote about what it was necessary and not necessary to do in her grandparents' time. Fill in the blanks with *had to* or *didn't have to*.

1   Everyone *(work)* _____had to work_____ very hard in those days. There weren't any machines to help on the farm and not many things to buy even if people could afford them. My grandfather *(plant)* ____had to____ his crops every year. He *(weed)* _____had plant_____ and water them all summer. In the fall he *(harvest)*

5   _____ them and take them to market. During the busy planting and harvesting times, everyone in the family, including small children, *(help)*

_____.

    My grandmother's life was not any easier. She *(prepare)* ___had to prepare___ meals every day from scratch. She couldn't pop a frozen dinner into the microwave.

10   She *(make)* _____ most of her own and her children's clothes and keep everything clean. She *(take)* _____ care of the younger children and see that the older ones did their chores and their homework.

    There was no running water or electricity on the farm in those days. The children *(pump)* _____ the day's water from the well every morning

15   before school. In the evening, after they had finished their chores, they *(do)* _____ their homework by candlelight.

Even though life was difficult in those times, there were some advantages. People *(worry neg.)* _____ about some of the things we think about now—pollution and the danger of nuclear war. People certainly *(think neg.)*
20 _____ about being bored. They had too much work to do.

USING YOUR SKILLS

Think about the advantages and disadvantages of life in your parents' or grandparents' time. Write or tell about what people *had to* do/*didn't have to* do then.

SUMMARY EXERCISES: EXPRESSING NECESSITY IN PRESENT/FUTURE AND PAST TIME

You may want to review pages 101–105 in Chapter 3 before doing the following exercises.

ASK AND ANSWER

Four young women, Liz, Ming, Keiko, and Anna, share an apartment. All of them work and no one has much time for housework. They have decided that they would save time if everyone took turns doing household chores on weekdays.
Here is the schedule of chores they made out for last week and next week.

LAST WEEK'S SCHEDULE

	Mon.	Tues.	Wed.	Thurs.	Fri.
Make breakfast	Liz	Ming	Keiko	Anna	Liz
Cook dinner	Ming	Keiko	Anna	Liz	Ming
Wash dinner dishes	Keiko	Anna	Liz	Ming	Keiko
Shop for food	Anna			Liz	
Take clothes to laundromat		Ming			Keiko
Clean living room					Anna

NEXT WEEK'S SCHEDULE

	Mon.	Tues.	Wed.	Thurs.	Fri.
Make breakfast	Ming	Keiko	Anna	Liz	Ming
Cook dinner	Keiko	Anna	Liz	Ming	Keiko
Wash dinner dishes	Anna	Liz	Ming	Keiko	Anna
Shop for food	Liz			Ming	
Take clothes to laundromat		Keiko			
Clean living room					Anna

With a partner, take turns asking and answering questions about last week's and next week's schedules.

Example

How often did Ming have to cook dinner last week? How often does she have to cook it next week?

USING YOUR SKILLS

A. What did you have to do to help around the house when you were a child? What do you have to do now? What were your other responsibilities then and now? Tell about them using *have to* and *had to*. Add any details needed to make your explanation clearer.

B. Compare your own responsibilities now and a few years ago. Are there some things that you have to do now that you didn't have to do then? Are there other things that you don't have to do now but had to do then?

FINDING OUT ABOUT . . .

Participles Used as Adjectives

Many present and past participles can be used as adjectives. These participial adjectives often express emotions.

■ *Present Participle Adjectives**

Examples	*Comments*
The story is *amusing*. an *amusing* story	The present participle *amusing* shows the effect the story has.
The commercials are *annoying*. Several *annoying* commercials interrupted the show.	The present participle *annoying* shows the effect the commercials have.

■ *Past Participle Adjectives*****

Examples	*Comments*
The child was *amused by* the story. The *amused* child moved closer to her father.	The past participle *amused* shows the reaction of the child to the story.
I was *amused by* the show but *annoyed at* the commercials.	An appropriate preposition must be used when past participle adjectives are followed by objects.

■ *Some Common Participial Adjectives*

Verb	*Present Participle Adjective*	*Past Participle Adjective*
amaze	amazing	amazed (at, by)
amuse	amusing	amused (at, by)
annoy	annoying	annoyed (at, with, by)
bewilder	bewildering	bewildered (by)
bore	boring	bored (by, with)
confuse	confusing	confused (by)
disappoint	disappointing	disappointed (at, with, by)
disgust	disgusting	disgusted (by, with)
embarrass	embarrassing	embarrassed (by)

*All present participles end in *-ing*.

**Most past participles that can be used as adjectives are regular (end in *-ed*). Some exceptions: *frozen* (the *frozen* lake), *broken* (a *broken* arm), *torn* (a *torn* sweater), and *grown* (a *grown* child).

exhaust	exhausting	exhausted (by, from)
fascinate	fascinating	fascinated (by, with)
frighten	frightening	frightened (by, of)
frustrate	frustrating	frustrated (by)
interest	interesting	interested (in)
irritate	irritating	irritated (by, with)
please	pleasing	pleased (by, with)
relax	relaxing	relaxed (from)
rest	resting	rested (from)
shock	shocking	shocked (by)
surprise	surprising	surprised (at, by)
tire	tiring	tired (of, from)*
worry	worrying	worried (about, by)

PRACTICING YOUR SKILLS

Say or write a few sentences giving your own opinion about several of the following topics. Use present participles and other adjectives. Avoid overused adjectives like *good*, *bad*, *nice*, and *wonderful*.

1. a movie or TV show

   I saw a *boring* movie on television last night. It was supposed to be *interesting*, but the plot was *confusing*, and the acting was *disappointing*. Worst of all, it was interrupted by *annoying* commercials every fifteen minutes.

2. a specific television, newspaper, or magazine ad
3. a book you have read
4. a game you have played or watched
5. foods you like and dislike
6. someone you know
7. famous people and their activities
8. your own or your friends' spare-time activities
9. different kinds of music
10. a favorite piece of music

Tired from: exhausted
  I'm *tired from* working all day.
 Tired of: bored, ready for a change
  I'm *tired of* watching TV. I think I'll take a walk.

ASK AND ANSWER

First work on your own, thinking about your answers to the following questions about feelings in particular situations. Then, working with a partner, ask and answer the questions. Use either past participle adjectives or other adjectives that describe feelings. Avoid overused words like *good*, *bad*, *nice*, *wonderful*. Try not to use any adjective more than twice in your answers.

How do you usually feel when . . .

1. you first wake up in the morning?

    For the first few minutes I feel *tired* no matter how much sleep I got the night before. But after I have a cup of coffee, I usually feel *rested* and *eager* to start the day.

2. someone gives you a compliment?
3. you listen to music you like?
4. you have to listen to music you don't like?
5. you think you have hurt someone's feelings?
6. you have to give a speech in class?
7. the speech is a great success?
8. you do something wrong and nobody knows?
9. you do something wrong and somebody finds out?
10. you try to do something again and again but don't succeed?
11. you have to take a test?
12. you get a better grade than expected on the test?

USING YOUR SKILLS

All of us have had experiences in which we were embarrassed by something we said or did. Perhaps a word we said was misunderstood by someone or a gesture we made was misinterpreted. After a period of time some of these moments are no longer embarrassing and may even seem amusing. Tell or write about an embarrassing moment in your life. Explain why you were embarrassed.

Expressions Using *be* + Past Participle

Several common expressions use *be* + past participle, followed by an object. Notice the prepositions used.

Are you *prepared for* the meeting tomorrow?

Are you *opposed to* the reorganization plan that will be discussed or in favor of it?

Other Expressions:

be acquainted with   something or someone

be involved in   something

be qualified for   something

be related to   someone

be married to / engaged to   someone

be divorced from   someone

be finished with / be done with   something

be ready for   something

ASK AND ANSWER

Work with a partner. Before you begin to talk, think about several questions for your partner to answer using the past participle expressions listed on this page or in the preceding section. Both the questions and the answers your partner will give should include an object and the appropriate preposition.

You may want to jot down some of your questions on a piece of paper before you begin.

Examples

What subjects are you *interested in*?   *Answer*: I'm *interested in* . . .

Are you acquainted with (someone)?   *Answer*: Yes, I'm *acquainted with* . . .

Passive Voice in Sentences Beginning with *it*

The passive voice can be used in sentences that begin with *it*.

Examples

It is said that a picture is worth a thousand words. (Active voice: People say that a picture is worth a thousand words.)

Before Galileo's time, it was thought that the sun orbited around the earth. (Active voice: ... people thought that the sun orbited around the earth.)

Comments

The passive form of verbs such as *say, think, believe, assume, report, confirm, hope, fear, deny, know* are frequently found in this construction.

PRACTICING YOUR SKILLS

A. Fill in the blanks with the passive form of the verb given in parentheses. Notice the use of the passive in sentences beginning with *it*.

1. Millions of people watched their television screens as the space shuttle *Challenger (launch)* _____was launched_____ from the Kennedy Space Center on January 28, 1986.

2. It *(hope)* _____ that the space shuttle would bring back a great deal of useful scientific information, and would help the public understand the value of space exploration.

3. It *(think)* _____ that the presence of a civilian crew member would help the public to understand the space program.

4. Christa McAuliffe, an elementary school science teacher, *(choose)* _____ to be the first civilian in space.

5. It *(believe)* _____ that she could help other teachers explain the science of space flight to children in their classes.

6. Almost as soon as the shuttle took off, it *(know)* _____ that something was wrong.

7. As people watched the Challenger veer off its course, a huge cloud of smoke *(could see)* _____ coming from the spacecraft.

8. Although everyone hoped that the crew *(could rescue)* _____, it *(fear)* _____ that the flight would end tragically.

9. In fact, all seven crew members *(kill)* _____ instantly. It *(say)* _____ that the Challenger explosion was the world's worst space disaster.

10. A presidential commission *(appoint)* _____ to investigate the cause of the disaster.

11. After testimony by many witnesses, it *(believe)* _____ that the most probable cause of the accident was a break in the seal of one of the booster rockets.

12. It *(confirm)* _____ that some scientists had been aware of the danger but had not been able to persuade others to delay the flight.

 B. Change the following sentences to sentences beginning with *it* and a verb in the passive voice.

  Example

1. Many people believe that carrying a rabbit's foot brings good luck.

   It is believed that carrying a rabbit's foot brings good luck.

2. People think that this belief originated in western Europe sometime before 600 B.C.

3. Many people say that the horseshoe is the most universal of all good luck charms.

4. People know that the Greeks introduced horseshoes to Western culture in the fourth century B.C.

5. However, people did not think that the horseshoe placed above a doorway brought good luck until the tenth century A.D.

6. Some people hope that finding a four-leaf clover will bring good luck.

7. Other people believe that breaking a mirror will bring seven years of bad luck.

USING YOUR SKILLS

Many people also consider it bad luck to spill salt, walk under a ladder, open an umbrella indoors, or have a black cat walk in front of them. Some people believe that the number 13 is an unlucky number and that Friday the thirteenth is an unlucky day. Most North Americans know about these superstitions whether or not they believe in them.

What is considered to be lucky or unlucky in your own country? Tell or write about some common beliefs.

Using *get* with Adjectives

Examples	*Comments*
It*'s getting dark* earlier every day.	Get can be used with many adjec-
I *get confused* when I try to learn too many things at once.	tives or past participles functioning as adjectives, especially in informal speech and writing. In this context
My parents *got married* in their early twenties.	*get* usually means "become."

Common adjectives that can be used with *get* are those describing weather and temperature (get wet/hot/cold/foggy/dark/light); certain emotions and states (get hungry/thirsty/nervous/angry/mad/bored/upset/confused/disgusted/sick/well); life events (get engaged/married/divorced/remarried/hired or fired from a job). Also, get finished/done.

PRACTICING YOUR SKILLS

Complete the sentences with the appropriate form of *get* + adjective.

1. It's supposed to rain this afternoon. It *(cloudy)* ___'s getting cloudy___ already. If you don't leave right away, you *(wet)* _____ on your way home.
2. One reason I don't want to *(married)* _____ until I've chosen a career is that I believe couples who marry too early are more likely to *(divorced)* _____ .
3. I *(mad)** _____ every time I think about what she did.
4. Some people I know have had a lot of problems recently: the father just *(fired)* _____ from his job, and two of the children *(sick)* _____ at exactly the same time.
5. I usually *(tired)* _____ in the middle of the afternoon if I don't sleep enough the night before.
6. I used to _____ very *(nervous)* _____ every time I had to open my mouth in class, and I still _____ a little *(anxious)* _____ if I have to talk for a long time.
7. I don't like jobs with a lot of repetition. I *(bored)* _____ doing the same thing every day.
8. Riding a motorcycle can be dangerous. If you are not careful, you could *(hurt)* _____ .

*In this context *mad* means "very angry."

USING YOUR SKILLS

A.   In the place you are now, at what time of day does it usually start to get light? dark? Will it be the same six months from now? If seasons change, in what month does it start to get warm? cold? How about other places you know?

B.   Do you know anyone who has gotten married (divorced, remarried) recently? Do you think people are getting married earlier or later in life than in your parents' generation?

LITTLE WORDS

Adjective + Preposition Combinations

Examples

I'm *afraid of* thunder.

He's *good at* tennis.

Do you think most people are *kind to* others?

Do you think most people are *grateful for* help?

He's *bad at swimming*.

She's *proud of learning* English.

Comments

Notice that certain prepositions usually follow certain adjectives. We say that a person is afraid *of* something, good *at* something, kind *to* someone, grateful *for* something.

Adjective + preposition combinations are often followed by gerunds (*swimming, learning*). A gerund has the same form as the present participle (verb + -*ing*) but is used in the same way a noun is used.

(For more about gerunds, see Chapter 10.)

There are many adjective + preposition combinations in English. Listed below are some of the most common ones.

afraid of (someone or something)

angry at/with (someone)

angry about (something)

anxious about (something)

anxious for (something)*

ashamed of (someone, something)

bad at (something)

capable of (something)

careful with/about (something)

careless with/about (something)

considerate of (someone)

courteous to (someone)

difficult for (someone)

eager for (something)

easy for (someone)

fond of (someone, something)

good at (something), good to (some-one)

grateful for (something)

happy about/with (something, some-one)

hard for (someone)

honest about (something), honest with (someone)

kind to (someone)

jealous of (someone)

mad at (someone), mad about (something)

patient with (someone)

polite to (someone)

proud of (something, someone)

sad about (something)

sorry for (someone), sorry about (something)

successful at (something)

sure of/about (something, someone)

worried about (something, someone)

See pages 244–245 for prepositions used with past participle adjectives.

PRACTICING YOUR SKILLS

Answer as many as possible of the following questions. Use full sentences in your answer in order to practice adjective + preposition combinations.

1. What have you done during the last few years that you are very *proud of*?
2. What do you feel *capable of* achieving in the next few years?
3. What has happened recently that you are *happy about*?
4. Is there anything you have done recently that you are *sorry about*? *ashamed of*?
5. Are you *afraid of* thunder (lightning, earthquakes, tornadoes, dogs, insects)?

Anxious about means "worried about."

I am *anxious about* the rise in crime.

Anxious for often has the same meaning as *eager for*.

I'm *anxious for* my vacation to start.

6. Is there something that most people are *worried about* but that you have never been *anxious about*?
7. Are you *fond of* animals?
8. Are you usually *kind to* people? *Considerate of* their feelings?
9. Are there some people you find it difficult to be *patient with*?
10. Are you *angry about* anything (*angry at* anyone) right now?
11. Are you ever *jealous of* people?
12. Are you *eager for* (*anxious for*) anything to happen soon?
13. Are you usually *careful with* your possessions? Is there anything you are *careless about*?
14. Are you *sure of* your answers?

CHECK YOURSELF

Without referring to the list, fill in the blanks with an appropriate preposition. Check your answers on page 436.

1. I was afraid _____ *of* _____ dogs until I got a puppy of my own. The little dog was eager _____ affection. It was easy _____ anyone to be fond _____ him. When he died in an accident, I was sad _____ it for months. Everyone in the family felt sorry _____ me.

2. I have to train new employees in my office. The work is hard _____ people to learn, and not everyone can be good _____ it right away. I try to be considerate _____ everyone's feelings and not get mad _____ anyone who is trying, but I can't always be patient _____ people who don't try.

3. I'm proud _____ learning to speak English as well as I do. It wasn't easy _____ me. I knew I was capable _____ doing it from the beginning, but I wasn't completely sure _____ my ability to stick with it. It's difficult _____ me not to be jealous _____ people who seem to learn without any effort.

4. Children in my country were trained to be polite _____ every adult. Even when we were angry _____ our parents, we would have been ashamed _____ saying so. I think it is important for children to be courteous _____ older people, and I'm grateful _____ being brought up that way.

5. It's sometimes difficult to be honest _____ everything you do. It's particularly difficult to be honest _____ yourself.

SENTENCE SENSE

Sentence Types and Sentence Problems

Which conversation sounds more natural?

"Had lunch yet? Want to get a sandwich?"
"Sorry. Don't have the time today."
"Tomorrow?"
"Sure. Right after class?"
"Great! See you then."

"Have you had lunch yet? Do you want to get a sandwich?"
"I'm sorry. I don't have the time today."
"Will you have lunch with me tomorrow?"
"Sure I will. Should we meet right after class?"
"That would be great! I'll see you then."

The first conversation probably sounds more natural. In everyday talk between friends, people use many incomplete sentences. The subject or verb or both may be missing. This incompleteness is not due to carelessness or lack of education but is normal in informal conversations among educated native English-speakers.

USING YOUR SKILLS

If you are studying in an English-speaking country, try to listen in on a few informal conversations between native English speakers. Do people speak mostly in complete or incomplete sentences? Report on what you hear to the class.

Using Complete Sentences When Writing

In written English it is customary to write in complete sentences. All sentences should include a subject and a complete verb.* Sentences must begin with a capital letter and end in appropriate punctuation.

---

*Imperatives (see pages 105–109) are considered complete sentences because the subject (*you*) is implied.

(You should) Stop.

Occasionally, skilled writers use incomplete sentences to create the effect of informality.

We lived on a farm.	statement
Would you like me to tell you about the place where I was born?	question
What a beautiful place it was! I hate cities!	exclamation

Statements of fact or opinion end with a period. (.) Questions end with a question mark. (?) Sentences expressing strong emotion (pleasure, surprise, anger) may end in an exclamation point. (!)

PRACTICING YOUR SKILLS

A. The following sentences are normal in conversation but would need to be changed if written. Add subjects and verbs when needed.

1. Like the country better than the city.

I like the country better than the city.

2. Grew up on a farm.
3. Family in region for generations.
4. Beautiful place.
5. Trees, flowers, rivers and streams everywhere.
6. A wonderful place to grow up.
7. Rode to school in a bus every morning.
8. To run in the fields and climb trees after school.
9. On weekends, swimming and fishing with my friends.
10. Not many neighbors.
11. Only a few families nearby.
12. But never lonely.

B. Identify the subject(s) and verb(s) in each of the following complete simple sentences.

1   I grew up in a medium-sized city. We lived in a small apartment on the fourth floor of a tall building. My aunt and her children shared the apartment with us. We didn't have much room. We were happy. We liked to be together. I had few toys. I always had plenty of children to play with. There was no park nearby. There were no backyards to
5 play in. We played on the street in front of the house. We didn't have much money. We always had enough to eat. We had one another's love.

▰▰▰▰▰ *Compound Sentences*

A composition composed only of simple sentences like the ones in the previous exercise can be monotonous. Most writers want to vary their writing by including other kinds of sentences. Compound sentences are especially useful in expressing ideas that are connected and are of approximately equal importance.

An independent clause contains a subject and complete verb. It can stand by itself as a simple sentence or can form part of a compound sentence. In a compound sentence, two or more independent clauses are joined in one of three ways.

1. With a coordinating conjunction (*and, but, or, so, yet, for,* or *nor*). A comma precedes the conjunction.

   We didn't have much room, *but we were* happy.
     s   v   s   v

2. With a semicolon (;)

   We were happy; we liked to be together.
     s   v   s   v

3. With a semicolon and transition word or phrase. A comma generally follows the transition. Some examples of transitions are *in addition, therefore, however.**

   I had few toys; *however, I* always *had* plenty of children to play with.
   s v   s   v

▰▰▰▰▰ *Combining Sentences with Coordinating Conjunctions:* and, but, or, so, yet, for

Note the meanings of the coordinating conjunctions used to show the logical relationship between ideas in compound sentences.

Examples	*Comments*
We lived in a small apartment, *and* my aunt lived with us.	*and* = addition

---

*This chapter will present an introduction to the use of transition words and their meanings. Additional treatment of common transition words can be found in the Sentence Sense section of Chapters 8 and 9.

We didn't have much money, *but* we always had enough.

but = contrast, concession*

I could play with my cousins, *or* I could play with my friends.

or = choice

There were lots of children, *so* I always had someone to play with.

so = result

There was no park nearby, *yet* we always found places to play.

yet = concession

We were happy, *for* we had one another's love.

for = reason**

PRACTICING YOUR SKILLS

Complete the following sentences with a clause (subject and verb). Tell about your childhood home or another place that was important to you as a child. You may change the sentences slightly to fit your own situation.

1. I think about _our house in the country_ often, and _I remember all the good times we had_.

2. I remember _____, and _____
    _____.

3. I no longer have the same feelings I had as a child, but _____.

4. I used to play with _____, or _____
    _____.

5. I have good memories of my life there, so _____.

6. My memories are of a time in the past, yet _I still remember that_.

7. I will never forget _____, for _____
    _____.

Continue constructing compound sentences with coordinating conjunctions, telling about a place you remember from childhood.

---

*Contrasting clauses are in direct opposition.

He's sick, *but* I'm well.

Clauses expressing concession present a result that is different from what is expected.

She's sick, *yet* she came to work today.

He's eighty years old, *but* he swims every day.

**For* is used as a coordinating conjunction only in rather formal styles of English. A more common way of expressing the same meaning is

We were happy *because* we had one another's love.

■■■■■■■ *Combining Sentences with the Coordinating Conjunction* nor

Examples	*Comments*
We weren't poor. We weren't rich.	*Nor* = negative addition
We weren't poor, *nor were we* rich.	*Nor* is used to connect negative clauses.
We didn't have expensive toys. We didn't need them.	When using *nor*, an auxiliary or *be* is placed before the subject, and the
We didn't have expensive toys, *nor did we* need them.	second negative is omitted.

PRACTICING YOUR SKILLS

Combine each set of simple sentences into one compound sentence using *nor*. In the second clause, remember to put *be* or an auxiliary before the subject and to omit the negative.

1. As a child, I didn't have many problems.
   I didn't worry much about my future.

   Example

   As a child, I didn't have many problems, nor did I worry much about my future.

2. I didn't think I would ever leave home.
   I didn't think I would come to a new country.

3. I haven't been sorry about my choice.
   I haven't been unhappy with my new life.

4. It hasn't been difficult to make new friends.
   I don't feel as lonely as I thought I would.

5. My hometown wasn't very large.
   It didn't offer many opportunities.

6. My town didn't have many schools.
   It didn't have a university where I could continue to study.

7. Until high school, I hadn't decided to be an engineer.
    I hadn't thought about going away to school.

8. I didn't want to leave my family.
    I didn't want to leave my friends.

9. I couldn't study engineering in my town.
    I couldn't stay with my family if I wanted to continue my education.

Joining Words or Phrases: Parallel Structure

And, *but*, *yet*, *or*, and *nor* can join units that are smaller than a sentence. However, the parts that are joined must have the same grammatical structure. For example, a noun must be joined with a noun, and an infinitive with another infinitive.

When you use parallel structures and coordinating conjunctions, it is often possible to avoid repeating unnecessary words.

Examples	*Comments*
My *aunt* and (my) *cousins* lived with us.	*noun — noun*
The *living room* and (the) *kitchen* were attached.	The second determiner can be omitted.
Was your village *large* or *small*?	*adjective — adjective*
I worked *quickly* yet *carefully*.	*adverb — adverb*
I liked *to swim* but not (to) *dive*.	*infinitive — infinitive* The second *to* can be omitted.
I *was studying* in the mornings and (I) (was) *working* in the afternoon.	*verb phrase — verb phrase* The second auxiliary and the second mention of the same subject can be omitted.
I *was studying* and *working*.	Punctuation note: No comma is necessary to separate two parallel units that are smaller than a clause. Commas are necessary, however, with more than two units. The comma preceding the conjunction is optional but often used.
I *was studying*, *working(,)* and *taking* care of my children.	

PRACTICING YOUR SKILLS

Combine the following into a single sentence using the conjunctions *and*, *but*, or *or*. Eliminate any unnecessary words. Use appropriate punctuation.

1. I decided to attend university. (and)
I decided to study engineering.

Example

I decided to attend university and study engineering.

2. There was a good university in the capital. (but)
The engineering school was small. (and)
Only 50 students were accepted each year.

3. I decided to study abroad. (and)
I began to consider schools in North America.

4. I wanted to go to a university in the United States. (or)
I wanted to go to a university in Canada.

5. No one in my immediate family had studied abroad. (but)
A friend of my brother was studying in the United States. (and)
A cousin of mine had worked in the United States.

6. My brother's friend sent me information about his school. (and)
My brother's friend sent me the addresses of several other schools in the United States.

7. I sent a letter to his school. (and)
I sent a letter to several other schools.

8. I applied to three universities. (and)
I waited anxiously to hear from them.

━━━━━━━ *Two-Part Conjunctions:* either/or, neither/nor, not only/but *(also)*, both/and*

Many two-part conjunctions can join either clauses or smaller grammatical units. The structures that follow them must be parallel. For example, if a verb follows *either*, a verb must follow *or*.

*Also called correlative conjunctions.

Examples	*Comments*
1. *Either* I could live in a single room, *or* two other students and I could share an apartment. (clauses)	*either/or* = choice
2. I could *either* live in a single room *or* share an apartment with two other students. (verb)*	
I could *neither* pay all my expenses myself *nor* expect my parents to pay them. (verb phrases)	*neither/nor* = negative addition (seldom used to combine clauses)
Neither my parents *nor* I could pay everything. (pronouns or nouns)	
I needed money *not only* for tuition *but also* for living expenses.** (prepositional phrases)	*not only/but (also)* = addition
I was *both* surprised *and* delighted when my government offered me a small scholarship. (adjectives)	*both/and* = addition (Not used to combine clauses)
Both my mother *and* father were happy about the news. (nouns)	Notice that two singular subjects connected by *and* require a plural verb.

PRACTICING YOUR SKILLS

A. Combine the following sentences, using two-part conjunctions. Be sure to use parallel structures. There is often more than one possible solution. (Teachers' note: In more advanced classes, you may want to display various corrected answers and discuss stylistic preferences.)

1. *(not only/but (also))* I was accepted by a large university in Connecticut.
I was accepted by a smaller university in Florida.

Examples

I was accepted not only by a large university in Connecticut but also by a smaller university in Florida.

Not only was I accepted by a large university in Connecticut, but also by a smaller university in Florida.

*Although both 1 and 2 are grammatically correct, writers in English generally prefer to use conjunctions to combine the shortest possible units, as in example 2.

**When *not only/but (also)* joins two complete clauses, *be* or an auxiliary is placed before the subject in the first clause.

Not only did I need money for tuition, *but* I *also* needed money for living expenses.

2. (*both/and*) The large university offered me a partial scholarship.
The other university offered me a partial scholarship.
3. (*neither/nor*) The university in Florida didn't offer me a full scholarship.
The one in Connecticut didn't offer me a full scholarship.
4. (*not only/but also*) I wanted to live comfortably while I was going to school.
I didn't want to have to get a job while I was adjusting to life in a new country.
5. (*not only/but also*) I would need to earn some money to travel to the United States.
I wanted to have enough money to travel around the United States in the summer.
6. (*Either/or*) I could borrow money and begin school the next semester.
I could live at home and work for a year and begin school later.

B. Complete the following in your own words. You may change the wording to fit your own situation.

1. After class we could either _____ or _____.
2. To celebrate my next birthday I'd like either to _____ or _____.
3. The next free weekend I want either to _____ or _____.
4. _____ is not only an interesting place to visit but _____.
5. If there is enough time we could not only _____ but also _____.
6. Both _____ and _____ are worth a visit.
7. Neither _____ nor _____ is very expensive.
8. Neither _____ nor _____ is very difficult to get to.

USING YOUR SKILLS

Write about a decision you need to make within the next year or so. What options do you have? What factors will influence your choice? Use a variety of sentence types and include several examples of coordinate and two-part conjunctions.

■■■■■■ *Introduction to Transitions*

Transitions are words and phrases that connect new ideas with ideas that have been stated previously. Many transitions are more frequent in writing than in conversation. Transitions can play an important role in helping to make the logical relationship between ideas clear to the reader.

SIMPLE SENTENCES

Examples	*Comments*
I needed to send the university letters of recommendation. *For example*, I needed a letter from a former teacher and from the principal of my high school. The university asked for two letters of recommendation. *Moreover*, they wanted me to send them all my transcripts.	Transitions like *for example* and *moreover* (addition) are usually placed at the beginning of a simple sentence. They show the logical relationship between the ideas in the new sentence and ideas in the previous sentence(s).
I sent my application immediately. *However*, the letters and transcripts had to be translated. The letters, *however*, needed to be translated. The letters needed to be translated, *however*.	A few transitions, particularly *however*, also appear in the middle or at the end of a sentence. Punctuation note: Commas follow transitions at the beginning of a sentence, are used before and after midsentence transitions, and precede end-of-sentence transitions.

COMPOUND SENTENCES

Examples	*Comments*
It took me a long time to prepare my application; *in fact*, I worked on it for over a week.	A semicolon and transition can be used to combine two simple sentences (independent clauses) into a compound sentence.

PRACTICING YOUR SKILLS

A. Note any possible logical relationships in each set of simple sentences. Then choose an appropriate transition word to combine each set of simple sentences into one compound sentence. In many cases more than one answer is possible, but do not use any transition word more than once. Add all necessary punctuation.

Addition	*Results*	*Contrast*	*Contrast-Concession*
in addition	therefore	nevertheless	however
moreover	consequently	nonetheless	
furthermore	thus		

1. I knew that applying to an American university would be complicated. I didn't know how complicated.

   Example

   I knew that applying to an American university would be complicated; however, I didn't know how complicated.

2. I was not sure that my high school principal would write me a letter of recommendation.
   He agreed to do so right away.
3. I needed to show proof of my ability in English.
   I signed up to take the TOEFL.
4. The TOEFL was a very long test, *moreover,*
   I had never taken a multiple-choice test before.
5. I needed to send my TOEFL results to each university.
   I had to fill out a form with their addresses.
6. I thought the exam was difficult.
   I did very well.
7. I waited to hear if I had been accepted.
   I worried about what I would do if I were not accepted.
8. It takes a long time for mail from the United States to reach my country. *thus,*
   It took several weeks to receive my acceptance letter.

B. Complete the following compound sentences in your own words. Talk about yourself or a classmate.

1. _____ decided to study _____; therefore, _____
   _____.
2. _____ needed to _____; moreover, _____
   _____.

3. _____ was always good at _____; consequently, _____.

4. _____ never been very good at _____;
nevertheless, _____.

5. Not many people know how to _____; however, _____
_____.

6. _____ learned to _____; furthermore, _____
_____.

USING YOUR SKILLS

Write a paragraph telling how you learned to do something that at first you thought you could not do. Tell about the problems you had and how you overcame the difficulties. Use a variety of sentence types and several of the transition words mentioned in this section.

Sentence Problems: Punctuating Compound Sentences Correctly

When two or more independent clauses are combined to form a compound sentence, they must be joined with appropriate connecting words and correct punctuation.

Correct

, + conjunction	We talked about his choices, *but* he still could not decide what to do next.
;	We talked about his choices; he still could not decide what to do next.
; + transition + ,	We talked about his choices; *however,* he still could not decide what to do next.

Incorrect: Run-on sentence

no punctuation	We talked about his choices he still could not decide what to do next.

Incorrect: Comma splice

comma only	We talked about his choices, he still could not decide what to do next.

PRACTICING YOUR SKILLS

Correct the following run-on sentences by adding appropriate connecting words and/or punctuation. In most cases several solutions are possible.

1. I needed to take the TOEFL it was not possible to take it in my home town.

Examples

. . . . the TOEFL. It . . . .

. . . . the TOEFL; it . . . .

. . . . the TOEFL, but it . . . .

. . . . the TOEFL; however, it . . . .

2. I could either take the exam in a nearby town, I could go to the capital.
3. The capital was only 100 miles away yet I had never seen it.
4. Moreover, my uncle and his family lived in the capital, I knew I could stay with them.
5. I took the train the night before the exam it was scheduled to arrive early in the morning.
6. I woke up to find that the train had stopped, we were nowhere near our destination.
7. A railroad employee told us that there had been a minor accident we were supposed to start again in a half hour.
8. With some luck we would arrive by noon, however, I couldn't be sure I would be at the exam by 1:00 P.M.
9. The train pulled into the station at 11:30 my uncle drove me directly to the exam site.
10. We were among the first people there so I even had time for a quick lunch.

■■■■■■■■ *Complex Sentences*

Complex sentences usually connect ideas of unequal importance. They are formed by joining an independent clause with a subordinate clause. A subordinate clause *cannot* stand by itself as a sentence. When an independent clause forms part of a complex sentence, it is called the main clause.

subordinate clause*   main clause

Before I took the test, I was a little nervous.

*Also called a dependent clause.

main clause   subordinate clause

I was nervous although I was a good student.

Punctuation note: When the subordinate clause comes before the main clause, a comma separates them.

Recognizing Subordinate Clauses

There are a limited number of subordinating words that introduce a subordinate clause and show the logical relation between it and the main clause. The best way to recognize subordinate clauses is to become familiar with the common subordinating words and their meanings.*

Common Subordinating Words That Express Logical Relationships

Cause: *because, since, as, inasmuch as*

Result: *so . . . that, such . . . that*

Purpose: *so that*

Conditions: *if, unless,*

Concession (unexpected result): *although, even though, though*

Opposition: *while, whereas*

Time: *before, after, until, when, while, as, whenever, since, as soon as*

LOOKING AT FORMS

Label the subject and verb in each clause of the following complex sentences taken from readings in this book. Circle the subordinating word, and underline the subordinate clause. Note the use of commas.

1. Sometimes people use words that are wrong because they sound better than the right ones.

*Subordinating words are examined in greater detail in several sections of this book. See individual words in index.

2. Once found, it cannot be lightly discarded, because lack of *querencia* is a kind of starvation.

3. When he has to leave, it is not for the promised land on the terrestrial horizon.

4. If a person wants to terminate the conversation, he may start shifting his body position.

5. It was the moment before the curtain parted or rose.

6. She kept on going until she said the last word.

PRACTICING YOUR SKILLS

All the following subordinate clauses would be considered incomplete sentences (fragments) in written English. Complete them by adding an independent clause (main clause) either before or after the fragment. Adjust capitalization and punctuation. Note: Talk about the preparation for a trip you have taken. You may change the cues in order to speak truthfully of your own situation.

1. Because I was going to visit someplace very different from my home.

    Examples

    Because I was going to visit someplace very different from my home, I didn't know what to expect.

    I didn't know what to expect because I was going to visit someplace very different from my home.

2. If I wanted to make my trip a success.
3. As the time drew closer.
4. Although I was going to be traveling by myself.
5. Until the day before I left.
6. While I was packing.
7. So that I wouldn't forget anything I needed.
8. When I got up that morning.
9. After my family drove me to the airport.
10. As soon as I got on the plane.

Summary Chart of Common Connecting Words and Phrases

Transitions	Subordinating Words	Coordinating Conjunctions
Time and Sequence		
first	before	
second (third, etc.)	after	
next	when	
then	whenever	
after that	while	
finally	as	
afterward	since	
previously	until	
before that	as soon as	
prior to that		
meanwhile		
at the same time		
during that time		
Additional Information		
in addition		and
moreover		
furthermore		
Opposition and Concession		
on the contrary	while	but
in fact	whereas	yet
however	though	
nevertheless	although	
nonetheless	even though	
Cause and Result		
therefore	because	so
consequently	since	
thus	as	
as a result	inasmuch as	
	so . . . that	
	such . . . that	
Purpose		
	so that	for

USING YOUR SKILLS

Write a paragraph telling about the preparation for a major event in your life—perhaps a trip you have taken. Tell about your feelings as well as your actions in preparing for the event. End your story before the event takes place. Use a variety of sentence types but include several complex sentences with subordinating words.

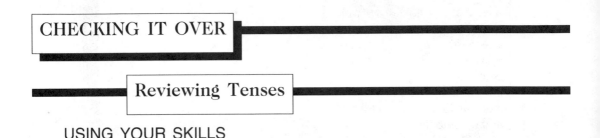

CHECKING IT OVER

Reviewing Tenses

USING YOUR SKILLS

The following excerpt is adapted from a newspaper article written in 1986. It uses present and future tenses to refer to current and upcoming events.

Rewrite the passage as if you were telling the story now. You do not know whether the system described is still in use. Change present and future tenses to appropriate past tenses. You will also need to change time phrases such as *now* and *next year*. Check your answers on pages 436, 437.

PUTTING A WORKER'S EXPERTISE ON THE COMPUTER

1   Aldo Cimino is an employee of the Campbell Soup Company, a large manufacturer of canned soups. Cimino has 44 years of experience with Campbell. He is one of the few employees who knows everything there is to know about one important stage in the manufacture of canned soups. He is an expert on the 72-foot-high "cookers" that fill up
5   to 850 soup cans a minute.

      Mr. Cimino retires next year, and Campbell worries that when he leaves they will lose all his years of experience. At the present time, when one of the maintenance workers has a problem with the cookers, he usually asks Mr. Cimino. Problems in this stage of the canning process need to be fixed in a short time or the soup must be
10   thrown away. Cimino, because of his experience, can generally determine the trouble and find a solution very quickly after asking the worker a few questions.

      In order not to lose valuable information when Cimino retires, Campbell is going to put his expertise into a computer program. Dozens of software engineers are going to interview Mr. Cimino and the workers and attempt to organize and codify a lifetime of
15   experience about canning. Their idea is to capture his expertise in an inexpensive computer system. The computer will contain answers to thousands of questions that workers in the plant now ask Mr. Cimino. Campbell hopes that next year, workers who have questions about what to do can turn to the computer for answers.

Reviewing the Passive Voice

PRACTICING YOUR SKILLS

A. Change some of the following active sentences into passive ones. Use a *"by phrase"* only if necessary. Note: Some sentences cannot be made passive. Other sentences may sound better in the active voice. Check your answers on page 437.

1. People used to wear blue jeans only for work.

    Example

    Blue jeans used to be worn only for work.

2. Nowadays people wear jeans everywhere.
3. People wear jeans to the opera.
4. People wear jeans to the theater.
5. Some people wear "designer jeans" that cost more than $50.
6. Blue jeans are not new.
7. Someone invented blue jeans in California in the middle of the nineteenth century.
8. Gold miners wore them first.
9. People discovered gold in California in the 1840s.
10. A few years later, thousands of people were searching for gold in the American West.
11. A seventeen-year-old tailor named Levi Strauss made the first blue jeans.
12. He made them from heavy canvas.
13. People were using canvas to make tents.
14. People were using canvas for covered wagons.
15. Before Strauss, no one was using canvas for clothes.
16. Later, Strauss used another fabric to make his popular overalls.
17. People made this softer and lighter fabric in Italy and France.
18. In France, people called it *serge de Nîmes*.
19. In the United States people pronounced "de Nîmes" *denim*.
20. Workers made the denim thread in the Italian town of Genoa.
21. French weavers called the town Genes.
22. "Genes" sounds like *jeans*.
23. Later, people called the clothes made from denim jeans.

B. Experiment with different ways of writing the sentences in Exercise A as three short paragraphs. Use both the active and the passive voice. You may connect some of the sentences, using coordinating conjunctions—*and*, *but*, and *or*.

USING YOUR SKILLS

A. In your country or region, are there holidays or other occasions when people wear special clothes or regional or traditional costumes? If so, describe the clothes and the occasions to someone who has never seen them. Use both the active and passive voice.

B. Do you think people should choose clothes for comfort? style? economy? practicality? To please themselves? To please others? To look the same as everyone else? To look different from anyone else? To show a person's position or role in society? Explain your ideas using both the active and passive voice.

CHAPTER 8

TIME AND TENSE

The Past Perfect Tense

Forming the Past Perfect Tense

Subject	had	Past Participle	
She	had	written	15 pages by ten o'clock last night.
I	had	read	the first three chapters when I fell asleep.

Using the Past Perfect Tense

The past perfect tense expresses an activity or situation that was completed before another event in the past or before a specific time in the past.

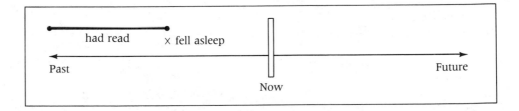

The past perfect is normally used with other past tenses, particularly the simple past tense. The past perfect expresses the event that took place in a more distant past.

I had read three chapters when I fell asleep.

The simple past tense can be used in both parts of the sentence when the context or a time expression such as *before* or *after* shows which event came first.

I *read* three chapters before I *fell* asleep.

However, the past perfect tense is needed when the exact sequence of events is not clear.

Past perfect

They *had finished* dinner when he arrived. (Meaning dinner was over by the time he arrived.)

Simple past

They *finished* dinner when he arrived. (Meaning they ate the rest of the dinner after he arrived.)

PRACTICING YOUR SKILLS

Fill in the blanks using the past perfect for the earlier event and the simple past for later event(s) in every sentence. Check your answers on page 437.

1. Before my family came to this country we *(learn)* _____had learned_____ some English in school, but none of us *(know)* _____knew_____ how to speak it well.

2. Even though we *(prepare)* ____had prepared____ ourselves for the move, there *(be)* ____was____ many things to get used to.

3. My father *(be)* ____had been (was)____ a lawyer in our country, but when we first came here he *(get)* ____got____ a job as a stock clerk in a manufacturing company.

4. My father *(be)* ____had been____ with the company for only three months when he *(get)* ____got____ his first raise.

5. When he *(become)* ____became____ assistant manager in 1985, he *(have)* already ____had have____ several promotions.

6. My mother *(work neg.)* ____hadn't worked____ before, but soon she *(start)* ____started____ to work in my cousin's store.

7. The first day of school my sisters and I *(feel)* ____felt____ like we *(study)* ____studied____ never _____ English before. We *(understand neg.)* ____didn't____ a word anyone said to us.

8. After several months, we *(understand)* ____understood____ almost everything and could speak a little bit. Our parents *(be)* ____was____ pleased with how much we *(learn)* ____had learned____ in such a short time.

USING YOUR SKILLS

Choose five dates that mark important events in your own life, such as the year you graduated from high school or the year you got your first interesting job. Tell briefly what you had already accomplished before those dates. Be careful to use the appropriate tenses to make the sequence of events clear.

■■■■■■■■ *Contrasting the Past Perfect and the Present Perfect Tenses*

Remember that the past perfect (*had* + past participle) is used to express an activity or situation completed before another event in the *past*. The present perfect (*has/have* + past participle) is used to express an activity or situation that took place any time before *now*. (See Chapter 5, pages 158–167, for more details on the present perfect.)

CHECK YOURSELF

Fill in the blanks with the appropriate tense—either present perfect or past perfect. Check your answers on page 437.

1. I *(write)* _____'ve written_____ four pages, and I'm ready to take a break now. I *(finish)* _____'ve_____ already _____finished_____ most of my work. Yesterday I didn't do much. I *(sit)* _____had_____ just _____sat_____ down at my typewriter when the telephone rang. After that there were many other interruptions. I *(complete)* _____ only half a page when I decided to give up for the day.

2. I don't feel well. I *(eat neg.)* _____ much for days, and I *(have)* _____ a splitting headache for several hours now. I *(call neg.)* _____ a doctor yet, but I think I will. It may just be nervousness. I *(be)* _____ under a lot of pressure recently. I felt exactly the same way a couple of months ago, when I *(start)* _____ just _____ my new job.

3. During the summer all the TV stations re-run programs, and it's hard to find anything you *(see neg.)* _____ already _____. I turned on my favorite series last night, but after a few minutes I realized I *(see)* _____ already _____ it twice.

The Past Perfect Progressive Tense

The progressive form of the past perfect tense can also be used to contrast earlier and later actions in the past. The progressive form stresses the duration of the earlier activity.*

Subject	had	been	*Base + -ing*	
She	had	been	writing	for several hours.

Contractions

I'd, you'd, he'd, she'd, we'd, they'd

ASK AND ANSWER

With a partner, practice asking and answering questions beginning with *How long*? in the past perfect progressive tense or past perfect tense. Use the sample dialogue and the information given in the chart below.

Example

A: How long had her parents been waiting at the airport when the plane landed?
B: They had been waiting for two hours and 45 minutes.

Subject	*Earlier Event*	*Later Event*	*Times*
her parents	wait / at airport	plane lands	6:00–8:45
the patient	wait / in the emergency room	doctor comes	4:00–5:15
you	work / at your first job	change jobs	1983–1985
country	be / at war	declare peace	1941–1945
president	be / in office	lose election	1976–1980
father	work / as dentist	retire	1950–1982
family	live / in apartment	buy house	1985–1987

---

*Non-action verbs such as *be, seem,* and *know* are not normally used with progressive tenses. See pages 48–50 for a list of nonaction verbs.

   correct: She had known his family for many years.
   not: ~~She had been knowing his family for many years.~~

USING MODALS

Expressions Using *would*

■■■■■ *Softening a Message:* would like

Examples

What *would* you *like* to drink? = What do you want to drink?

I*'d like* some coffee = I want some coffee, please.

I*'d like* it with cream.

Comments

Would ('d) like is a polite way of saying *want*. It is followed by a noun, noun phrase, pronoun or infinitive (*to* + base)

■■■■■ *Expressing Preference or Choice:* would rather

Examples

Would you *rather* sit near the window?

I*'d rather* sit at this table.

I*'d rather not* sit near the kitchen.

Comments

Would ('d) rather expresses a choice or preference. It is followed by the base form of the verb.

HOW IT SOUNDS

After pronouns, the contracted form of *would* (I*'d,* you*'d,* he*'d,* she*'d,* we*'d,* they*'d*) is almost always used in speech and informal writing.

In normal rapid speech it is often difficult to distinguish between a sentence such as "I*'d* like coffee" (I want coffee, please) and "I like coffee."

Practice hearing the differences by listening to your teacher say one of the following sentences chosen at random. Indicate whether the sentence you hear is from Group 1 or Group 2.

	1		2

1

I'd like coffee.
I'd like milk in my coffee.
I'd like to see you.
We'd like to travel.
They'd like to visit us.

2

I like coffee.
I like milk in my coffee.
I like to see you.
We like to travel.
They like to visit us.

ASK AND ANSWER

A. First, circle the food or beverage you prefer in the exercise below. If you do not like either of the choices given, add your own.

Then, working with a partner, ask and answer questions about each other's preferences. You may use either of the dialogues as a model, making changes when necessary.

Dialogue 1. A: *Would* you *rather* have coffee or tea?
            B: I*'d like* some coffee, please.

Dialogue 2. A: *Would* you *rather* have sugar or sweetener in your coffee?
            B: Neither. I*'d like* it without either.

Choice 1	*Choice 2*	*Another Choice*
⟨coffee⟩	tea	_____
with sweetener	with sugar	*without sweetener or sugar*
orange juice	grapefruit juice	_____
poached eggs	scrambled eggs	_____
butter	margarine	_____
skim milk	whole milk	_____
white bread	whole wheat bread	_____
cooked cereal	cold cereal	_____
soup	salad	_____
vegetable soup	chicken soup	_____
french dressing	italian dressing (on salad)	_____
baked potato	french fries	_____

B.   First, circle the activity you prefer. (You may substitute another activity for one of those given.) Then, with a partner, ask and answer questions about each other's preferred activities. Use the dialogue as a model, but add information of your own whenever possible.

A: *Would* you *rather watch* the news on television or read it in the newspaper?
B: *I'd rather read* the newspaper. You find out much more about what is happening in the world.

1.   eat at home / go out for dinner
2.   cook your own meals / have someone cook for you
3.   spend evenings at home with a few friends / go to parties
4.   walk in the country / walk in the city
5.   work in the garden / sit in the garden
6.   swim in salt water / swim in fresh water
7.   wear comfortable clothes / wear fashionable clothes
8.   take an easy but boring class / take a difficult but interesting class
9.   live in a warm climate / live in a cool or changeable climate

C.   In this exercise you will make and refuse suggestions and invitations. Notice how *would (n't) like* is used in the following dialogue.

A: *Wouldn't* you *like* to have dinner with us tonight?
B: *I'd love* to, but I have to study.*

With a partner, take turns making and refusing invitations or suggestions. Use the dialogue as a model.

1.   watch a movie on TV / study for an exam
2.   go for a walk / pick up my child after school
3.   have a cup of coffee after class / go to my next class
4.   stop by our house on your way home / work late
5.   take a vacation this summer / earn money for school
6.   eat out tonight / save money
7.   take a break / finish my report

*I'd love to, meaning "I'd like to very much," is used frequently in informal speech and writing.

■■■■■■■■ *Asking Permission:* Would you mind if I . . . ?

Examples

Would you mind if I *used* your telephone?

No, go ahead. It's in the kitchen.

Would you mind if I *parked* here for a minute?

Yes, I would. This space is reserved. I'm afraid you'll have to find another one.

Comments

Would you mind if . . . is a polite way of asking permission. It is followed by a verb that is the same as the past tense.*

Notice that *no* (I wouldn't mind) may be used to give permission.
Yes, (I would mind) may be used to refuse permission.

ASK AND ANSWER

One person should take the role of an employee, the other the boss. The employee will ask permission using *Would you mind if. . . ?* The boss will either give or refuse permission, adding additional comments when possible.

1. take my break soon.

Employee: Would you mind if I took my break soon?
Boss: No, I don't mind as long as you finish typing that letter before lunch.
Employee: No problem. I'll get to it right after the break.

2. move my desk closer to the window
3. use the telephone to call home
4. wear jeans to work
5. eat lunch at my desk
6. bring my child to work with me on school holidays
7. leave as soon as I finish
8. come later and leave later
9. come later and leave earlier

*In informal conversation, the verb is more likely to be in the present tense.

    Would you mind if I *use* your telephone?
 or
    Do you mind if I *use* your telephone?

■■■■■■ *Polite Requests with* Would you mind

Do you

Examples	Comments
Would you mind waiting a few minutes? *No.* (I don't mind.) I'm not in a hurry. *Would you mind letting* me copy your test? *Yes, I would mind.* I don't think that's fair.	Polite requests for someone to do something can be made with *Would you mind* + gerund (verb + *-ing*). Notice that *no* can be used to consent to a request. *Yes* may indicate a refusal.

ASK AND ANSWER

A. Work with a partner. In many situations the following imperatives might be considered too abrupt or rude. Take turns "softening" them by changing them into requests beginning with *Would you mind . . . ?* Your partner may either consent to or refuse your request.

1. Explain to me how I should fill out the form.

    Would you mind explaining to me how I should fill out the form?
    Of course not. What do you need to know?

2. Tell me where I should write my name.
3. Show me where I should sign it.
4. Write down that information for me.
5. Repeat that number.
6. Tell me who can answer my question.
7. Translate this sentence for me.
8. Speak a little more slowly.
9. Show me where it is on the map.
10. Tell me how I can get there by public transportation.

USING YOUR SKILLS

With a partner, role-play the following situations. Use *Would you mind . . . ?*

1. The electricity has just gone off in your apartment. You are not sure what to do. You knock on your neighbor's door.

2. You are not sure you understand the teacher's last assignment. You would like another student to explain it to you.

3. You are calling your friend, but his mother answers the phone and tells you he is too busy to talk now. It's important that you talk to him tonight.

4. Someone has just told you her name, but you are not sure you know how to pronounce it. It might help if she wrote it down. You want to remember the name but you don't want your new friend to think you weren't paying attention.

■■■■■■■ *Unfulfilled Intentions:* **would have**

Examples	*Comments*
I *would have written* you sooner, but I didn't know your address.*	*Would have* + past participle is used to express past intentions that were never carried out.

PRACTICING YOUR SKILLS

A. Ming has good intentions, but she doesn't always budget her time well. At the beginning of each week, she makes a long list of things she wants to do. At the end of the week, she often finds that she hasn't done half of what she intended and she needs to explain to herself why not. Construct sentences about Ming's unfulfilled intentions using *would have* + past participle.

1. I wanted to catch up on all my work.

   I would have caught up but the teacher assigned new work every day.

2. I wanted to exercise for a half hour every day.
3. I wanted get my hair cut.
4. I wanted to clean out all the cabinets in the kitchen.
5. I wanted to buy presents for several of my relatives.
6. I wanted to read several new books in English.

B. You probably plan more realistically than Ming does, but perhaps there are some things you intended to do recently but weren't able to. Construct several sentences about your own unfulfilled intentions.

---

*Would have (would've) sounds like *would of* in rapid speech.

■━━━■ *Expressing (Unfulfilled) Past Desires and Preferences*

Examples	*Comments*
My mother *would have liked* to be an engineer, but at that time engineering schools did not accept women.*	*Would have liked* is followed by an infinitive (*to* + base) or a noun. It usually means that someone did not get whatever was desired.
I *would rather have taken* my vacation last month, but I had to work.	*Would rather have* + past *participle* expresses preferences in the past. It usually means that someone did not get whatever was preferred.

PRACTICING YOUR SKILLS

All of us can think of times when we made poor choices or when circumstances prevented us from doing what we wanted to do. Construct several sentences about your own regrets or complaints. Use *would have liked* or *would rather have.*

Examples

I *would have liked* to travel around the United States last summer, but I had to study.

I *would rather have seen* another movie, but my friend had already seen it.

FINDING OUT ABOUT . . .

Causatives and Related Forms

Let, make, and *have* express the idea of causing or allowing someone to do something.

In the active voice, *let, make,* and *have* are followed by an object and the base form of another verb.

---

*It is also possible to say "She would have liked to have been an engineer."

Subject	Let / Make Have	Object	Base
I	*let*	my friend	*borrow* my car.
The mother	*lets*	the child	*play* outside.
His boss	*made*	him	*finish* the work.
The doctor	*makes*	his patients	*stay* in bed.
I	*had*	the barber	*cut* my hair.
I always	*have*	the mechanic	*check* the oil.

Let means to permit or allow someone to do something.

Make expresses the idea of force or strong persuasion.

Have, used in this way, usually expresses the idea of arranging or paying for someone to perform some service.

Help can be followed by either the base form or the infinitive form (*to* + base).

I *helped* my friend *finish* her work. or I *helped* my friend *to finish* her work.

PRACTICING YOUR SKILLS

Add several different endings to each of the following sentences. Remember to use the base form of the verb following *let, make,* or *have,* and either the base or infinitive form after *help.*

1. I let my friend *borrow my typewriter*.
   use my dictionary.
2. The parents let their four-year-old child . . .
3. The parents let their sixteen-year-old child . . .
4. When I was a child my parents didn't let me . . .
5. The boss makes all her employees . . .
6. The union doesn't let the company . . .
7. An employment office helps clients . . .
8. Some teachers make students . . .
9. I had the camera store . . .
10. The customs office makes everyone entering the country . . .
11. My friend helped me . . .

USING YOUR SKILLS

A. Every family with young children must decide on certain rules that their children will follow. Most families also require children to help with some household tasks. Some families are permissive, letting children make many of their own rules. Other families are very strict. What do you think is the better policy?

1. Working on your own, write two sets of rules, one for a six-year-old boy and another for a thirteen-year-old girl. Think about reasons for your choices.
2. Discuss your answers with a small group of your classmates. Do you and your classmates agree or disagree? If possible, construct a set of rules that reflect the group's thinking.

B. Should universities make all students take certain courses? Let students choose all their own courses?
C. Should governments make all children attend elementary school? high school? university?
D. At what age should governments let people vote?
E. Should governments make all employers pay employees a minimum wage? Make employers hire and promote employees without regard to race, religion, or gender?

■■■■■■■ Make *Followed by an Adjective*

Subject	Verb	Object	Adjective
Potato chips always	*make*	him	*thirsty.*
She	*makes*	me	*angry.*
The ride	*made*	the child	*sick.*

Make followed by an adjective (*thirsty, angry, sick*) expresses the idea that something or someone causes someone to feel or behave in a certain way.

PRACTICING YOUR SKILLS

Complete these sentences. Use one of the adjectives suggested or supply your own.

tired	sick	hungry	healthy	dizzy	thirsty	impatient
happy	sad	late	strong	weak	irritable	anxious

1. The rush hour traffic sometimes makes me . . .
2. Skipping breakfast in the morning always makes me . . .
3. Vigorous exercise makes me . . .
4. Compliments make me . . .
5. Long car rides make me . . .
6. Spicy food makes me . . .
7. Waiting in line makes me . . .
8. _____ makes me . . .
9. _____ makes me . . .

Causative have *in the Passive Voice*

Notice the difference between the active and passive voice versions of sentences with *have*.

ACTIVE VOICE

Examples

I *had* the mechanic *check* the engine.

I *had* the barber *cut* my hair.

Comments

Have someone do something.

PASSIVE VOICE

Examples

I *had* the engine *checked.* (by the mechanic)

I *had* my hair *cut.* (by the barber)

Comments

Have something done (by someone).

The passive voice is often used to talk about paying to have a service done. In most cases we want to emphasize the service being done rather than the person who does it. The *"by* phrase" is usually not used.

ACTIVE VOICE

Examples

Mike is a wonderful auto mechanic. I always *have* him *check* the engine.

I *had* Jerry *cut* my hair. He always does a better job than Steve.

Comments

Emphasizes the person who does the service.

PASSIVE VOICE

Examples

I *have* the engine *checked* frequently.

I *had* my hair *cut*.

Comments

Emphasizes the service.

PRACTICING YOUR SKILLS

Change active to passive. Do not use a *"by* phrase."

1. I had the mechanic check the oil.   I had the oil checked .
2. I had the jeweler clean my watch.
3. I had the cleaner dry clean my winter clothes.
4. I had the camera store develop my film.
5. I had the shoemaker put new heels on my shoes.
6. I had the store clean my typewriter.
7. I had the repairman repair the gear shift of my bicycle.
8. I had someone type my term paper.
9. I had the optician adjust my glasses.
10. I had the dentist fill my tooth.
11. I had the dental hygienist clean my teeth.

USING YOUR SKILLS

A. If you own a car, check the service manual. It will probably tell you that you should have your car checked at regular intervals even if it is running well. According to your manual, how often should you have the following done?

    oil checked / changed   engine tuned
    spark plugs cleaned / replaced   air and fuel filters replaced
    tires replaced   brakes checked

B. If you do not own a car, tell about something else you own that needs professional maintenance or repair (a typewriter, bicycle, watch, camera, TV).

◼◼◼ Get *as a Causative*

ACTIVE VOICE

Examples

I *got* my friend *to drive* me home.

I *got* my roommate *to cook* dinner.

Comments

Get someone to do something is similar in meaning to *have someone do something*. *Get* is more informal than *have* and is more likely to be used when we talk about persuading a friend to do something rather than paying a professional for services. Notice that the infinitive (*to* + base) is used after *get*.

PASSIVE VOICE

I *got* my hair cut = I *had* my hair cut.

I *got* my bike fixed = I *had* my bike fixed.

In the passive voice, *get* may replace *have* with no change in meaning.

Get is more informal than *have*.

USING YOUR SKILLS

Are you usually successful in getting other people to help you do some of the things you need to do? Explain.

Verbs of Perception

When certain verbs of perception are followed by another verb, the second verb must be in either the present participle (verb + *-ing*) or the base form. Common verbs used in this pattern are *feel, hear, listen to, look at, notice, observe, overhear, see, smell, watch, witness.*

Examples

Last night while I was lying in bed, I *heard* the rain *beating* on the roof. I *saw* the branches of a tree outside my window *moving* in the wind.

Comments

The present participle is usually chosen to indicate an action in progress now or in the past.

I remember last night's storm. I *heard* the rain *beat* on the roof. I *saw* the branches of a large tree *move* in the wind.

The base form can also be used, especially when we want to emphasize that the action is completed.

In many cases, either the present participle or base can be used with little or no difference in meaning.

PRACTICING YOUR SKILLS

Complete the following sentences using a second verb in either the present participle or base form. (In some cases either form may be used.) Use one of the verbs suggested.

blow   cook   gossip   play   care   flash   turn   roar

1. During the storm I felt the wind _____*blow/blowing*_____ , heard the thunder _____ , saw lightning _____.
2. I like to listen to Segovia _____ the guitar.
3. I was embarrassed when I overheard two people _____ about someone I know.
4. It's wonderful to look at a great dancer _____ in the air.
5. I get hungry just as soon as I smell dinner _____.
6. Psychologists who study development observe parents _____ for their children.

USING YOUR SKILLS

Each of us has times when we are particularly aware of our perceptions. For example, on a camping trip we may be aware of all the new sights, smells, and sounds around us. If we are awake in the middle of the night, we may hear sounds we have never been aware of before and see the world around us a little differently.

Recall a time in your own life when you were particularly aware of your own perceptions. Describe as vividly as possible what you saw, heard, and felt at that time.

Making Comparisons with Adjectives and Adverbs

Examples	*Comments*
San Francisco is *as interesting as* New York.	*as . . . as* compares things (or people) that are alike in some way.
San Franciscans speak *as glowingly* about their city *as* New Yorkers do about New York.	
New York *is busier than* San Francisco.	Note the forms that are used to compare two things (people, groups) that are different in some way.
Life in New York is *more hectic than* life in San Francisco.	
People in New York move *faster than* people in most other places.	
New York is *the largest* city in the United States.	Note the forms that are used to compare three or more things (people/groups) that are different.
Some people consider San Francisco *the most beautiful* city in the United States.	
Sometimes it's difficult to know which city to talk about *the most enthusiastically*.	

SIMPLE FORM	COMPARATIVE	SUPERLATIVE	
Adjectives			
large	larg*er than*	*the* larg*est*	For one-syllable adjectives and two-syllable adjectives ending in *-y*, add *-er* to form the comparative and *-est* to form the superlative. Use *the* with the superlative.
tall	tall*er than*	*the* tall*est*	
funny	funn*ier than*	*the* funn*iest*	
Adjectives or Adverbs			
fast	fast*er than*	*the* fast*est*	A few adverbs have the same form as adjectives. She's a *fast* worker. (adjective) She works *fast*. (adverb)
hard	hard*er than*	*the* hard*est*	
late	lat*er than*	*the* lat*est*	
early	earl*ier than*	*the* earl*iest*	
Adjectives			
careful	*more* careful *than*	*the most* careful	Most two-syllable and all three-syllable adjectives and adverbs use *more . . . than* for the comparative and *the most* for the superlative.
difficult	*more* difficult *than*	*the most* difficult	
Adverbs			
quickly	*more* quickly *than*	*the most* quickly	
carefully	*more* carefully *than*	*the most* carefully	
Adjectives			
good	*better than*	*the best*	A few common adjectives and adverbs have irregular forms.
bad	*worse than*	*the worst*	
far	*farther than*	*the farthest*	
	further than	*the furthest**	
Adverbs			
well	*better than*	*the best*	
badly	*worse than*	*the worst*	
far	*farther than*	*the farthest*	
	further than	*the furthest**	

*Farther, farthest are used to talk about physical distance.

   San Francisco is farther from Chicago than New York is.

Further, furthest usually mean "additional."

   Do you have any *further* questions?

PRACTICING YOUR SKILLS

A. Using the information from the chart, fill in the blanks using an appropriate comparative form.

	New York City	*San Francisco*
Population (1980)	7,071,639	676,974
Area (square miles)	304	46
Terrain	flat	hilly
Latitude	40 degrees north	37 degrees north
Average temperature in January	24–35 degrees F	44–58 degrees F
Average temperature in July	68–81 degrees F	55–76 degrees F
Average annual snowfall	29 inches	0
Living costs	very expensive	expensive

1. The population of New York is ____*larger than*____ the population of San Francisco. (large)
2. San Francisco is _____ in area _____ New York is. (small)
3. Both cities are crowded, but New York is _____ San Francisco. (crowded)
4. New York is _____ San Francisco. (flat)
5. San Francisco is _____ New York. (hilly)
6. New York is slightly _____ north _____ San Francisco. (far)
7. In January, New York is _____ San Francisco. (cold)
8. In July, San Francisco is usually _____ New York. (cool)
9. For people who like to live in an even climate, San Francisco is _____ New York. (good)
10. For people who love snow, San Francisco is _____ New York. (bad)
11. Both cities are expensive, but life is _____ in New York _____ in San Francisco. (expensive)

B.   Construct several sentences comparing two places you have lived in or visited. Emphasize the differences between them. Talk about their climate, location, and physical characteristics. Also, tell which city you think is more beautiful, more interesting, more glamorous, more comfortable to live in. Do others in the class share your opinion?

▰▰▰▰▰ *Comparisons with* as . . . as

1.   *As* + adjective + *as* and *as* + adverb + *as* can be used to talk about people or things that are the same in some way.

    I'm *as tall as* my mother. We're both 5′3″.
    I talk *as fast as* my sister does. We both talk a mile a minute.

2.   *Almost* and *nearly* are used when the comparison is not exact.

    My younger sister is *almost as tall as (nearly as tall as)* I am.

3.   *Just* is often used to indicate that the two parts of the comparison are exactly alike.

    I work *just as hard as* my boss does.

4.   *Not as* + adjective/adverb + *as* can be used to talk about differences.

    I'm *not as tall as* my older brother.
    Rent outside New York City is *not as expensive as* rent in the city.

PRACTICING YOUR SKILLS

A.   *As* + adjective + *as* is used in several common expressions.

    Without my glasses, I'm *as blind as* a bat.
    I can never get my sister to change her mind. She's *as stubborn as* a mule.

    Complete the following with an *as* + *adjective* + *as* comparison.

1.   I won't disturb you while you're studying. I'll be _____. (quiet / a mouse)

2. He was so embarrassed at having to talk in front of the class that he turned
_____. (red / a beet)

3. I haven't eaten all day. By now I'm _____. (hungry / a bear)

4. I'll never stay at that hotel again. The bed was _____. (hard / a rock)

5. For a moment she thought that she was going to fall. She turned
_____. (white / a sheet)

6. The dancer created the illusion of weightlessness. She was
_____. (light / a feather)

7. After my exams are finished, I won't have any obligations. I'll be
_____. (free / a bird)

B. Again, make a comparison between two places you know. This time, emphasize similarities as well as differences. Use (*not*) *as* + adjective + *as*.

possible adjectives: attractive cosmopolitan exciting fascinating friendly glamorous historic modern old picturesque

Examples

My city is as fascinating as the capital city.

It's not as cosmopolitan as New York.

▬▬▬ *Using Superlative Adjectives*

The superlative form (*the coldest, the most fascinating*) is needed to compare three or more things, people, or groups.

PRACTICING YOUR SKILLS

Fill in the blanks with the superlative form of one of the following adjectives.

cold	far	hot	low
comfortable	fascinating	large	populous
crowded	high	long	small

1. The ___*hottest*___ temperature ever recorded in the United States (134 degrees F) was in Death Valley, California, in 1913.

2. The _____ United States temperature (−80 degrees F) was recorded in Prospect Creek, Alaska.

3. The _____ mountain in the United States is Mount McKinley, in Alaska (20,320 feet).

4. The Mississippi River is the _____ river in the United States (3,741 miles).

5. The _____ point in the United States is Death Valley, California (282 feet below sea level).

6. Alaska is the _____ of the 50 states in area. (570,833 square miles).

7. The place in the United States that is the _____ north is Point Barrow, Alaska.

8. The _____ state is Rhode Island (1,055 square miles).

9. With more than 26 million people in 1986, California has become the _____ state.

10. New Jersey has more people per square mile than any other state. It is the _____ .

11. The _____ city to live in is _____ .

12. The _____ city to visit is _____ .

■■■■■■■■ *Using* one of + *Superlative Adjective* + *Plural Noun*

Notice the use of *one of* and the superlative. A plural noun is needed when we talk about "one of many."

The Mississippi is *one of the longest* rivers in the world.

One of the most beautiful buildings in my country is _____ .

PRACTICING YOUR SKILLS

Construct sentences using *one of* + superlative adjective + plural noun. Talk about people, places, and events in your country.

1. popular / sport

   One of the most popular sports in my country is basketball.

2. great / writer
3. popular / place to visit
4. old / city
5. historic / site

6. large / industry
7. crucial / export (import)
8. important / natural resource
9. famous / actor or singer
10. distinguished / scholar or scientist
11. characteristic / food
12. good / university
13. heroic / person in my country's history
14. picturesque / celebration
15. important / holiday

USING YOUR SKILLS

Two travel writers were asked to list the most glamorous cities in the world.

Eugene Fodor	Kate Simon
1. Paris	1. Venice
2. New York	2. Leningrad
3. London	3. New York
4. Rio de Janeiro	4. San Francisco
5. Hong Kong	5. Kyoto

Make your own list of the five most beautiful, exciting, glamorous cities in the world. Explain your choices. You may talk about cities you have actually visited or ones that you have only heard or read about. If one of your classmates has been to any of the cities on your list, find out his/her opinion.

Using less than, the least

Less than and *the least* have the opposite meaning from *more than* and *the most*.

Adjectives

San Francisco is *less* expensive *than* New York.

One of *the* most beautiful but *least* visited National Parks is King's Canyon.

Adverbs

I love music, but I'm *less* talented *than* my sister.

Unfortunately, I'm *the least* skillful musician in my family.

PRACTICING YOUR SKILLS

Who has an opinion? Who disagrees? State your opinion using *less than* or *the least*. Add information to support or explain your opinion.

1. Which course would you find less interesting, a math course or a literature course?
2. What job would you find less challenging, working in a office or working in a store?
3. What kind of food do you find less appealing, food from your own country or American food?
4. What is the least pleasant household chore that you have to do regularly?
5. What is the least challenging job you've ever had? (least challenging course you've ever taken?)
6. What's the least relaxing vacation you've ever taken?
7. Which is the least expensive good restaurant in town?
8. What is the least useful product you have seen advertised recently?

SUMMARY EXERCISES: COMPARATIVE AND SUPERLATIVE ADJECTIVES AND ADVERBS

A. Construct questions about common last names using information from the chart below. Use a variety of comparative forms.

TEN MOST COMMON NAMES (UNITED STATES)	**TEN MOST COMMON NAMES (GREAT BRITAIN)**
1. Smith	1. Smith
2. Johnson	2. Jones
3. Williams	3. Williams
4. Brown	4. Brown
5. Jones	5. Taylor
6. Miller	6. Davies (pronounced the same as Davis)
7. Davis	7. Evans
8. Wilson	8. Thomas
9. Anderson	9. Roberts
10. Taylor	10. Johnson

B. Using the list below ask and answer questions about who you would rather work for. Compare your answers with your classmates'.

CHOOSE YOUR BOSS		
Supervisor A	*Supervisor B*	*Supervisor C*
very friendly to everyone	somewhat distant at first but people say she is friendly when you get to know her	polite but rather impersonal
loses temper occasionally	never gets angry	gets angry only about important things
works regular hours	usually works late	works late only when there is a great deal of work to do
office door is always open	easy to make an appointment to see her	visits workers' desks
explains work clearly	does not always explain work clearly the first time	gives both written and oral instructions
does not like to be asked too many questions	answers questions when asked	anticipates questions
dresses casually	dresses fashionably	wears conservative business clothes
has worked in same job for 10 years	began two years ago as trainee, was rapidly promoted	has worked for 15 years in many different companies

1. Who would you least like to work for? Why?
2. Compare the other two supervisors. Explain the differences between them using a variety of comparative forms. Which of the two would you rather work for?
3. If you have worked at two or more jobs, tell about the boss (supervisor) you liked best and why.
4. If you have been a boss or a supervisor of other employees, compare different ways of working with employees.

LITTLE WORDS

Prepositions + Noun Combinations

Many prepositions appear in fixed expressions or idioms. For example, we always say someone is *in* a hurry, that workers are *on* strike. We do not choose *in* and *on* because of their meaning but because those prepositions always occur in those expressions.

There are many such fixed expressions using prepositions in English. Below are several common expressions in which the preposition *in* or *on* is used with nouns. Practice using them in sentences of your own.

Using in, on *with Nouns in Fixed Expressions*

1. We say *in* a language (*in* English, Spanish, Russian, Chinese, etc.)

    The dictionary gives definitions *in* English and *in* Spanish.

2. We say *in* a book (a newspaper, a magazine, essay, story, etc.), but *on* the radio, *on* television, *on* the telephone.

    Many people prefer to watch the news *on* television; others like to read the more detailed accounts that appear *in* the newspapers.

3. We say *in* the rain (snow, sun), *in* good (bad, nice, rainy, snowy, sunny, cloudy, clear) weather, but *on* a clear (sunny, cloudy) day.

    In bad weather I usually drive to work; *on* a clear day, I like to walk.

4. We say *in* to refer to an item of clothing that someone is wearing.

    The man *in* the red sweater is in two of my classes.

5. We say *in* a loud (soft, high, low, clear, steady, unsteady, etc.) voice, *in* a whisper.

    Maxine spoke *in* a loud voice. Another child spoke *in* a whisper.

6.   We say *in* a good (bad, terrible, pleasant, etc.) mood.

I always wait until my mother is *in* a good mood before I tell her any bad news.

7.   We say *in* style, *in* fashion, *in* good (bad, poor) taste. *Out of* style, *out of* fashion to mean the opposite.

Not everything that is *in* style is *in* good taste.

8.   We say *in* (good, bad, poor) health when we refer to people: *in* (good, bad, wonderful, terrible, etc.) condition/shape when we refer to things and sometimes people.

My grandfather walks two miles every day to stay *in* good health. He's *in* good shape for his age.

If you can find a used car *in* good condition, you should buy it.

PRACTICING YOUR SKILLS

Use the preposition + noun combination you learned in this section to answer the following questions.

1.   What is your major source of news: newspapers, radio, TV? *In* what language do you usually read (watch, listen to) the news? *In* what language do you talk about the news?

2.   What are some kinds of leisure activities you usually do *in* different kinds of weather?

3.   Do you usually speak *in* a loud voice or a soft one? How does your voice change when you are nervous, excited, angry, *in* a good or bad mood?

4.   How do you feel about following fashions in clothing? Is it important for you to stay *in style*? Are there some things that are *out of* style that you like anyway?

5.   What do you do to stay *in* good health? What would you advise others to do?

SENTENCE SENSE

Expressing Cause and Result

Using because *or* since *to Introduce Causes*

Either *because* or *since* can be used to show the cause of an action or situation.

Examples

Sometimes people use words that are wrong *because* they sound better than the right ones.

Since there are many words with similar meanings, I sometimes choose the wrong one.

Comments

Because and *since* introduce a clause (subject and verb) indicating cause; another clause expresses the result.

Either clause can come first. A comma is used when the dependent clause comes first.

PRACTICING YOUR SKILLS

Determine the cause and result in each set of sentences. Then combine each set into one sentence using *because* or *since*. Pay attention to your use of commas.

1. Thousands of new words are added to English every year. Dictionaries must publish new editions periodically to keep up with the way people use language.

   Since / Because thousands of new words are added to English every year, dictionaries must publish new editions periodically to keep up with the way people use language.

2. In 1986, one publisher decided to publish a second edition of its unabridged dictionary. Definitions of many words were out of date, and there were no entries for many commonly used words.
3. *Compact disc* and *VCR* were not defined in the first edition. These things had not been invented yet.
4. No one could find a definition for *reggae* in the 1966 edition. The word for the popular Jamaican music was not introduced until 1968.

5. The word *chocoholic* to describe people who are addicted to chocolate is a recently invented word. It cannot be found in the earlier edition.

6. Revising a dictionary is a complicated task. It took nine years to complete the new edition.

7. No single person can keep up with new words in computer science, medicine, business, or the arts. Hundreds of experts in 180 different fields were asked to write or edit definitions.

8. In some controversial fields, several authorities were consulted on a single word. The experts did not always agree on definitions.

9. Fifty thousand new words were added. The second edition is 500 pages longer than the first.

10. It takes a lot of space to give definitions for 315,000 words. The new dictionary weighs 13½ pounds.

11. People go to the library to look up words they cannot find in smaller dictionaries. Libraries must purchase major new unabridged editions as soon as they appear.

12. Most people need to consult an unbridged dictionary only occasionally. They can get by with a much smaller and more convenient dictionary for every day use.

▬▬▬▬▬ *Using* because of*

Examples	*Comments*
Because of new discoveries in science, new words were invented to express new ideas.	*Because of* introduces phrases telling the cause.
	A clause expresses the result. When the phrase precedes the clause, a comma is usually needed.

PRACTICING YOUR SKILLS

Add *because of* before the phrase and combine it with an appropriate result clause to form a sentence. Add a comma when necessary.

Because of the inclusion of 50,000 new words, the second edition is even larger than the first.

or

The second edition is even larger than the first *because of* the inclusion of 50,000 new words.

---

*Due to is also used to introduce phrases stating cause. This usage not considered acceptable by some authorities.

Phrases	*Clauses*
inclusion of 50,000 new words	Many people do not own one.
amount of time needed to write definitions	The second edition is even larger than the first.
failure of experts to agree	More than one expert had to be consulted in many cases.
size and expense of the average unabridged dictionary	It took nine years to complete the task.
many new inventions in 20 years	Many new words were invented to describe them.
number of editors and experts who had to be hired	The second edition cost several million dollars to produce.
need to include both popular words and technical words	Dictionary editors look at words in both popular magazines and technical journals.

▰▰▰▰ *Transitions to Introduce Results*

The following words and phrases—arranged in increasing order of formality—are used to introduce results. The more formal transitions (especially *thus* and *hence*) are rarely used in spoken English.

as a result	consequently
for this (that) reason	thus
therefore	hence

Examples	*Comments*
There are many things I have learned to do on my own. *As a result,* I feel confident that I can do almost anything I want to do.	Transitions help relate ideas in one sentence to those in the next sentence or clause.
I refused to listen to my parents' advice; *consequently,* my table manners are atrocious.	Transitions are usually followed by a comma.
Some children are disciplined very severely; *therefore,* they are extremely afraid of making a mistake.	The two sentences may be joined with a semicolon.

PRACTICING YOUR SKILLS

A.   You have been asked to talk about your own best qualities. You are modest enough to believe that most of your good qualities are a result of the way your parents and other adults treated you as a child. Construct sentences about yourself using each of these connectors used in everyday speech — *because, since, as, because of, as a result, for this (that) reason* — to talk about cause and result.

Examples

I'm a hard worker *because* I saw my parents work hard all their lives.

My parents always told my sisters and me that we were smart enough to learn anything if we tried hard enough. *As a result*, all of us have done well in school.

B.   Although it is almost impossible to prove the influence of people's childhood experiences on their personalities as adults, many people have opinions on the matter. Choose five of the childhood situations listed below and write as many sentences as possible for each of your choices. Use a variety of cause-and-result connectors: *because, since, because of, as a result, for this (that) reason, therefore, consequently*. When you have finished, share your answers with a partner, small group, or the class, and discuss differences in opinion.

1.   Growing up in a large family.

Because children who grow up in a large family must learn to share, they usually find it easier to cooperate with others when they become adults.

Parents with large families cannot spend a great deal of time supervising each child; *for that reason*, children in such families learn to take care of themselves at an early age.

2.   being an only child.
3.   being the youngest (oldest, middle) child in a family
4.   being raised by one parent only
5.   being raised in a nuclear (extended) family*
6.   having strict (permissive) parents
7.   being raised in a family where traditional male and female roles are important (unimportant)
8.   being raised in society that is rapidly changing
9.   being raised under the threat of nuclear war

*In a nuclear family, only parents and children live together. In an extended family, other relatives live in the same household and often share responsibility for the care of children.

USING YOUR SKILLS

A.   Working in a small group, imagine that you and your classmates are sociologists who have just finished some research in which you have studied a hundred families over a period of 25 years. When you first began your research, all the children in the families were less than five years old. They are now adults. The purpose of your study was to establish a connection between childrearing and later development of good and bad personality traits. You believe that your research team found a connection and have just written a report of your findings. Write a summary of your report. Use a variety of connecting words, including those that are common in more formal writing: *therefore, consequently, thus, hence.*

■■■■■■■ *Cause and Result with* so . . . that, such . . . that

When *so . . . that* and *such . . . that* are used to enclose other words or phrases, they give the cause of a situation or action and are followed by a clause stating the result. *That* is sometimes omitted, especially when speaking.

SO . . . THAT

Examples	*Comments*

I was *so tired (that)* I could barely
      ADJ
 move. (Because I was very tired, I could barely move.)
	so . . . (that)
	   ADJ

She spoke *so fast (that)* I could barely
      ADV
 understand a word.
	so . . . (that)
	   ADV

There were *so many people (that)* it
      NOUN
 took me a long time to find my friends.
	so many or *few* . . . . *(that)*
	     COUNTABLE NOUN

I had *so much fun (that)* I decided to
      NOUN
 stay later then I had planned.
	so much or *little* . . . . . . *(that)*
	     MASS NOUN

SUCH ... THAT

She was *such an interesting speaker*
    ADJ NOUN
(that) her audience applauded at the end of her talk. (Because she was a very interesting speaker, her audience applauded at the end of her talk.)

such . . . . *(that)*
 ADJ + NOUN

PRACTICING YOUR SKILLS

A. Fill in the blanks with the names of friends or famous people. Then complete the sentences in your own words.

1. ____Woody Allen____ was so funny that ____the audience never stopped laughing____.

2. _____ tells such good jokes that _____.

3. _____ is so intelligent that _____.

4. _____ speaks so convincingly that _____.

5. _____ plays so many different kinds of music that _____.

6. _____ has such a beautiful voice that _____.

7. _____ has so much confidence that _____.

  Continue constructing sentences about people you know based on the model.

B. Fill in the blanks with either *so* or *such*. Then complete the sentences with a result clause.

1. There were _____*so*_____ many people who wanted to hear the speaker *that very few of us could find seats*.

2. It was _____*such*_____ a large audience that *people had to stand in the back of the room*.

3. The room was _____ crowded that _____.

4. There were _____ few chairs that _____.

5. It was _____ a small room that _____.

6. When she started to speak, the room was _____ noisy that _____ _____.

7. However, she spoke in _____ an eloquent way that _____.

C. Think about a speech or performance that impressed you very much. Jot down adjectives, adverbs, and adjective + noun combinations to describe what you remember. Then, construct several sentences about the event using *so* or *such* and a result clause.

Example

Event: rock concert

famous band; well-publicized concert; hot, crowded, noisy, packed auditorium; difficult to find seat; uncomfortable but very much fun; good sound system; talented keyboard player, played skillfully; amazing drummer, played wonderfully; played many different styles of music

It was such a famous band that people lined up to buy tickets the night before.
The auditorium was so crowded that it was hard to find a place to stand.

D. Follow the directions for the previous exercise. However, this time describe a place that impressed you greatly.
E. Follow the directions for the previous exercise. However, this time describe a person that you either like or dislike.

Expressing Purpose

Using so that, (in order) to *to Express Purpose*

Either *so that* or *(in order) to* are used to connect a situation or event and its purpose.

Examples

She is changing jobs *so that* she can do more interesting work.

He went back to school *so that* he could finish his degree.

Comments

So that is followed by a clause. Modal auxiliaries such as *can, could, may, might, will, would* are used in the second clause.*

---

*Do not confuse *so that* used to introduce a purpose with the coordinating conjunction *so* (page 257), meaning result. A modal auxiliary usually signals purpose.

Compare:

I wanted a better job, so I began taking courses in night school. (result)

I wanted a better job so that I could earn more money. (purpose)

She is changing jobs *in order to* do more interesting work.

He went back to school *to* finish his degree.

(In order) to is followed by the base form of a verb (no subject).

PRACTICING YOUR SKILLS

A. The advertisement on page 310 is addressed to people who have left school. It lists a large number of reasons why they may want to return. Construct ten sentences using *so that* or *(in order) to* to talk about the reasons you or your friends have for going to or returning to school. You may use reasons from the advertisement or make up your own.

Examples

I'm going to school (in order) to get a masters in computer science.

My friend's mother is returning to school so that she can get her B.A. before her daughter does.

B. In a poll published in *Newsweek* magazine in 1986, a group of American working women were asked if they worked primarily to earn money or for some other reason.

	Worked Mostly to Earn Money	*Worked Mostly for Other Reasons*
Total working women	56%	41%
College grads	36%	59%
No college	65%	33%
By occupations		
Blue Collar	60%	37%
Clerical and sales	68%	29%
Professional and business	40%	57%

1. Construct several sentences interpreting the poll. Use *so that* or *(in order) to* in your answers.

2. Construct several sentences of your own using *(in order) to* or *so that* to talk about people you know and some of their reasons for working. Use a different reason in each sentence.

"Someday I'm going back to school to...

☐ GET A MASTERS IN COMPUTER SCIENCE
☐ TAKE ANOTHER CRACK AT CHAUCER
☐ START WORK ON MY NURSING DEGREE
☐ SHOW THAT HIGH SCHOOL TEACHER WHO SAID I'D NEVER MAKE IT PAST 12TH GRADE
☐ START A PROGRAM FOR THE HOMELESS
☐ BONE UP FOR THE CPA REVIEW
☐ FINISH COLLEGE
☐ STUDY CONVERSATIONAL ITALIAN
☐ EARN CREDITS TOWARD MY TEACHING CERTIFICATE
☐ DISCOVER HOW GOOD MY MATH IS
☐ TAKE THOSE SCIENCE COURSES I'LL NEED FOR MED SCHOOL
☐ FINISH MY DISSERTATION ON THE FRENCH REVOLUTION
☐ BECOME A CLINICAL PSYCHOLOGIST
☐ GET A DOCTORATE IN CHILD DEVELOPMENT
☐ GET MORE FUN OUT OF LIFE
☐ STUDY MUSIC

☐ IMPROVE MY LEGAL WRITING SKILLS
☐ FIND A MORE MEANINGFUL CAREER
☐ LEARN TV PRODUCTION
☐ GET A PhD IN CHEMISTRY
☐ GET A MASTERS IN INDUSTRIAL RELATIONS
☐ TAKE A BUSINESS COURSE
☐ TAKE A COURSE IN FAMILY RELATIONS
☐ LEARN HOW TO RUN A RADIO STATION
☐ IMPROVE MY MANAGEMENT SKILLS
☐ BECOME A DENTIST
☐ STUDY LATIN-AMERICAN ANTHROPOLOGY
☐ GET A DEGREE IN CRIMINAL JUSTICE
☐ STUDY WESTERN CIVILIZATION
☐ BECOME A LABOR NEGOTIATOR
☐ TAKE A COURSE IN WOMEN'S STUDIES
☐ OPEN A HOSPICE FOR AIDS PATIENTS
☐ TEACH PHILOSOPHY
☐ TUTOR INNER-CITY HIGH SCHOOL STUDENTS

☐ IMMERSE MYSELF IN THE CLASSICS
☐ FINISH MY GRADUATE WORK IN SOCIOLOGY
☐ ENTER A PRE-PROFESSIONAL HEALTH SCIENCES PROGRAM
☐ STUDY CREATIVE WRITING
☐ GET READY FOR RETIREMENT
☐ ACQUIRE A SPECIALTY IN PERINATAL NURSING
☐ GET MY DOCTORATE IN SOCIAL WORK
☐ LEARN HOW TO MAKE A MOVIE
☐ TAKE A MARKETING COURSE
☐ GET MY DEGREE IN POLITICAL SCIENCE
☐ LEARN TO HANDLE MONEY
☐ STUDY COMPARATIVE RELIGIONS
☐ GET A MASTERS IN HEALTH LAW
☐ BECOME A DENTAL HYGIENIST
☐ TAKE SOME COURSES IN PASTORAL COUNSELING
☐ GET MY B.A. BEFORE MY DAUGHTER GETS HERS "

LOYOLA UNIVERSITY OF CHICAGO
More school to go back to.

USING YOUR SKILLS

What factors are important to you in choosing a job? What do you hope to achieve through your work? Write a short essay about the work you do or are planning to do and your goals. Use a variety of ways of expressing cause, result, and purpose in your essay.

Expressing Contrast and Concession

A number of words and phrases emphasize either direct opposition or an unexpected result.

Notice how words in italics in the following sentences from "A New Understanding of the Past" (pages 153, 154) help show the contrasts that are emphasized in the article.

> [Researchers] once considered these 250 centuries to be a period in which the ancestors of modern man made little progress. *However,* in the past decade, researchers have begun to conclude that *on the contrary* this period, the late ice age, was a time that witnessed a great explosion of civilization. *In fact,* the people of this time are probably the inventors of language, music, art, and the foundations of trade.
>
> *Although* the Cro-Magnon's total brain size is no bigger than that of their more primitive predecessors, the frontal lobes of the Cro-Magnon brain are larger and more developed. . . . *While* Neanderthals died before their mid-40s, there is evidence that some Cro-Magnons lived into their sixties.

While, whereas

Examples

While most Neanderthals died young, some Cro-Magnons lived long enough to pass on their knowledge to the next generation.

Neanderthals were heavy boned and muscular *while* Cro-Magnons were slimmer in appearance.

The Neanderthals' small frontal lobes limited their capacity for symbolic thought, *whereas* the Cro-Magnons could use their superior brains to improve their lives.

Comments

While and *whereas* connect clauses showing ideas in direct opposition and may usually be attached to either clause.

While is used in both conversation and writing.

Whereas is used only in formal English.

PRACTICING YOUR SKILLS

A.   Combine sentences using *while*. *While* may be attached to either clause. When the subordinate clause comes first, a comma is needed.

1.   English is written from left to right.
Arabic is written from right to left.

English is written from left to right *while* Arabic is written from right to left.
While English is written from left to right, Arabic is written from right to left.

Arabic is written from right to left *while* English is written from left to right.
While Arabic is written from right to left, English is written from left to right.

2.   Computers process information in sequence.
The human brain processes many different kinds of information at the same time.

3.   In the United States, distances are measured in miles. In most parts of the world distances are measured in kilometers.

4.   In temperate climates there are hot and cold seasons.
In tropical climates there are dry and rainy seasons.

B.   Continue the exercise by constructing complex sentences about several of the following topics, using *while* to show ideas in opposition.

1. prehistoric civilization / modern civilization
2. technological societies / nontechnological societies
3. animal intelligence / human intelligence
4. science courses / humanities courses
5. lecture courses / discussion courses
6. high school courses / college courses
7. dictionaries / encyclopedias
8. bilingual dictionaries / monolingual dictionaries
9. your language / English
10. the most prestigious jobs in your country / the most prestigious jobs in the United States (or another country you know well)
11. the most important unsolved problem in your country / the most important unsolved problem in the United States (or another country you know well)

USING YOUR SKILLS

Select a topic that you are familiar with from the previous exercise. Write an essay emphasizing contrasts. Use *while* and *whereas*.

▰▰▰▰▰▰ Instead of

Examples

Instead of bringing a bottle of wine, you should give the hostess a small bouquet of flowers.

You should always present gifts with your right hand *instead of* your left hand.

Comments

Instead of is followed by a noun, noun phrase, or a gerund, not a clause.

PRACTICING YOUR SKILLS

Complete the following sentences.

1. Let's have some tea instead of _____ *coffee* _____ .
2. You should study in the library instead of _____ .
3. You should take a science course next semester instead of _____ .
4. You should use a bilingual dictionary instead of _____ .
5. Let's walk instead of _____ .
6. You can give the hostess some candy instead of _____ .

USING YOUR SKILLS

If a North American were to visit your country without knowing some of the customs, he or she would probably be misunderstood in many social situations. What North American social customs would be considered unusual or rude in your home country? Give advice about appropriate behavior for a visitor who is invited to someone's home. Use *instead of* or *while*.

Examples

While Americans sometimes bring a homemade food specialty when invited to dinner, in my country such a gift would be rude because it would imply that the guest did not expect to be fed well.

Instead of arriving exactly on time, you should be a little late.

■■■■■■■■ **On the contrary, in fact**

Examples	*Comments*
Some people think that nursing is an unrewarding job; *on the contrary*, it provides the satisfaction of knowing that you are helping people.	*On the contrary* introduces an idea or opinion in direct opposition to what has been said previously.
Some people think that improvements in medicine mean that fewer health care workers are needed; *in fact*, health care is one of the fastest growing professions.	*In fact* indicates that the previous information is wrong.

ASK AND ANSWER

Ask a partner the following questions about an average day in the United States. Your partner must guess an answer even though he or she probably will not know. Respond with *in fact* and the correct answer (found on the bottom of this page).*

Example

A: On a typical day how many Americans go to the movies?

B: I'd guess a million.

A: In fact 3 million Americans go to the movies on a typical day.

On a typical day in the United States . . .

1. how many babies are born?
2. how many twins or triplets are born?
3. how many telephone calls are made?
4. how many long-distance telephone conversations take place?
5. how many cups of coffee are drunk?
6. how many couples get married?
7. how many people go to school?
8. how many people celebrate their sixty-fifth birthday?
9. how many people go to hear a major symphony orchestra?
10. how many people die?

*1. 9,077 babies 2. 360 twins or triplets 3. 679,000,000 telephone calls 4. 50,000,000 long-distance telephone conversations 5. 500,000,000 cups of coffee 6. 5,962 couples 7. 41,000,000 children and adults go to school. 8. 5,041 people turn 65. 9. 38,690 people attend a symphony concert. 10. 5,200 people die. Statistics *from* Mike Feinsilber and William B. Mead, *American Averages: Amazing Facts of Everyday Life* (New York: Doubleday, 1980).

USING YOUR SKILLS

What are some common misconceptions that people have about your country or your language? Explain what people think; then tell what you believe to be true. Use *on the contrary* and *in fact*.

████████ **On the other hand**

Example	*Comments*
Nursing is not as well paid as some other professions; *on the other hand,* it provides the satisfaction of knowing that you are helping others.	*On the other hand* relates facts or ideas that are different but not always in direct contrast.

USING YOUR SKILLS

A. Write or talk about a job or profession that you are considering, focusing on its advantages and disadvantages. Use *on the other hand.*

B. Write or talk about a current social or political issue that you have not yet made up your mind about. Try to give several sides of the issue. Use *on the other hand* to present various opinions.

████████ *Expressing Concession (Unexpected Result)*

Some words and phrases emphasize facts or ideas that are different from what we might expect.

Although he doesn't eat well, he is healthy.

I had a wonderful time *even though* I don't usually like parties.

Despite his not eating well, he is healthy.

I usually don't like parties; *however*, I had a wonderful time.

████████ **Though, even though, although**

Examples	*Comments*
(Even) though he eats a lot, he doesn't gain weight.	*Though, even though,* and *although* are followed by a clause (subject and verb). All are used in speech.

Examples	*Comments*
It is possible in restaurants to ignore food that has dropped on the floor *although* it would be kinder to call the waiter's attention to the fact that there is a fish on the floor.	*Although* is preferred in more formal styles of written English. A comma is used when the dependent clause precedes the main clause.

PRACTICING YOUR SKILLS

A. Connect the following sentences, using *though, even though,* or *although* to express an unexpected result.

1. It was very noisy. I slept soundly.

/*(Even) though*/*although* it was very noisy, I slept soundly.

2. He has a good reputation. I have never been able to trust him.
3. She's the best driver I know. She had an accident.
4. I don't remember everything in the lecture. I take good notes.
5. They told the truth. Not a single person believed them.
6. Some people are good spellers. They need to use a dictionary sometimes.
7. His mother is getting older. She hasn't lost any of her energy.
8. I can't remember his name. I've met him several times.
9. She's been searching for several weeks. She hasn't found a job yet.

B. Combine sentences. If the result is expected, use *because* or *since*. If the result is unexpected, use *though*, *even though*, or *although*.

1. The food was wonderful. Everyone ate a great deal.

Because/*since* the food was wonderful, everyone ate a great deal.

2. My family still hasn't received the package. I mailed it several weeks ago.

My family still hasn't received the package *though (even though*/*although)* I mailed it several weeks ago.

3. The car is in good condition and the tank is full of gas. It doesn't run.
4. I've worked overtime. I have some extra money.
5. Many people were impressed with the candidate. She didn't win the election.
6. I had worked hard from morning to night. I fell asleep as soon as my head hit the pillow.
7. I was tired. I managed to finish all the work I had to do.

8. The sky was cloudy all day. It didn't rain.
9. I had read the book before. I remembered most of the important information.
10. She proofread her essay carefully. She made only a few mistakes.
11. I took two aspirin an hour ago. I still have a headache.

In spite of, despite*

Examples

He never gains a pound *in spite of* the enormous amount of food he eats every day.

Despite their "primitive" qualities, the brains of dolphins and whales evolved in a rare manner.

Comments

In spite of and *despite* also express an unexpected result but are followed by phrases.

PRACTICING YOUR SKILLS

Connect the following phrases with their unexpected results. Add *despite* or *in spite of* before each phrase.

Example

In spite of/despite her injured foot, she managed to finish the race in second place.

Phrases

her injured foot

the heavy traffic
the cold weather
his anger
the noise
their unfamiliarity
  with many of the words
her rapid speech
their late start

Clauses (unexpected result)

They managed to understand most
of the article.
He managed to talk in a calm voice.
I was able to follow the conversation.
They finished the work in plenty of time.
She finished the race in second place.
I appreciate winter.

I could hear the concert.
The trip never takes more than a
half hour.

Despite the fact (that) and *in spite of the fact (that)* are followed by clauses (subject and verb).

Despite the fact that/In spite of the fact that he eats an enormous amount of food every day, he doesn't gain any weight.

▬▬▬▬▬ *Concession:* however, nevertheless, nonetheless

These transition words introduce a concession. They are similar in meaning to *yet* or *but . . . still* but are more formal in style. *However* is used in both speech and writing. *Nevertheless* and *nonetheless* are common only in formal writing.

Examples	*Comments*
My uncle is no longer young; *however*, his mind is as active as it was when he was 20.	*However* may appear at the beginning or end of a sentence or clause. Note the punctuation used.
He needs his rest, however.	In some cases, *however* may be placed in the middle of a sentence. Commas seperate it from the rest of the sentence. Placing it at the end or in the middle of the sentence makes it more emphatic.
Most men in their sixties, *however*, are not as healthy as he is.	
Many states have passed laws to prevent air pollution; *nevertheless/ nonetheless*, the air over most large cities continues to worsen.	*Nevertheless* and *nonetheless* usually begin a sentence or clause.

PRACTICING YOUR SKILLS

A. Rewrite these sentences using *however*. If it is possible to place *however* in more than one position in your sentences, give as many stylistic variations as you can, paying attention to the punctuation used.

1. Passengers wearing seat belts may still be injured in a serious accident, but they are much less likely to be killed.

Passengers wearing seat belts may still be injured in a serious accident; *however*, they are less likely to be killed.

Passengers wearing seat belts may still be injured in a serious accident; they are less likely to be killed, *however*.

Passengers wearing seat belts may still be injured in a serious accident; they are, *however*, less likely to be killed.

2. My uncle is not a citizen, but he still has to pay taxes.

3. My government has tried several approaches to solving the problems of farmers, yet food production has not kept up with the needs of a growing population.

4. My friend's study habits don't seem very efficient to me, yet she gets good grades.

5. Medical science has made great progress over the past few years, but it still has not found the cure for the common cold.
6. Modernization has brought about many necessary changes in my country, yet I feel it is important to maintain our traditional culture.

B. Rewrite two sentences from the previous exercise using *nevertheless* and two sentences using *nonetheless.* Check your punctuation.

SUMMARY EXERCISES: CONTRAST AND CONCESSION

A. Construct sentences interpreting the chart below, emphasizing contrasts between answers given in 1977 and 1985 and in answers given by men and women in each year. Use *while, whereas, instead of, on the contrary, in fact,* and *on the other hand*.

Changing Attitudes Toward Women's Roles

	Women		Men	
	1977	1985	1977	1985
It is much better for everyone if the man is the achiever and the woman takes care of the home and family.	62.3%	46.1%	67.9%	49.5
It is more important for a wife to help her husband's career than to have one herself.	59.1	36.4	50.4	35.9
A working mother can establish just as warm and secure a relationship with her children as a mother who does not work.	54.4	66.7	40.9	52.5
A preschool child is likely to suffer if his or her mother works.	61.5	46.0	71.5	61.5

Sources: National Opinion Research Center;
University of Michigan Population Studies Center

B.   Combine the following sets of sentences into a single sentence using one of the following: *however, nevertheless, nonetheless, although, even though, despite,* or *in spite of*. There are several possibilities for each set of sentences. Compare your answers with those of others in the class. Although your sentences should all have approximately the same meaning, do you see any differences in style or levels of formality?

1.   Progress has been made recently.
Working women lack some advantages that men have.

Although/Even though progress has been made recently, working women lack some advantages that men have.

Despite/In spite of the progress that has been made recently, working women lack some advantages that men have.

Progress has been made recently; *however/nevertheless/nonetheless* working women lack some advantages that men have.

2.   There are many more jobs open to women than there were previously.
Women's salaries are not equal to men's salaries.

3.   A man in some companies may receive a high salary.
A woman with the same job may get less pay.

4.   In some fields women have equal access to beginning jobs.
They are less likely to be promoted than their male counterparts.

5.   Most elementary school teachers are women.
Most elementary school principals are men.

6.   More and more women need to work in order to support their families.
Some employers still think that male employees are the only breadwinners.

7.   Some women with young children would prefer to work part time or at a job with flexible hours.
Such jobs are not easy to find and often have low salaries and few benefits.

8.   More women with young children are working outside the home.
There are not enough good day-care centers.

9.   Day-care workers need to be sensitive and highly skilled.
Salaries for day-care workers are generally very low.

10.   Some people think that large companies should provide on-site day care for workers.
Only a small number of corporations have done so.

C.   The chart below compares women's salaries to those of men in the United States, Australia, and several countries of Western Europe. With your classmates, construct as many sentences as you can describing the information given. Use a variety of expressions from this section to express relationships between facts.

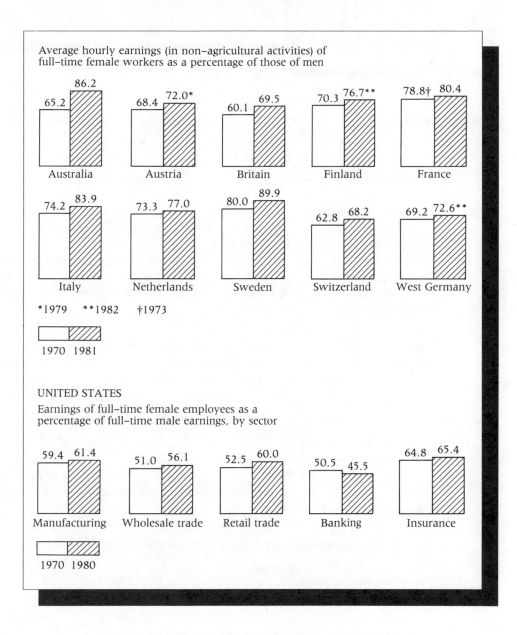

Average hourly earnings (in non–agricultural activities) of full–time female workers as a percentage of those of men

Australia 65.2 86.2
Austria 68.4 72.0*
Britain 60.1 69.5
Finland 70.3 76.7**
France 78.8† 80.4

Italy 74.2 83.9
Netherlands 73.3 77.0
Sweden 80.0 89.9
Switzerland 62.8 68.2
West Germany 69.2 72.6**

*1979   **1982   †1973

1970 1981

UNITED STATES

Earnings of full–time female employees as a percentage of full–time male earnings, by sector

Manufacturing 59.4 61.4
Wholesale trade 51.0 56.1
Retail trade 52.5 60.0
Banking 50.5 45.5
Insurance 64.8 65.4

1970 1980

D. Have job opportunities for women changed in your country? If so, what changes have been made and what is still to be done?

E. Write or talk about a reform movement or social change in progress in your country. What has been achieved? What is still to be done?

CHECKING IT OVER

Review of Tenses, Passive and Active Voice

PRACTICING YOUR SKILLS

A. In the following selections from Jack Agueros' memoir of growing up in a Puerto Rican community in New York City, the simple past, the past perfect, and *would* + base are used to talk about past time in the active voice. (Verbs in the passive voice are in italic type.) Fill in the blanks with an appropriate verb form. Check your answers on page 437. Note: In some cases a choice other than the one made by the author is possible. Discuss any differences with your teacher and classmates.

1 My house _____*had*_____ books, not many, but my   have
   parents _____ me to read. As I   encourage
   _____ a good reader they   become
   _____ books for me and never   buy
5 _____ me money for their purchase. My father   refuse
   once _____ a bookcase for me. It   build
   _____ an important moment, for I   be
   _____ always _____ that my   believe
   father _____ not too happy about my being a   be
10 bookworm.

The passage continues with Agueros' account of family celebrations.

   The atmosphere at home _____ always warm.   be
   We _____ to be a popular family. We   seem
   _____ frequently, with two standing parties a   entertain
   year—at Christmas and for my birthday. Parties
15 _____ always large. My father   be
   _____ the beds and _____   dismantle / move
   all the furniture so that the full two rooms *could be used*
   for dancing. My mother _____ up a storm,   cook

20   particularly at Christmas. *"Pasteles," "lechon asado," "arroz*
      con gandules," and a lot of *"coquito"* to drink (meat-stuffed
      plantain, roast pork, rice with pigeon peas, and coconut nog).
      My father always _____ in a band. They   bring
      _____ without compensation and   play
      _____ guests at the party. They   be
25   _____ and _____ and   eat / drink
      _____ while a victrola _____   dance / cover
      the intermissions. One year my father _____   bring
      home a whole pig and _____ it in the foyer   hang
      doorway. He and my mother _____ it by   prepare
30   rubbing it down with oil, oregano, and garlic. After preparation,
      the pig *was taken down* and *carried* over to a local bakery
      where it *was cooked* and *returned* home. Parties always
      _____ on till daybreak, and in addition to the   go
      band there _____ always volunteers to sing   be
35   and declaim poetry.

B.   The verbs in italic type are in the passive voice. Change them to the active.
          Which do you prefer in this passage?

C.   Most of the sentences in the passage are in the active voice. Try substituting
          the passive voice when possible. Do you prefer any of the substitutions?

VOCABULARY

bookworm: a person who reads a lot
standing: regularly scheduled
dismantle: take apart
cook up a storm: cook a great deal of special food
without compensation: without pay
victrola: old-fashioned record player

CHAPTER 9

TIME AND TENSE

There are three more ways of talking about future time in English: the future progressive tense, the future perfect tense, and the future perfect progressive tense. Although used much less often than the future tenses discussed in Chapter 3, these additional future tenses are often used when we want to relate one event in the future to another event or time in the future.

The Future Progressive Tense

Forming the Future Progressive Tense

The future progressive is formed with *will* + *be* + verb + *-ing*.

Subject	will	be	Verb + -ing	
We	will	be	writing	our final exam next week.
I	will	be	studying	most of the weekend.

Using the Future Progressive Tense

1. The future progressive is often used when we look ahead to actions that will be in progress at a specific time in the future.

    At this time next week, I *will be finishing* my last exam.
    On July 2, I *will be returning* home.

2. Like other progressive tenses, the future progressive is usually used only with action verbs. With most nonaction (stative) verbs, use *will* + verb instead. (See pages 48–50 for a list of the most common nonaction verbs.)

    When I return, my own country *will seem* strange to me.
    Not
    ~~will be seeming strange~~

3. *May, might, could,* and *should* can be used when we are not certain that the action will take place. *Should* reflects a higher degree of certainty than either *may, might,* or *could.*

I'm applying to graduate school. I should be getting my M.A. in a few years.

Five years from now I could still be studying, or I might be working.

PRACTICING YOUR SKILLS

Where will you be and what will you be doing at this time tomorrow? Perhaps you are quite certain what you will be doing; perhaps there are several possibilities. Complete the following sentences in the future progressive. Use *will* if you are certain of what you will be doing at the time mentioned. Use *should* if you are less certain. Use *may, might,* or *could* if you are mentioning one of several possibilities.

1. At 7:30 tomorrow morning, *I'll be eating breakfast*.
   I might still be sleeping.
2. At 8:30 tomorrow morning, . . .
3. At 10:30 tomorrow, . . .
4. At 5:30 P.M. tomorrow, . . .
5. At 7:00 P.M. tomorrow, . . .
6. At midnight tomorrow, . . .
7. Next Tuesday at noon, . . .
8. On my next birthday, . . .
9. On this date next year, . . .

USING YOUR SKILLS

Tell or write about a specific event you are looking forward to: a visit from an old friend, a party, the last day of class. Use a variety of future tenses, including the future progressive to tell what you think you will be doing on that date.

The Future Perfect Tense

Forming the Future Perfect Tense

The future perfect is formed with *will* + *have* + past participle.*

Subject	will	have	Past Participle	
I	will	have	written	all my exams by next week.
I	will	have	finished	all my other work before then.

Using the Future Perfect Tense

The future perfect is used to describe events or actions that will be completed before a specific time or before another event in the future.

By the time I finish my computer course, I *will have learned* how to use four different programming languages.

By the end of the year, NASA *will have launched* three more space vehicles.

PRACTICING YOUR SKILLS

What are your short-range and long-range goals for the future? Tell several things you plan to have accomplished before the times mentioned.

1. By the end of this week, *I will have answered several letters*.
   I will have balanced my checkbook.
2. By the end of the year, . . .
3. By (five years from now), . . .
4. In my lifetime, . . .

---

*Past participle is the traditional term for the form of the verb that is always used after the auxiliary *have* in English. The name sometimes confuses students because they think the past participle can be used to talk only about past time. This is not true. The past participle is used to talk about present and future events as well as past ones.

USING YOUR SKILLS

Sometimes in applying for a job or admission to college, people are asked to write a letter or a short essay describing their plans for the future and explaining how they intend to carry out those plans. Practice writing such a letter or essay. Decide if you are writing for an employer, a college admissions officer, or some other person, and write accordingly.

The Future Perfect Progressive Tense

Forming the Future Perfect Progressive Tense

The future perfect progressive is formed with *will* + *have* + *been* + verb + *-ing*.

Subject	will	have	been	*verb* + -ing	
She	will	have	been	writing	for the newspaper longer than any other employee.
They	will	have	been	working	long enough to get a pension.

Using the Future Perfect Progressive Tense

The future perfect progressive may be substituted for the future perfect when the action described is one that will be in progress at a specific time in the future and will probably continue beyond that time.

By the end of this year my father *will have been working* at the same job for 40 years, but he still has another five years to go before he retires.

By next July we *will have been making* mortgage payments on our house for ten years, but it will be another ten years before we have finished paying.

USING YOUR SKILLS

A.   Many Americans know the story of Rip van Winkle. In the famous story by the American author Washington Irving, a man falls asleep for 20 years. When he wakes up, the world has changed so much that he can no longer recognize it.

With your classmates, imagine what the world will be like 20 years from now. Use any appropriate future tense in your answers.

medicine in the year 20_____

computers in the year 20_____

space travel in the year 20_____

people's jobs in the year 20_____

family life in the year 20_____

Is there anything that you think will be the same in 20 years?

B.   Choose one topic you and your classmates discussed or a topic of your own and write a short essay (150–250 words) explaining your own ideas about the changes you think will have taken place 20 years from now.

USING MODALS

Review of Modals with Present/Future Reference

Modals and Modal-like Expressions	Usual Meanings	Examples
am / is / are able to	ability (present)	She *is able to* speak a little Italian now.
will be able to	ability (future)	She *will be able to* speak Italian better in a few months.
can	asking permission (informal) requesting someone to do something (informal)	*Can* I borrow your notes? *Can* you speak more slowly?

	ability	She *can* read Italian.
	impossibility (negative)	The car *can't* be out of gas. I just filled the tank.
could	asking permission	*Could* I make an appointment to see you?
	requesting someone to do something	*Could* you help me?
	possibility	It *could* be my cousin calling.
	(neg) impossibility	It *couldn't* be my sister at the door. She's out of town.
had better	strong advisability	You*'d better* finish your work soon. It's important.
have/has to	necessity	You *have (got) to* finish your
have/has got to	necessity (informal)	work this evening. It's necessary.
don't/doesn't have to	lack of necessity	You *don't have to* do any extra work. That's not necessary.
may	asking permission	*May* I use your telephone?
	possibility	It *may* be my friend calling.
might	possibility	It *might* be my aunt calling.
must	necessity	You *must* see a doctor right away. You look sick.
	probability, logical deduction	Dinner *must* be ready. I can smell it.
must not	prohibition, necessity not to do something	You *must not* drive after you drink.
ought to	advisability, obligation	I *ought to* get more exercise.
	expectation (future probability)	The incumbent *ought to* win the election. She's ahead in all the polls.
shall*	offer, suggestion	*Shall* I close the door?
should	advisability, obligation	Everyone *should* see a doctor from time to time.
	expectation (future probability)	Dinner *should* be ready soon. It's almost time.

Shall is sometimes substituted for *will* in the simple future tense.

   I *shall* return soon.

This usage is uncommon in American English.

is / am / are supposed to	expectation (future probability) advisability, obligation (sometimes unfulfilled)	It's *supposed to* be hot tomorrow. Children *are supposed to* be seen and not heard.
will	requesting someone to do something	*Will* you repeat the question, please?
would	requesting someone to do something	*Would* you turn down the radio, please?
would like	"softened" demand or request	I *would ('d) like* to see a menu, please.
would rather	preference, choice	We *would ('d) rather* have our coffee later.
would you mind	asking permission (polite) polite request	*Would you mind* if I used the telephone? *Would you mind* getting me a cup of coffee?

PRACTICING YOUR SKILLS

Requests and Permission

A.   Work with a partner. Role play the following situations involving making requests or asking permission. Use a variety of forms: *can, could, may, will, would, would you mind.*

1.   You left the house this morning in such a rush that you left all your books and homework on the kitchen table. You have a few minutes before class and you see somebody who is in your class.

2.   You stop the teacher as she is entering the classroom. You want to ask her if you can turn in your homework later in the afternoon.

3.   You are calling a friend's house at dinnertime because it is important that you speak with him as soon as possible about a personal matter. Someone else answers the phone.

4.   You may have to be absent from class two days next week when someone in your family will have surgery. You want to ask the teacher for next week's assignment so you can keep up with the work.

5.   Your car won't start. Before you take it to the mechanic, you would like a friend who is good with cars to look at it.

6. An old friend is coming to visit you next week. You want to ask your boss if you can have several afternoons off if you promise to make up the work the following week.
7. There is someone at school that you would very much like to meet. You would like a mutual friend to introduce you.
8. You are trying to make an appointment with the dentist as soon as possible because you have a toothache. Her receptionist offers you an appointment for three weeks from now.
9. It's your turn to clean up after dinner, but you have a date in ten minutes. Your roommate isn't very busy.

Advisability and Necessity

B. A North American friend of yours will be living in your home country together with his or her spouse and children for a year. Your friend has asked you for advice to help plan the trip. They will be leaving in a few months.

1. What should they do now? After they arrive? Construct ten or more sentences using *should*, *ought to*, and *had better* to give practical advice that will make their trip easier.
2. Arrangements will be made to introduce the family to a great many people as soon as they arrive. They are not familiar with many of the customs of your country and would like to know what to do in various social situations. For example, they need to know polite ways of introducing themselves, how to accept or refuse invitations, what to do when eating in a home or restaurant. Construct five or more sentences giving rules for appropriate behavior in various social situations. Use *should* or *be supposed to*.
3. Sometimes a gesture that is acceptable in one country will be considered rude or offensive in another. For example, in the United States it is perfectly polite to use either the right or the left hand when giving something to someone. In some countries it is offensive to use the left hand. What are some things a visitor to your country *must not* do?

Obligation and Preference

C. Use the cues given to help you construct sentences about what you *have to* do and what you *would rather* do during the next few weeks. You may change the cues to fit your own situation. Add sentences of your own.

1. do laundry   chat with friend

   I have to do my laundry, but *I'd rather chat with my friend*.

2. get up early	sleep late.
3. clean the refrigerator	go swimming
4. balance my checkbook	read the newspaper
5. work late	spend the evening with friends
6. go to the dentist	shop for clothes

Probability and Possibility

D. You are the kind of person who doesn't like to make definite plans until the last minute. Respond to the following questions with "I'm not sure," and add a sentence using *may*, *might*, or *could* to talk about one or more possibilities.

1. What are you going to eat for dinner tonight?

I'm not sure. I might cook some spaghetti, or I may just have a sandwich.

2. Are you going home after class?
3. What are you going to do after you finish your homework?
4. What time are you going to get up tomorrow morning?
5. Do you want to see a movie tomorrow night?
6. What are you going to do this weekend?
7. What courses are you going to take next semester?
8. Where are you going to live next year?

Ability

E. You are looking for a job and you want to assess the skills and abilities you have that would help you find one. Compile as long a list as possible of your skills and abilities, major and minor. Don't be modest. Use *can* and *be able to*.

Examples

I can speak three different languages.

I can use two different word-processing systems.

I am able to get along with others well.

FINDING OUT ABOUT . . .

Making Comparisons Using Nouns*

Using more + *Noun* + than

Examples	*Comments*
There are *more people* in New York *than* in San Francisco.	Comparisons of nouns are formed with *more* + noun + *than*.
There is a lot *more traffic* in the center of the city *than* in the suburbs.	Both countable nouns, like *people*, and mass nouns, like *traffic*, are used in this pattern.

PRACTICING YOUR SKILLS

Use the cues to construct a question with *more* + noun + *than*. Address your question to the student on your right. That student should answer the question and also construct a question for the next student. Substitute names of specific places where possible.

1. people / city X — city Y

   Examples

   A: Are there *more people* in Los Angeles *than* in Boston?

   B: There are *more people* in Los Angeles.

2. universities / this city — another city
3. books / university library — public library
4. shoppers downtown / on weekdays — weekends
5. cars on the highway / at 5:00 A.M. — at 8:00 A.M.
6. restaurants / downtown — suburbs
7. cold weather / here — farther north
8. job opportunities / in the city — in a small town
9. things to do in the evening / near the university — in another part of town
10. tourists / in the capital city — in another city
11. snow / at high altitudes — at low altitudes
12. time to relax / in the city — in the country.

*See Chapter 8, pages 291–299 for comparisons centered around adjectives and adverbs.

13. industry / in the city—outside the city
14. pollution / in places with heavy industry—in places with light industry
15. crime / in large cities—in smaller cities

■■■■■■ *Using* fewer than/less than

Examples	*Comments*
There are *fewer* jobs in small towns *than* in the cities.	*Fewer than* can be used to compare countable nouns.*
Small towns usually have *less* industry *than* urban centers.	*Less than* is used with mass nouns.**

PRACTICING YOUR SKILLS

Construct several sentences comparing two small towns or suburbs that you know. Which place has fewer people, stores, houses, movie theaters, restaurants, schools? Which place has less traffic, industry, pollution, crime?

■■■■■■ *Using* as + much/many + noun + as

Examples	*Comments*
I can make *as much* money working part time in a factory *as* I can working longer hours in an office.	*As* + *much/many* + noun + *as* can be used to talk about two people, things, or groups that are the same.
There are as *as many* factory jobs *as* office jobs.	*Many* is used with countable nouns. *Much* is used with mass nouns.
There are *not as many* jobs in the summer *as* (there are) in the winter.	*Not as* + *much/many* + noun can be used to express differences.

PRACTICING YOUR SKILLS

A. What is important to you in choosing a job? Construct several sentences comparing two jobs you have had or might want to have in the future. Use a variety of comparative forms centering on nouns. Here are some possible things to consider in making your comparison.

Less is often used with countable nouns in informal English.
**See pages 70–72 for lists of common mass nouns.

money	free time
benefits (insurance, sick pay, etc.)	independence
variety	chances to use your skills
challenge	opportunities for learning
opportunity for advancement	contact with co-workers
length of vacation	contact with the public
choice of vacation time	commuting time

Examples

I made more money in the job I had last year than I do now, but I didn't like the work as much. There was less variety and fewer opportunities for advancement.

B.   What are some similarities or differences between typical working conditions in your country, in North America, and in your classmates' countries?
        Here are some possible questions.

How many hours a week do people usually work? How many days a week?

What are the typical salaries for some jobs?

Do women generally work at the same jobs as men? Earn the same salaries?

How long is the usual vacation? Do workers choose their vacation times?

Do most people belong to unions?

Do people change jobs frequently? Stay in the same job most of their lives?

▬▬▬▬ *Using* the same (as), similar (to), different (from)

Examples	*Comments*
Fast food restaurants in New York sell exactly *the same food as* fast food restaurants in San Francisco.	Notice the use of prepositions: the same *as,* similar *to,* different *from.**
Modern buildings in European cities are *similar to* modern buildings in large North American cities.	
In most cities there are only a few older buildings that look *different from* all the other buildings.	

*In informal speech people often say *different than*.

■■■■■■■■■ *Using* like, alike

Examples

One modern building *looks like* another.

Fast food restaurants in New York and Paris may *look alike*.

Comments

Look, be, feel, taste, and a few other verbs can be used with *like* and *alike* to express similarity.

Note the difference in the way *like* and *alike* are used.

like

x + verb + *like* + y

He *looks like* his brother.

One fast food hamburger *tastes* just *like* any other.

alike

x and y + verb + *alike*

He and his brother *look alike*.

All fast food hamburgers *taste alike*.

PRACTICING YOUR SKILLS

Fill in the blanks with *the same as, similar to, different from, like,* or *alike*. In some cases more than one answer may be appropriate.

1. *There* is pronounced ____the same as____ *their*.
2. What does Thai food taste _____? Is it _____ Chinese food?
3. Will I be able to recognize your brother when I see him? Does he look _____ you?
4. The pronunciation of *feel* is _____ the pronunciation of *fall*.
5. *Principal* and *principle* are pronounced _____.
6. Some of the courses I'm taking now are_____ ones that I took in my own country.
7. Do modern buildings in your country look _____ buildings in other parts of the world?
8. Do you think most modern buildings look _____?
9. Do you think a dinner in one fast food restaurant tastes _____ a dinner in any other fast food restaurant?

USING YOUR SKILLS

Read the following paragraph. What do you think?

A HOMOGENIZED WORLD?

All over the world, big city life is becoming more and more the same. The same international corporations build similar steel and glass towers in Sydney, Australia, and São Paulo, Brazil. Turn on the radio in any large city and you hear the same rock and roll music even though it may be sung in different languages. Blue jeans are an international
5 fashion. Fast food restaurants have sprung up everywhere. You can buy the same pair of blue jeans or eat the same hamburger and french fries in Tokyo and New York.

Do you agree or disagree with the writer of the paragraph? State your own views. Be sure to give examples that support your opinion.

▬▬▬▬ *Using Superlatives with Nouns*

Examples	Comments
The capital is the city with *the most tourists*.	*The most* + noun can be used to compare three or more things or people.
The western region of my country has *the fewest visitors*.	*Least* and *fewest* mean the opposite of *most*.
The month with *the least rain* is August.	*Fewest* is used with countable nouns.*
	Least is used with mass nouns.

ASK AND ANSWER

A. Work with a partner from another country if possible. Ask and answer questions based on the cues. Use the superlative form *the most* or *the least / fewest*. Add questions of your own.

1. tourists

Which region of your country has the most tourists?

Which area has the fewest tourists in winter?

2. cultural attractions (museums, orchestras, theaters)
3. universities
4. modern buildings
5. places of historic interest
6. public parks
7. places to shop
8. restaurants
9. rain in spring, summer, etc.
10. traffic
11. pollution

SUMMARY EXERCISES: COMPARATIVE AND SUPERLATIVE

Includes review of material in Chapter 8.

Look carefully at the information about the three apartments and three potential tenants.

*In informal speech, *least* is frequently used with countable nouns.

Working in small groups, first decide which two apartments each of the tenants should consider. Compare and contrast those two apartments with the one not chosen. Why are they better choices? (Use a variety of comparative and superlative forms in your answers.)

Compare and contrast the two apartments your group has chosen for one set of tenants. What should their final choice be?

CHOOSING AN APARTMENT

Apartment 1	*Apartment 2*	*Apartment 3*
in large modern building	in 15-year-old medium-sized building	in small remodeled older building
elevator	elevator	no elevator
parking in building	parking on street	street parking (difficult to find)
supermarket in building	shopping ½ mile away	a few shops nearby
small living room and bedroom	large living room and one small and one large bedroom	small living room and two medium-sized bedrooms
small very modern kitchen with dishwasher	large kitchen with workable older appliances	medium-sized kitchen — tenant must buy stove and refrigerator
near park and school	one mile from park, a few blocks from elementary school	has back yard, one mile from elementary school
owned and managed by large realty company	managed by neighborhood realty company	owner lives in building.
rent: $650 a month	rent: $450 a month	rent: $350 a month

Possible Tenants

1	2	3
Family with two small children and cat. Have moderate income.	Young married couple. Plan to have children in a few years. Combined salaries give them an above-average income.	Three unmarried college students. Work part time. Have below-average income.

Note: None of the tenants has seen any of the apartments. They must decide which two they will look at. Later they will decide if they want to rent one of them.

LITTLE WORDS

Inseparable Verb and Preposition Combinations

English contains many examples of verbs which are normally followed by particular prepositions. Listed below are several common verb + preposition combinations.*

(dis) agree with	look for
belong to	object to
depend on / upon	plan on
dream about / of	succeed in
hope for	talk about
insist on / upon	talk to
laugh about	think about
listen to	

PRACTICING YOUR SKILLS

After reviewing the verb + preposition combinations listed above, complete the following sentences by using an appropriate preposition. Use the name of a friend or classmate as subject.

1. *Yolanda* is very active in student affairs. *She* belongs *to* several different organizations.

2. _____ and I like to talk _____ current affairs. Even though he/she disagrees _____ me on almost every issue, I like to talk _____ him/her whenever I can.

3. _____ dreams _____ becoming famous some day.

---

*Teacher's note: Only a sample of the many combinations that exist can be covered in this and the following chapter. Students who need more work with verb + preposition (particle) combinations should be advised to purchase a dictionary that covers them in detail. Generally speaking, English dictionaries prepared especially for learners of English such as the *Longman Dictionary of American English* or the *Oxford Advanced Learner's Dictionary* provide more information about these vital expressions than do most bilingual dictionaries or dictionaries prepared for native speakers of English.

4. _____ has very firm opinions. He/She always insists _____ stating a point of view and is not bothered when anyone objects _____ his/her ideas.

5. _____ plans _____ continuing his/her education. He/She is thinking _____ applying to several different schools and hopes _____ a scholarship to at least one of them.

6. _____ is looking _____ a job that pays well and is interesting.

7. _____ is very reliable. You can always depend _____ him/her to keep promises.

8. Since _____ is both talented and hard working, I think he/she will succeed _____ anything he/she chooses to do.

9. I like to listen _____ my friend speak. He/she has such a nice voice.

10. _____ never takes him/herself too seriously. He/she laughs _____ his/her problems.

Verb and Preposition Combinations with Idiomatic Meanings

In the previous examples, the meaning of the verb + preposition combination was clear from the meaning of the individual words. However, in many cases verbs and prepositions combine to produce expressions with new meanings. Compare the following.

Examples	*Comments*
She *ran into* the room and closed the door.	The verb and preposition keep their basic meaning.
I *ran into* someone I hadn't seen for years. ((*run into*: meet by chance)	The combination has a meaning that cannot be guessed from the meanings of the individual words.

The following are among the many verb + preposition combinations that have an idiomatic meaning.

count on: rely on, depend on
drop by: visit without advance notice
get along with: have a good relationship with
get over: recover from

get together (with): meet
look like: resemble
put up with: tolerate
take care of: care for
run into: meet by chance

PRACTICING YOUR SKILLS

Fill in the blanks with an appropriate verb + preposition expression from the above list.

1   Some people don't realize that my cousin and I are related. I don't (resemble) _____*look like*_____ her very much even though we have the same color hair. We have different personalities, but we (have good relations with) _____ each other very well. We often (meet)

5   _____ to chat. Sometimes she'll (visit) _____ my apartment on her way home from work. We live in the same neighborhood, so sometimes we will (meet by chance) _____ each other at the supermarket.

   We have good times together, but even more important is the fact that
10   she's always been someone I could (rely on) _____ to help me. When I was sick last year she (cared for) _____ me. She walked my dog while I was in the hospital. Even after I was home it took me a long time to (recover from) _____ my illness, and I was feeling so bad that I probably wasn't a very pleasant person to be with. My cousin
15   (tolerated) _____ me nevertheless. I'll always be grateful to her.

SENTENCE SENSE

Transitions That Show Time

Many transition words and phrases help show the relationship between events in time. Time transitions usually occur at the beginning of a sentence and are usually followed by commas. Some of the most common time transitions are shown below.

Pointing Ahead in Time	*Pointing Backward in Time*	*Simultaneous*
first, second, third (etc.)	previously	meanwhile
next	before that	at the same time
then	prior to that	during that time
after that		
finally		

USING YOUR SKILLS

A. When we teach someone how to do something, it is often important to show each step in the process in its proper order. For example, if you were teaching a beginning cook how to make a stew, you would need to explain which ingredients must be added first. If you were showing an employee how to use a new machine, it would be important to show which button must be pressed first. If you were teaching a friend how to operate your camera, you would want to be sure that he or she knew what to do and in what order.

For this exercise use the following instructions. (Teachers' note: In large classes divide students into groups.)

First, write down at least five activities you are good at and could teach to someone else. Think about skills you have developed at work or in school, or hobbies.

Next, put a check next to those activities that involve procedures that must be done in a fixed order.

Then, tell your group the activities you have chosen. *Meanwhile*, you will have an opportunity to listen to the ideas of others.

After that, choose one activity that you could teach and one or more activities that you would like to learn.

Then, write out instructions for the activity you know about, using time expressions to show sequence.

Finally, check to see if your instructions are clear by showing your instructions to a classmate who would like to learn about your activity. If necessary, use his or her questions to revise your instructions.

B. Many folktales and children's stories have complicated plots telling the adventures of the hero or heroine. Write or tell a story from your culture. Use transition words to help you show the sequence of events in time.

Connecting Clauses with Time Words—Review of Tenses in Complex Sentences

In the following sections, note the time expressions used to connect clauses. Pay attention to the tenses that normally are used in each clause.

Focus on Present or Unspecified Time

ACTIONS IN SEQUENCE: *BEFORE, AFTER, UNTIL, WHEN*

Examples

(a) *Before* I start to study, I organize my work space.

(b) *After* I put all my books and papers in order, I can start.

(c) I can't work *until** I have arranged my desk.

(d) *When* I have put everything in order, I can start.

Comments

Before, after, until, and *when* are used to join actions in sequence.

Before precedes the event that happens last. *After, until,* and *when* precede the event that happens first. Either the independent or the subordinate clause can come first in the sentence. If the subordinate clause precedes the main clause, a comma is used (a, b, d).

Usual tenses:
The simple present tense is often used in both clauses (a, b). The present perfect tense is sometimes used in the subordinate clause (c, d). The present perfect emphasizes the idea that one action is completed before the other begins.

SIMULTANEOUS OR OVERLAPPING ACTIONS: *WHILE, AS*

(e) *While / as* I prepare dinner, I usually plan my schedule for the evening.

While or *as* may be used to talk about actions that happen at about the same time.

**Till* is used in speech and very informal writing.
    I can't work *till* I've arranged my desk.

(f) My roommate and I usually talk about the day's events *while / as* we're eating dinner.

(g) My little cousin is making a lot of noise *while / as* we're talking on the phone.

Usual tenses:
Main clause: the simple present tense indicates timeless or habitual actions (e, f). The present continuous suggests that the actions are happening at the moment of speaking (g).

Subordinate clause: either the simple present (e) or present progressive (f, g) can generally be used. The present progressive suggests a relatively long continuous activity.

SIMULTANEOUS HABITUAL ACTIONS: *WHENEVER, WHEN*

(h) *Whenever* I have too much work to do, I get a little nervous.

(i) *When* I look up something in the dictionary, it's never where I look for it first.

Whenever means "any time that."

In some cases (i), *when* can mean the same as *whenever*.

Usual tenses:
The simple present in both clauses (h, i).

CONNECTING THE PAST WITH THE PRESENT: *SINCE*

(j) I've had the same study routine *since* I was a high school student.

(k) I've been studying after dinner ever *since* I was in high school.

Since connects a past action with the present.

Usual tenses:
Main clause: present perfect (j) or present perfect progressive (k). Subordinate clause: past tense.

PRACTICING YOUR SKILLS

Complete the following sentences in your own words. Talk about what you usually do when you study. If necessary, change part of the exercise in order to speak about your own situation.

1. I've been studying a great deal since *I decided to apply to graduate school*.
2. When I don't have much time, I . . .
3. Before I sit down at my desk, I . . .
4. Until I get started, I . . .
5. Whenever I can't read my class notes, I . . .
6. I like it quiet when I . . .

7. I (don't) like to listen to the radio while I . . .
8. I've been studying the same way since I . . .
9. Whenever I need to remember something, I . . .
10. I usually wait to take a break until I . . .
11. Before I start to write an essay, I . . .
12. While I'm writing, I . . .
13. I don't like to stop until I . . .
14. After I've completed the first draft, I . . .
15. Before I hand in my essay, I . . .
16. After I've finished everything, I . . .
17. I've felt more confident about my work since I . . .

USING YOUR SKILLS

A. Tell what you usually do when you read newspapers or magazines. Do you read them from beginning to end, or do you skim the headlines and then turn to the sports page? Which section do you read first, next, last? Are there any sections that you don't read at all?

B. Most of us have certain things that we almost always do in a certain order in the morning, before we go to bed, or when we come home from school or work. What part of your day is most governed by routines? What do you do? Tell or write about your routines using transition words and clause connectors.

C. If you are enrolled in a university program, you are probably aware that certain courses must be taken in a certain sequence. For example, a more specialized course will often require the completion of a more general course as a prerequisite. Explain the rules that exist at your university for your field of study. Imagine you are talking to a new student.

D. Write a paragraph describing education in your country to someone who is totally unfamiliar with the system. Show the sequence in which a typical student attends various schools and learns different subject matter. Pay attention to time words and tense usage.

E. If you work (or have worked in the past), does your job involve procedures that must be done in a certain order? If so, explain the order in detail, as if you were talking to a new employee you were training to do your job.

■■■■■■■■ *Focus on Future Time*

ACTIONS IN SEQUENCE: *BEFORE, AFTER, UNTIL, WHEN*

Examples

(l) I will take several more courses *before* I choose a major.

(m) *After* I have taken a few more math courses, I might decide to major in math.

(n) I'm not going to choose a major *until* I am a junior.

(o) *When* I am more certain about my interests, I will choose.

(p) *When* I begin my sophomore year, I will be thinking seriously about the choice.

Comments

Before precedes the later event. *After, until,* or *when* precede the earlier event.

Usual tenses:
Main clause: future-oriented tense (l, n, o, p) or modal (m).
Subordinate clause:
Simple present or present perfect tense (l, m, n, o, p). (Do not use a future tense.)

BY THE TIME (THAT), WHEN

(q) *By the time/When* I graduate, I will have taken most of the courses in the math department.

The future perfect tense may be used in the main clause of sentences beginning with *by the time (that)* or *when* to emphasize that one future event will be completed before the other.

PRACTICING YOUR SKILLS

A. Construct sentences about your future using the patterns given. Pay attention to the tenses you use in each clause.

1. Before _____*I graduate*_____, I _____*will begin to look for a job*_____.
2. I _____ before _____.
3. After _____, _____.
4. _____ after _____.
5. Until _____, _____.
6. _____ until _____.
7. When _____, _____.
8. _____ when _____.
9. By the time that _____, _____.
10. _____ by the time that _____.

B. Interview a classmate about his or her future plans. Use the format of the previous exercise to report what you have learned.

USING YOUR SKILLS

Write a paragraph telling about an important decision you must make. Tell what you plan to do to prepare for the decision and what you think will happen afterwards.

■■■■■■■■ *Focus on Past Time*

ACTIONS IN SEQUENCE:
WHEN, BEFORE, AFTER, UNTIL, BY THE TIME (THAT)

Examples	*Comments*
(r) I had already studied English for several years *when* I first came to the United States.	Usual tenses: When describing two events that happened in sequence in the past, the past perfect is often used to describe the earlier event, the simple past to describe the later event.
(s) *Before* I came, I had read many books in English.	
(t) *Until* I arrived, I had scarcely had a chance to hear people speak English.	The simple past tense is often used in both clauses with *before*, *after*, and *until* if the sequence of events is clear (After I *lived* in the United States for a few months, it became easier to understand people).*
(u) *After* I had lived in the United States for a few months, it became easier to understand people.	
(v) *By the time (that)* I enrolled in the university, I had learned to understand almost everyone.	

HABITUAL ACTIONS IN THE PAST—SIMULTANEOUS OR OVERLAPPING: *WHEN/WHENEVER*

(w) I practiced speaking *whenever/ when* I met anyone who knew English.	*When* or *whenever* can be used to talk about repeated or habitual actions.
(x) I used to / would go to American movies *whenever / when* I had a chance.	Usual tenses: Main clause: simple past or habitual past (*used to / would* + base). Subordinate clause: simple past.

*Sentences with *when / whenever* are sometimes used to indicate that the first event causes the other event. In these cases the meaning is similar to that of conditional sentences with *if* (see page 360).

If / when / whenever I met anyone who knew English, I practiced speaking.

SIMULTANEOUS SINGLE OR CONTINUOUS ACTIONS IN THE PAST:
WHILE, (JUST) AS, WHEN

(y) I had many opportunities to practice English *while / when* I was living with an American roommate.

(z) He hung up the phone *(just) as* I entered the house.

(aa) *While* my roommate was doing graduate work, I was finishing my undergraduate degree.

While, as, and *when* can be used to talk about actions or situations that took place at (about) the same time in the past. *While* is common with long actions, events, and situations.

(Just) as is common with short actions.

Usual tenses:
The simple past can be used in both clauses, especially when referring to single short actions (z). The past progressive can be used in one clause (y) or both clauses, (aa) usually to indicate a long, continuous action or background event.

PRACTICING YOUR SKILLS

A. Use the cues to construct two-clause sentences using each of the following sentence connectors *when*, *before*, *after*, *until*, and *by the time (that)* at least once to talk about sequenced events in the past. Write or tell about yourself or someone you know. Use the simple past in one clause and the past perfect tense in the other.

1. attend nursery school for two years / start kindergarten

   After my sister had attended nursery school for two years, she started kindergarten.

   My sister didn't start kindergarten until she had attended nursery school for two years.

2. reach the age of six / begin elementary school
3. learn to read / learn to write
4. write in your own language / write in a foreign language
5. finish elementary school / begin high school
6. study algebra / study calculus
7. take the entrance exam / be admitted to a university
8. take general courses / take specialized courses
9. choose a major / graduate
10. get a B.A. / do graduate work

B. Working with your classmates or in small groups, complete as many sentences as possible telling how people's lives were changed by the inventions listed below. (Teachers' note: As a preparation for this exercise, individual students can be assigned to look up the history of one or more invention in the library and share information with their classmates.)

1. Before _____ was invented, _____.
2. After _____ was invented, _____.
3. Until _____ was invented, _____.

Twenty Great Inventions of the Past 500 Years

c.	1590	microscope	1876	telephone
	1608	telescope	1895	X ray
	1698*	steam engine	1896	wireless telegraph
	1790*	sewing machine	1903	airplane
	1800	electric battery	1904*	radio
	1810*	electric light	1920*	television
	1826*	photography	1930	turbojet engine
	1831	electric generator	1934	splitting of uranium atom
	1837	typewriter	1946	first practical electronic computer
	1867*	motion pictures	1947	transistor

C. Complete the following sentences about the first 15 years of your life.

1. When I was very young, . . .
2. Before I started school, . . .
3. Until I learned how to talk, . . .
4. By the time I was five years old, I could . . .
5. After I had gone to school for a few years, . . .
6. Whenever I had some free time, . . .
7. While I was growing up, my parents . . .
8. By the time I was ten, I could . . .

Continue constructing sentences about your childhood until the age of 15.

ASK AND ANSWER

Begin this exercise by making a list of what you were doing at several different times in the past few days. Show the day and time for each entry. *(Example: Mon-*

*Date given is a key date in the discovery. Important work was done earlier or later.

day, 7:00–7:30 A.M.—got children ready for school. Every weekday, 5:00 P.M.— began work.) Next, work with your partner to find out what he or she was doing at each of the times on your list. Finally, work together to construct two-clause sentences using *while, when, (just) as* that show what the two of you were doing at any given time.

Examples

At 7:00 A.M., while Mischa was sleeping, I was getting my children ready for school.

When Young He finished her work at 5:00, my job was just beginning.

USING YOUR SKILLS

A. Write a paragraph describing your own educational background. Describe the schools you have attended and the subjects you studied as you grew older. Establish the sequence of events through careful use of time words and expressions and attention to the use of past-time verb tenses.

SUMMARY EXERCISES

A. Below are some of the significant events in the life of Maxine Hong Kingston. A selection from her book *The Woman Warrior* is on pages 138, 139.

1940 born Maxine (Ting) Hong in Stockton, California. Her parents had recently immigrated from China.

1962 married Earll Kingston, an actor

1962 received B.A. from the University of California (Berkeley)

1964–65 graduate study

1965 received teaching certificate

1967 taught English and mathematics, Sunset High School, Hayward, California

1967 taught English at Kahuka High School, Kahuluu, Hawaii

1970–77 taught language arts at the Mid-Pacific Institute, Honolulu, Hawaii

1976 published *The Woman Warrior*, a memoir of her childhood

1976 won the National Book Critics Circle Award for the best nonfiction book published in 1976

1977 and after professor of English, University of Hawaii

1980 published *China Men*, her second book, which tells about the lives of her father and other male relatives

1970s and 1980s   published articles and short stories in several magazines

1981   won the American Book Award for nonfiction

1989   published *Tripmaster Monkey*, a novel about a Chinese-American playwright.

1. Write a one-paragraph biography of Maxine Hong Kingston similar to one that could appear on the jacket of the book she wrote. Do not use any dates in your paragraph but indicate the sequence of events by your use of time transitions and connecting words.
2. Check in the library for biographical information on a contemporary author whose books you admire. Summarize the important events in the author's life in a paragraph using time transitions and connecting words.
3. Imagine you have just published your first book and have been asked to prepare a biographical paragraph about your life. Write the paragraph you would like to see published.

B. Work in pairs. One student will be looking at the chart on page 355 and questions on this page. The other will be looking at the chart on page 356 and questions on the next page.

Scientific studies have shown that there are predictable stages that babies go through as they learn their native languages. Much communication occurs before a baby actually learns to speak. The chart on page 355 tells about a typical baby learning English as a first language during the first year of life. The chart on page 356 follows language development into the second and third year. Take turns asking and answering questions. Do not look at each other's charts.

Questions to ask your partner about the development
of communication skills in the 2nd and 3rd year.

1. What can the average baby do by the time he or she is 14 months? 17 months? 19 months? 21 months? 24 months? 36 months?
2. Name some things the typical child can do after he or she is a year and a half old but before his or her second birthday.
3. How large a vocabulary does the typical child have after his or her third birthday?
4. When does the typical child begin to produce gibberish sentences that include some real words? real two-word sentences? real three-word sentences?
5. Until what age is a child likely to say "John cookie?" "Me cookie?" By what age can a child say "I want cookies?"

Language Development: The First Year

Average age at which linguistic advances first occur. Individual patterns vary, but large discrepancies should receive professional attention.

Age in Months*	Milestone
0.25	Makes some response to sound
1.25	Smiles in response to stimulation
1.6	Coos; makes long vowel sounds
4	Turns toward speaker
	Says "ah-goo"
	Makes razzing sound
5	Turns toward ringing bell
6	Babbles
7	Looks up sideways toward ringing bell
8	Says "dada" and "mama" indiscriminately
9	Plays gesture games like peek-a-boo
	Looks directly at ringing bell
	Understands word "no"
11	Uses "dada" and "mama" as names
	Responds to one-step command and gesture indicating activity
	Says first word
12	Says gibberish "sentences" without using real words
	Says second word

*After age 2 months, ages have been rounded off to nearest month.

Source: Clinical Linguistic and Auditory Milestone Scale, developed by Arnold J. Capute, Bruce K. Shapiro, and Frederick B. Palmer

Questions to ask your partner about the development of communications skills in a baby's first year.

1. Do most babies say their first word by the time they are six months old? 11 months old? When do they say their second word?
2. What kind of sounds does a typical baby make when it is seven weeks old? 4 months old? 6 months old?
3. What kinds of things show that the baby is aware of language before it says its first word?
4. Name some of the things a baby can do after it is 9 months old but before it is a year old.
5. When a baby is 10 months old, is it possible that it would call its father "mama" or its mother "dada"?

Language Development: Years Two and Three

Average age at which linguistic advances first occur. Individual patterns vary, but large discrepancies should receive professional attention.

Age in Months	Language Milestone
13	Says third word
14	Responds to one-step command without gesture
15	Says 4 to 6 words
17	Says gibberish sentence with some real words
	Can point to five body parts
	Says 7 to 20 words
19	Forms 2-word combinations
21	Forms 2-word sentences
	Has 50-word vocabulary
24	Uses pronouns (I, me, you) indiscriminately
30	Uses pronouns (I, me, you) discriminately
36	Uses all pronouns discriminately
	Has 250-word vocabulary
	Uses plurals
	Forms 3-word sentences

Source: Arnold J. Capute, Bruce K. Shapiro and Frederick B. Palmer.

C. Using the information given on pages 355 and 356, write a paragraph telling about the development of communication skills in the average child. Substitute your own language's words for "mama" and "dada." Use time transition words and clause connectors and appropriate present-tense forms to make the sequence of events clear.

D. Imagine someone you know has just given birth to a new baby. Name the baby and then write a paragraph telling the baby's parents what they can expect their baby to understand and say in the next three years. Use time transitions and clause connectors and appropriate future-oriented tense forms to make the sequence of events clear.

E. Imagine that a child in your family has just turned three. Name the child and write a paragraph describing the stages in his or her language development until now. Use transition words, clause connectors, and appropriate past-oriented and present perfect verb tenses.

CHECKING IT OVER

Reviewing Various Ways of Talking about Future Time

PRACTICING YOUR SKILLS

Newspapers often publish articles on trends and predictions for the future. The following paragraphs are similar to such a newspaper story.

THE AMERICAN FAMILY IN THE YEAR 2000

1   If present trends continue until the year 2000, nine out of ten Americans will marry, but they will marry later than they did in the 1950s and 60s. The majority will have children, but they will have children later. Also, they most likely will have fewer children than their parents and grandparents. American divorce rates will remain high (in 1980

5   there were 109 divorced people for every 1,000 married ones), but most who divorce will be remarrying within a year or two of the divorce.

Are these trends going to affect American life drastically? Many family experts see hopeful signs in the trends. They believe that by the year 2000, Americans will have learned to adapt better to the continual and rapid change characteristic of modern soci-

10   ety. The family will remain the most important unit of American society, but it will be a family ready to adapt to changing times.

Most of the sentences talk about events in the future. Five different tenses are used to talk about future time.

1.   Underline all verb tenses in sentences that talk about future time.
2.   Write out examples of the verb tenses used in the story. Check your answers on page 438.

Give three examples of the simple present tense: _____,
_____, _____.

Give four examples of *will* + verb: _____, _____,
_____, _____.

Give one example of *going to* + verb: _____.

Give one example of the future progressive: _____.

Give one example of the future perfect: _____.

3.   Do you think there are cases in which another tense could be substituted without changing the meaning?

USING YOUR SKILLS

Has family life changed in your own country? Compare your generation with your parents' generation. Do you think family life in your country will change by the year 2000? the year 2010? Talk or write about your ideas.

Reviewing Prepositions

PRACTICING YOUR SKILLS

Most of the prepositions have been removed from the following selection from Sidney J. Harris' essay "What True Education Should Do." Replace them. Check your answers on page 438.

~~of~~, of, of, of, of, of, of, of into, into, into, into, in, in, from

1   When most people think ___*of*___ the word "education," they think _____
a pupil as a sort of animate sausage casing. _____ his empty casing, the teachers
are supposed to stuff "education."

But genuine education, as Socrates knew more than two thousand years ago, is
5   not inserting the stuffings _____ information _____ a person, but rather eliciting
knowledge _____ him; it is the drawing out _____ what is _____ the mind.

"The most important part _____education," once wrote William Ernest Hocking,
the distinguished Harvard philosopher, "is this instruction _____ a man _____
10   what he has inside _____ him.

And, as Edith Hamilton has reminded us, Socrates never said, "I know, learn
from me." He said, rather, "Look _____ your own selves and find the spark _____
truth that God has put _____ every heart, and that only you can kindle to a flame."

VOCABULARY

animate: living
eliciting: bringing out

USING YOUR SKILLS

Do you agree with Socrates' definition of education? Explain your views.

CHAPTER 10

Conditional Sentences

Conditional sentences usually consist of two clauses.

if clause (condition)	*result clause*
If it rains,	we won't go.

The result clause can come first.

We won't go	if it rains.*

There are many different kinds of conditional sentences. The major types are presented here. Notice how the differences in verb forms signal differences in meaning.

Type IA: Factual Conditions, Present (Habitual) Time

Examples

If she *writes* several mornings a week, she *is* satisfied.

She *is* happy if she *finishes* a page every few hours.

If/When you mix red and green paint, you *(will) get* brown.

If/When the temperature *is* above 32 degrees F, snow *(will melt) melts.*

Comments

The simple present tense is used in both the "*if* clause" and in the result clause to express a habitual activity or situation.

Either the simple present tense or the future tense can be used in the result clause to express facts or results that are certain to take place. Either *if* or *when* can be used to state the condition.

PRACTICING YOUR SKILLS

A. Complete these sentences in your own words, using the present tense in both clauses to express a habitual activity or situation.

*Note on punctuation: When the *if* clause (subordinate) comes first, a comma separates it from the result (independent) clause. When the result clause comes first, no comma is necessary.

1. If I don't eat breakfast, *I'm hungry by the middle of the morning*.
2. If I don't have much work to do, . . .
3. If I have some money left over after I pay my bills, . . .
4. If I meet a friend, . . .
5. If I get some mail, . . .
6. If there isn't much traffic, . . .
7. If I like someone right away, . . .
8. If I don't have to get up early, . . .

B. Use either the simple present or the future tense to complete these sentences, which tell about facts or results that are certain to take place.

1. If you mix blue and yellow paint, *you get (will get) green*.
2. If you consume more calories than you burn, . . .
3. When the temperature drops below freezing, . . .
4. If you add two even numbers together, . . .
5. If you multiply a number by 100, . . .
6. When a volcano erupts, . . .

C. Construct several sentences of your own about conditions and certain results.
D. Most of us work well and are happy when conditions around us are good, but all of us have to cope with less than perfect conditions sometimes. Tell how you make the best of a bad situation. Answer the following questions for yourself and share some of your answers with a partner or all your classmates. Add additional details whenever possible. Answer in full sentences to practice using the conditional.

1. What do you usually do if you are nervous about something?

    Examples

    If I'm nervous about something, I usually try to talk about it with a friend. That usually helps me to be calm enough to do what I need to do.

    If I'm nervous about something, I try to find a quiet place to sit and think about my problem. There are times when I need to be alone.

2. What do you usually do if you are tired but can't rest?
3. What do you usually do if people around are not encouraging?
4. What do you usually do if you disagree strongly with people but do not want to hurt their feelings?
5. What do you do if you have more work than time?
6. What do you do if you have difficulty concentrating on work you need to do?

    Add sentences of your own telling how you cope with difficulties in your life.

USING YOUR SKILLS

Use some of the ideas from the previous exercise to write a paragraph giving advice about coping with everyday difficulties. Tell what works for you and explain how it might work for others.

■ *Type IB: Factual Conditions, Future Probability, or Possibility*

Examples

If she *writes* every day next week, she *will/'ll finish* by the weekend.

She *might finish* even earlier if nothing *goes* wrong.

Comments

The simple present tense is used in the *"if* clause," and *will* or another modal auxiliary *can/may/might* + base is used in the result clause to talk about an event that is probable or possible in the future.*

PRACTICING YOUR SKILLS

Supply the appropriate form of the verb in the following sentences, which talk about possible or probable results.

1. If you _____*brush*_____ your teeth frequently, you_____*'ll have*_____ fewer cavities. (brush, have)
2. You _____ less difficulty sleeping if you _____ less coffee. (have, drink)
3. If parents _____ children sweet foods, they _____ bad eating habits. (give, develop)
4. If you _____ less and _____ more for the next few months, you _____ weight. (eat, exercise, lose)
5. Smokers _____ longer and healthier lives if they _____ smoking. (live, quit)
6. You _____ more energy if you _____ a good breakfast in the morning. (have, eat)

*In many languages a future-tense form is used in both clauses to express this meaning. Remember that in English, the present tense is used in the *if* clause.

ASK AND ANSWER

Take turns asking your partner about some of the following possibilities. Use complete sentences in your answers to practice using the conditional.

1. What will you do if it's sunny tomorrow?

If it's sunny tomorrow, I'll walk to the lake.

2. What will you do if you have some free time later in the week?
3. What will you do if you have a problem with tonight's homework?
4. What will you do if someone calls tonight?
5. What will you do if you finish your work early?
6. What will you do if you decide not to eat at home tonight?

USING YOUR SKILLS

A. Before we make major decisions, we usually think about the possible good and bad results. For example, one student might be thinking of reducing the number of hours she works.

If I work fewer hours, I'll have more time to study.

Think about one or two major decisions you are actually considering for your future: a move to another place, a change of jobs or schools, marriage, a trip, an expensive purchase, etc. Explain the possible results of the actions you are considering.

B. Although most North Americans do not believe in the following superstitions, many people know about them and may refer to them in conversation.

1. If you break a mirror, you will have seven years of bad luck.
2. If you find a four-leaf clover, you will be lucky.
3. If your nose itches, you will kiss a fool.
4. If a black cat crosses your path, you will have a bad day.
5. If you walk under a ladder, something bad will happen to you.

Are any of these superstitions known in your home country? What other superstitions or folk beliefs do people know about? Do some people take superstitions seriously? Share your ideas and opinions with your classmates.

■■■■■ *Unless*

Unless usually has the same meaning as "if . . . not"

Unless you hear from me, I'll be there at six. =
If you don't hear from me, I'll be there at six.

She'll finish soon *unless* something goes wrong. =
She'll finish soon if something doesn't go wrong.

PRACTICING YOUR SKILLS

Complete the following sentences in your own words.

1. Unless it rains tomorrow, <u>we'll go to the park</u>.
2. I'll buy some groceries on my way home, unless . . .
3. Unless I have more time, . . .
4. I'll write a check tomorrow, unless . . .
5. Unless the class is canceled, . . .
6. Unless they change their plans, . . .
7. I'll be home this evening unless . . .

Add sentences of your own.

■■■■■ *Type II: Nonfactual Present or Future Time*

Note the verb forms used to express conditions that speakers know are un-
true or unlikely to happen. Although the verb form in the *if* clause is the same
as the one used in the past tense, do not forget that these sentences refer to
present or future events.

Examples

If she *wrote* 24 hours a day, she
would/'d finish sooner.
Fact: She won't write 24 hours a
day.

I *could* buy a car if I *had* enough
money.
Fact: The speaker doesn't have
enough money.

Comments

The subjunctive is used in the *if*
clause to talk about nonfactual or
improbable conditions. This subjunctive looks the same as the simple past tense. *Would/could/might* +
base are used in the result clause.

If she *were* a professional writer, she *would* still *need* more time.
If she *was* a professional writer . . . (informal)
Fact: She is not a professional writer.

In formal English, *were* is used with both plural and singular subjects. In informal speech and writing, *was* is often used after singular subjects.

ASK AND ANSWER

Take turns asking and answering the following questions with one of your classmates or in a small group. Add additional comments to explain your answer. Answer in full sentences to practice using the conditional.

1. If you weren't here in class, what would you be doing?

   If I weren't here in class, I would be home practicing the piano. I love to play, but I seldom have enough time.

2. If you could travel anywhere you liked, where would you go? How would you travel, and what you would do when you reached your destination?
3. If you could live anywhere you wanted, in what city would you choose to live? In what kind of house or apartment?
4. If you could have any job you wanted?
5. If you could learn anything you wanted to learn?
6. If you could meet anyone in the world?
7. If you had twice as much money as you do now?
8. If you were ten years older or ten years younger?

PRACTICING YOUR SKILLS

Which of the following *don't* you have? Construct conditional sentences telling what you would do if you did.

1. a dog

   I don't have a dog. If I had one, I would take it for a walk every evening.

2. a car
3. a typewriter
4. a home computer
5. musical talent
6. a lot of free time

7. time for a vacation
8. athletic talent
9. good working habits
10. the power to make the world better

CHECK YOURSELF

Examine the following sentences. Underline the verbs used in each clause. Indicate whether the speaker is referring to a factual or possible event in the future or to a nonfactual or improbable one. Check your answers on page 438.

Examples

If I buy a car next summer, I'll choose a compact with four doors and front-wheel drive. (factual)

1. If I go to graduate school, I'll study chemistry.
2. If there were a good movie in town, we could go tonight.
3. He'd lose some credits if he changed schools.
4. If they have children, they'll need a larger apartment.
5. I'd like to go hiking with you if I didn't have to work this weekend.
6. If the senator is elected, he will try to increase aid for education.
7. I'd feel less worried about paying my bills if I had a scholarship.

■■■■■■■■ *If I Were You . . .*

People often give advice or warnings using the conditional expression "If I were you . . ."

If I were you, I would try to stop smoking. There is more and more evidence that smoking is bad for your health.

PRACTICING YOUR SKILLS

Give advice about what to do in each of the following situations, using "If I were you."

1. A friend thinks his exam was graded incorrectly, but he is afraid to ask the teacher.

2. A friend is having difficulty understanding the teacher's lectures.
3. A friend gets a traffic ticket. She doesn't think she deserves it.
4. A friend has just bought a new cassette tape player. He can't seem to get it to work and has difficulty reading the instructions.
5. A friend is considering buying a used car. He doesn't know much about cars.

Type III: Nonfactual Conditions Referring to Past Events

Note the verb forms used to refer to situations or events that did not take place in the past.

Examples	*Comments*
If she *had written* every day last week, she *would/'d have finished* a few days ago. Fact: She didn't write every day last week.	A form that is the same as the past perfect tense is used in the *if* clause.
We *could have moved* to a larger apartment if we *had/'d saved* our money. Fact: We didn't save our money.	*Would/could/might* + *have* + past participle are used to express past time in the result clause.
If she *had/'d known* someone in the city, she *might* not *have been* so lonely. Fact: She didn't know anyone.	

PRACTICING YOUR SKILLS

A. Change the following sentences, which tell about causes and results, to conditional sentences.

1. I didn't buy the sweater because it didn't fit me.

   I would have bought the sweater if it had fit me.

2. She is sick because she didn't take care of herself.
3. I didn't finish because I was tired.
4. They didn't eat because they weren't hungry.
5. The car didn't start because you left the headlights on.

6. We didn't get a chance to talk because it was so noisy in the room.
7. I didn't have time to see the exhibit before it closed because I was so busy.
8. He got into a lot of trouble because he didn't listen to my advice.

B. Although we may be happy with most of the decisions we have made in our lives, we may sometimes think about other choices that we did not make. Complete the following sentences in your own words. Add comments to explain your choices.

1. If I had decided to study in another city, I would have chosen San Francisco. I like the mild but changeable climate and I love being near the ocean. I'm happy here, but I would have been even happier there.
2. If I had decided to prepare for a different career, I would have chosen . . .
3. If I could have spent my last vacation differently, . . .
4. If I could have gotten to know someone better, . . .

Talk about other choices you could have made in your life but didn't.

USING YOUR SKILLS

Working in a small group, choose an important person in history who is known to each of you. Then, working together, try to construct as many sentences as possible telling what would have happened if the person had never lived. How would history have been different?

Note: The exercise can also be done with each group choosing a crucial event in history or an important invention.

CHECK YOURSELF

Examine each sentence and underline the verbs. Then, indicate whether the sentence refers to factual (possible) events or nonfactual (impossible or improbable events) and the time of the events referred to in both the *if* clause and the result clause. Check your answers on page 438.

1. If you <u>hadn't told</u> me, I <u>would</u> never <u>have guessed</u>.

Nonfactual, past-time events referred to in both clauses.

2. If you have a problem, I can help you.
3. I'll call home this weekend if I don't get a letter from my parents.

4. If I had my life to live over, there are a few changes I would make.
5. If you make one or two mistakes, it isn't very serious.
6. If I make a list of all the things I need to do every week, it keeps me organized.
7. It would be easier for him to learn if he were more relaxed.
8. If my grandmother were alive today, she would be surprised to see so many women working outside the home.
9. If you'd had the car fixed when you were supposed to, it might not have broken down.
10. You'll understand the lecture if you listen carefully.

SUMMARY OF THE MAJOR TYPES OF CONDITIONAL SENTENCES USING *IF*

Type	Time Referred to	Tense of If Clause	Tense of Result Clause	Example
(IA) factual	present habitual	present	present	If she *writes* regularly, she *is* satisfied.
(IB) factual	future	present	*will/can/may/ might* + base	If she *writes* regularly, she *will finish* her paper soon.
(II) nonfactual	present or future	same as past tense but *were* used with all subjects when verb is *be*.	*would/could/ might* + base	If she *wrote* regularly, she *would finish* her paper soon. If she *were* a famous writer . . .
(III) nonfactual	past	same as past perfect tense	*would/could/ /might* + have + past participle	If she *had written* regularly, she *would have finished* her paper last week.

■ *Otherwise*

Otherwise is a transition word used to contrast reality with something the speaker wishes were true if conditions were different.

PRESENT TIME

Examples

I don't have enough time to talk now; *otherwise* we *could have* a chat.

I don't have enough money to quit my part-time job; *otherwise* I *would go* to school full time.

Comments

The modals *would, could,* and *might* + base are often used after *otherwise.*

PAST TIME

I didn't have enough money with me at the restaurant last night; *otherwise* I *would have paid* for both of our meals.

Would, could, and *might* + *have* + past participle are used after *otherwise* to talk about what would have happened if conditions had been different in the past.

PRACTICING YOUR SKILLS

The statements below are factual. Add *otherwise* and a statement telling what would happen if conditions were different.

1.   I have to finish my work; *otherwise I'd love to have a cup of coffee with you*.
2.   I'm a little tired right now; . . .
3.   It's too cold to stay outside very long; . . .
4.   It's very late; . . .
5.   My parents' apartment is very small; . . .

Talk about what would have happened if conditions had been different in the past.

6.   There was a lot of traffic on the road; *otherwise I would have been on time*.
7.   It's a good thing they were wearing safety belts; . . .
8.   He wasn't well prepared for the exam; . . .
9.   She wasn't feeling very well then; . . .

■■■■■■■■ *Nonfactual Conditions with if Omitted*

When *were* or *had* is used to talk about nonfactual conditions, *if* may be omitted and the subject and verb inverted. This usage is common only in formal style.

PRESENT TIME

Were people to learn more about history, they would understand the present better.

If is omitted and *were* is placed before the subject.

PAST TIME

Had the government been better informed, they wouldn't have signed the treaty.

If is omitted and *had* is placed before the subject.

PRACTICING YOUR SKILLS

Chain drill or pairs: One student should complete the sentence. Another student should restate the sentence, omitting *if* and inverting the subject and verb. Sentences 1–6 are in present time, sentences 7–12 in past time.

1. If scientists were to discover a cure for cancer soon . . .

If scientists were to discover a cure for cancer soon, many lives would be saved.

Were scientists to discover a cure for cancer soon, many lives would be saved.

2. If nuclear weapons were to be destroyed . . .
3. If everyone in the world were to be well fed . . .
4. If the world's leaders were to understand one another better . . .
5. If the people of the world were to know more about one another . . .
6. If medical care today were the same as it was a hundred years ago . . .
7. If Columbus had sailed in the opposite direction, . . .

If Columbus had sailed in the opposite direction, he wouldn't have discovered the New World.

Had Columbus sailed in the opposite direction, he wouldn't have discovered the New World.

8. If dinosaurs had learned to survive . . .
9. If human beings had never learned to speak . . .
10. If Beethoven had been born deaf . . .
11. If Einstein hadn't been able to complete his education . . .
12. If industry hadn't been able to produce microchips cheaply . . .

USING YOUR SKILLS

A. Who else is in your family? Are you an only child, or do you have brothers and sisters? If so, are they older or younger than you are? Whatever the facts are, imagine what it would be like if the situation were different. For example, if you are the oldest child in your family, imagine what it would be like to be the youngest. Tell or write about how your life would have changed. Use a variety of conditional sentence types in your answer.

B. Imagine that a few years before you were born, your parents had decided to move to a different country than the one you grew up in. How would your life have been different? How would you be different now? Use a variety of conditional sentence types in your answer.

Expressing Wishes

Hopes and Wishes

Note the difference in meaning and form in the following sentences.

I *hope* my cousins *can* visit me soon.	Fact: I want my cousins to visit me, and it is possible that they will.
I *wish* my cousins *could* visit me soon.	Fact: I want my cousins to visit me, but I know they can't.

Hope is used when we think that something we want to happen is possible. *Wish* is often used when we want something to be true but know that it cannot be. When *wish* is used to express a nonfactual or unlikely situation, special verb forms follow.*

---

*Wish does not have this meaning when it is used in certain expressions

    I *wish* you a very happy birthday.

    I *wish* you well in your new job.

or as a substitute for *want*

    I *wish* to see the manager. (Meaning: I *want* to see the manager.)

WISHES ABOUT THE FUTURE

Examples

She wishes (that) she *could* graduate next semester.

or

She wishes (that) she *were going to* graduate next semester.
Fact: She isn't going to graduate next semester.

Comments

A past modal *(would, could, might)* or verb form that is the same as the past tense is used to talk about future and present wishes. In formal English, *were* is used for all forms of *be.*

WISHES ABOUT THE PRESENT

I wish (that) it *weren't* so cold.
Informal: I wish (that) it *wasn't* so cold.
Fact: It is cold.

I wish (that) I *saw* my family more often.
Fact: I don't see them often.

In informal speech, many English-speakers use *was* after *I, he, she,* and *it.*

WISHES ABOUT THE PAST

I wish (that) it *hadn't been* so cold yesterday.
Fact: It was cold yesterday.

I wish my family *had come* to visit me last summer.
Informal: I wish my family *would have come* to visit me last summer.

A form that is exactly the same as the past perfect *(had* + past participle) is used to express wishes about past events that did not take place.

Would + *have* + base is sometimes used in conversation but is not acceptable in more formal style.

PRACTICING YOUR SKILLS

A. Even people who are satisfied with their lives may spend time wishing for a life that is more exciting or glamorous then their own. The graph on page 374 shows the result of a survey taken in 1984 by the Roper Organization. They interviewed 2,000 American adults, asking them what they daydreamed about.*

---

*Daydreams are unrealistic pleasant thoughts or ideas we have while awake.

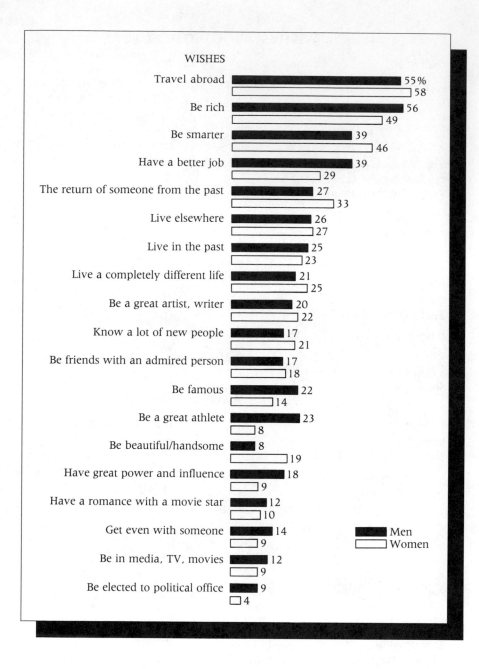

WISHES

	Men	Women
Travel abroad	55%	58
Be rich	56	49
Be smarter	39	46
Have a better job	39	29
The return of someone from the past	27	33
Live elsewhere	26	27
Live in the past	25	23
Live a completely different life	21	25
Be a great artist, writer	20	22
Know a lot of new people	17	21
Be friends with an admired person	17	18
Be famous	22	14
Be a great athlete	23	8
Be beautiful/handsome	8	19
Have great power and influence	18	9
Have a romance with a movie star	12	10
Get even with someone	14	9
Be in media, TV, movies	12	9
Be elected to political office	9	4

Construct at least ten sentences of your own explaining and commenting on the information given in the graph on page 374. Use *wish* and appropriate verb forms.

Examples

According to the survey, 55 percent of American men and 58 percent of American women wish they could travel abroad.

About half of the people interviewed wished they were rich.

Do you daydream? Do you share any of the wishes of the people interviewed in the Roper survey? Write or tell about a wish of your own.

B. Four international students are having a "gripe session."* Even though all of them are reasonably happy with their lives in the English-speaking university they all attend, they sometimes find that they feel better when they can complain to one another about some of the things that go wrong. Sometimes talking about their situation helps them to find things they hope to change. Even when they complain about things that cannot be changed, talking about their complaints often makes them feel better.

For each complaint, add a wish, a hope, or both. Remember that hopes refer to possibilities and wishes refer to situations that the speaker knows will probably not change.

1. Everyone speaks English very fast.

I wish everyone spoke slowly.

I hope I will be able to understand people better after I've been here longer.

2. Very few people here speak my language.
3. Most people here don't know much about my country.
4. The cafeteria never has food from my country.
5. I don't always understand what my professors expect me to do.
6. Tuition is more expensive than in my country.
7. A lot of customs here are different.
8. I don't know how to meet people here.
9. I'm not always sure what to do when I meet someone new.
10. I sometimes get homesick.

Do you have gripes of your own? What part of the situations you dislike can be changed and what probably cannot? Explain your hopes and wishes.

*A *gripe* is a complaint. A *gripe session* is an informal meeting in which people talk about their complaints.

C. Several people were asked to talk about situations or events in the past that they now regret. Construct as many sentences as possible to tell each person's story. Use *wish* + past participle.

1. When I first came I was too timid to speak to anyone. I spent all my time studying English, but I didn't ever speak with anyone. (Marta, age 22)

   Marta wishes she hadn't been so timid.

   She wishes she hadn't spent so much time by herself.

   She wishes she had tried to talk to people.

   She wishes she had realized other people were shy too.

2. I didn't exercise when I was young. I was never interested in sports. I didn't pay much attention to what I ate until I was middle aged. Now that I'm older, it's hard to develop good health habits. (Henry, age 66)
3. When I was a young man I was so concerned with being successful and making enough money to support my family that I didn't take time to enjoy life much. I loved my children but didn't spend much time with them when they were young. (Chung, age 45)
4. The first woman I fell in love with didn't even know I was fond of her. I was so concerned with being macho that I didn't pay any attention to her feelings. She's now married to another man. (Tony, age 24)
5. When my children were young, I needed to work but I didn't know how to look for a job or how I could find good child care. I had a number of terrible jobs and I worried about my children a lot. It took me a long time to find a solution. (Blanca, age 34)

USING YOUR SKILLS

All of us make some choices in life that we now regret. Write or tell about a choice you made but wish you hadn't. You may talk about school, work, or a personal decision.

USING MODALS

Review of Modals with Past Time Reference

MODALS AND MODAL-LIKE EXPRESSIONS

	Usual Meanings	Examples
was / were able to	ability	She *was able to* run a mile in five minutes when she was younger.
could	ability	My brother *could* read before he started school.
could have	possibility	I *could have* left my keys in my other coat pocket.
could not have	impossibility	I *couldn't have* left them in the office. I wasn't there this morning.
had to	necessity, obligation	I *had to* get a new visa. My old one had expired.
didn't have to	lack of necessity, obligation	I *didn't have to* get a new passport. I could use my old one.
may have	possibility	He *may have* forgotten the appointment.
might have	possibility	I *might have* left my keys in the car. I'm not sure.
must have	probability, logical deduction	You *must have* worked hard on your essay. It's very good.
must not have	improbability	She *must not have* studied very hard. She got a poorer grade than usual.
ought to have	(unfulfilled) advisability, obligation (unfulfilled) expectation	I *ought to have* written sooner, but I was very busy. The bus *ought to have* come by now.

should have	(unfulfilled) advisability, obligation	She *should have stayed* home and rested when she was sick.
	(unfulfilled) expectation	They *should have been* here by now. They left an hour ago.
was / were supposed to have	(unfulfilled) advisability, obligation	We *were supposed to* have finished it by now.
	(unfulfilled) expectation	It *was supposed to* have been warmer today.
would have	(unfulfilled) intentions	He *would have* gone to medical school, but he had to work instead.
would rather have	(unfulfilled) preference	She *would rather have* taken another job, but she needed to earn more money.

PRACTICING YOUR SKILLS

Ability in the Past

A. Work with a partner. Tell your partner all the things you *could do/were able to* do at the following ages. Don't be modest.

By the time I was five years old I could count to 100.

By the time I was ten I could . . .

By the time I was fifteen I could . . .

Continue listing your accomplishments at five-year intervals. Which are you most proud of?

B. Present your partner to the class as a person of high achievement. Emphasize the skills that he or she is most proud of.

C. Compare the situation of people in your country now with the situation in the past. What has changed for the better? For the worse? Use *can('t)*, *could(n't)*, *am / are / is / was / were (not) able to*.

Many more people are able to finish high school now. When my father was young, only a small number of people could go to school.

In some sections of the country people cannot drink the water without purifying it. Twenty years ago you could drink water from any lake.

Past Necessity and Lack of Necessity

D. Respond by telling what you or someone else *had to* do or *didn't have to* do in each of the situations. Add situations of your own.

1. The car broke down.

I had to get it towed to the nearest garage.

2. There wasn't much money left at the end of the month.
3. There was a sudden heavy rainstorm.
4. The apartment wasn't large enough.
5. The library closed early during the break.
6. You could pay with a personal check or credit card.
7. The second assignment was optional.
8. Most schools required an entrance exam.

Past Necessity or Obligation and Preference

E. Tell some things you have had to do recently that you didn't particularly enjoy. Tell what you would rather have done at that time.

Example

I had to get a part-time job last semester to pay my bills. I would rather have had more time to study.

Possibility / Impossibility: Present and Past

F. Working with your classmates, suggest several possibilities connected with each of the following events. Use *may*, *might*, or *could* for possibilities that are present, future, or timeless. Use *may have*, *might have*, or *could have* to express possible reasons or causes in the past.

1. They are late.

They might be here soon.

They may have been caught in traffic.

2. No one answers the phone at my friend's house.
3. The library wasn't very crowded.
4. The mail hasn't come yet.
5. The teacher looks worried.
6. The food in the cafeteria is getting better.
7. One student is not in class.

G. Respond to the following situations by making a statement using *couldn't have* to express impossibility.

1. The library wasn't open last night.

   I couldn't have studied there.

2. My friend was sick all last week.
3. The bike had a flat tire.
4. The mail isn't delivered on Sundays.
5. I didn't tell anyone my secret.
6. There was a lot of work and very little time.
7. His family doesn't live in this city.
8. A few years ago I didn't speak English very well.

Probability

H. Work with a partner. Take turns repeating the comment given (filling in the blanks with the name of someone you know). Your partner should respond with a cause or explanation using *must have*.

1. A: _____*Sylvie*_____ worked full time while attending school last semester.

   B: She must have needed to earn money.

2. _____ didn't get the letter on time.
3. The book I wanted is not in the library.
4. _____ left school early yesterday.
5. _____ has lost a lot of weight.
6. There wasn't as much traffic as I expected.
7. _____ is looking very good these days.
8. _____ English has improved a great deal.

Unfulfilled Expectation

I. Work with your classmates. For each of the following stories, tell what you think the person *should have done / ought to have done*. It is too late to change now, but the next time might be better.

1. Ling didn't do well on her first job interview. She didn't know what to wear. She didn't try to find out anything about the job before the interview. She hadn't thought about what she wanted to say, and she hadn't updated her résumé. When the interviewer asked her a question, she got very nervous.

   She should have asked for advice.

   She ought to have gotten information about the company before the interview.

2. Paulo didn't take the time to look at the university catalogue or to speak with his adviser before he signed up for classes last semester. He is not very happy with some of his courses and will probably have to stay in school an extra semester before he can complete his degree.

3. Sofie and her husband bought a used car last year. The salesman was very enthusiastic and seemed nice. They didn't ask many questions or ask to test-drive the car before they bought it. The car is now in the repair shop for the third time.

4. Daoud and Abdul decided to room together last semester. They didn't know each other very well. Daoud likes to play loud music and give parties. Abdul is very quiet and needs to study very hard to enter medical school next semester.

5. When the city government approved plans for widening a busy highway, they didn't realize the inconvenience it would cause to motorists and to the people who lived nearby. Because of poor planning, the construction work took twice as long as it was supposed to.

FINDING OUT ABOUT . . .

Gerunds and Infinitives

In this chapter we will be looking at some of the ways gerunds (verb + -*ing*) and infinitives (*to* + verb) are used in English sentences.

Both gerunds and infinitives are formed from verbs, but neither can take the place of a verb in a sentence. Both gerunds and infinitives act like nouns in English sentences.

I like *food*.   noun

I like *to eat*.   infinitive (*to* + verb)

I enjoy *eating*.   gerund (verb + -*ing*)

Gerunds after Prepositions

Only nouns or gerunds can follow prepositions like *about*. Infinitives cannot be used.

I'm thinking about a trip. (noun)
I'm thinking about traveling. (gerund)

Not

~~I'm thinking about to travel.~~

Many common expressions end in prepositions and can be followed by a gerund.

Examples

I'm *looking forward to starting* my new job.*

I will *be responsible for training* new workers.

I *believe in encouraging* workers to ask questions.

Familiarize yourself with the following expressions commonly followed by a gerund. (Only a few of the many fixed expressions ending in prepositions and followed by gerunds are given here.)

be capable of	apologize for	keep on
be in charge of	(dis)approve of	look forward to*
be (dis)satisfied with	believe in	object to*
be in favor of	care about	put off
be in danger of	complain about	thank for
be used to*	concentrate on	think about
be responsible for	dream of	worry about

PRACTICING YOUR SKILLS

A.   Complete these sentences, using a gerund and additional words as necessary. You may add another sentence to explain your answer.

1. Right now I'm (not) looking forward to _____*finishing this term*_____ .
2. At this time I'm (not) worried about . . .
3. In the next few months I plan on . . .
4. I (don't) care about . . .
5. In my spare time I often think about . . .
6. It's sometimes difficult for me to concentrate on . . .
7. I'm capable of . . .
8. I dream of . . .
9. I believe that most people in my country are opposed to . . .
10. Personally I'm in favor of . . .
11. It's easy / difficult for me to believe in . . .

*To is a preposition in many fixed expressions. Do not confuse the preposition *to* with the *to* used in infinitives. Like all other prepositions, *to* is followed by a gerund.

I am looking forward *to meeting* you.

Not

~~I am looking forward to meet you.~~

12. I don't like it when people complain about . . .
13. I've never been in danger of . . .
14. I think it is important to thank people for . . .
15. It's also important to apologize for . . .
16. When I'm with friends, I like to talk about . . .
17. At work (at home) I'm responsible for . . .
18. Sometimes I put off . . .

▬▬▬▬▬ *Choosing Gerunds or Infinitives after Verbs*

Some verbs must be followed by gerunds. Other verbs are followed by infinitives. A few verbs can be followed by either.

▬▬▬▬▬ *Gerunds Used as Objects of Verbs*

Note the use of the gerund as an object after *enjoy, miss,* (don't) *mind,* and many other verbs.

Subject	Verb	Gerund (Object)	
I	*enjoy*	*reading*	detective novels.
My husband	*misses*	*eating*	foods from his native country.
I don't	*mind*	*sharing*	my book with you.

Familiarize yourself with the following verbs, all of which are followed by gerunds, before doing the exercises on the next pages.

anticipate	delay	postpone
appreciate	dislike	practice
avoid	enjoy	quit
be worth	finish	recommend
can('t) help	imagine	spend time
consider	involve	suggest
continue	miss	try (experiment)*

*When *try* means *attempt,* it is followed by an infinitive. Note the difference in form and meaning.

Why don't you *try changing* the batteries? That might be the problem.

He *tried to climb* Mount McKinley but he wasn't able to.

PRACTICING YOUR SKILLS

A.   Construct sentences about the following activities. Tell which ones you *enjoy*, *dislike*, or *don't mind* doing. Add other activities to the list.

Examples

I *enjoy getting up* early.

I *dislike flying.*

I *don't mind* driving.

1. writing essays
2. playing chess
3. taking tests
4. flying
5. shopping
6. giving parties
7. attending parties
8. staying up late
9. getting up early
10. talking about myself
11. talking about world affairs
12. listening to other people
13. reading the sports page
14. reading the financial section
15. reading the front page

B.   Construct sentences using the gerund form of the verb given.

1.   I can't help (think) *thinking about my new job* .
2.   Can you imagine (find) . . .
3.   Would you consider (go) . . .
4.   It's not easy to quit (smoke) . . .
5.   The travel agent recommended (visit) . . .
6.   I don't need to spend time (practice) . . .
7.   I suggest (take) . . .
8.   Why don't you try (put) . . .

USING YOUR SKILLS

A.   Different people have different ways of working or studying. Some people enjoy working by themselves in a quiet place with no interruptions. Others work better with people around them.

Use the questions below to help you talk about your own work or study habits. Add details about your own circumstances to your answers.

1.   What kind of place do you enjoy working in?
2.   Is there any part of your work routine that you avoid doing?
3.   Do you ever delay starting a difficult task?
4.   Do you appreciate receiving help from others?
5.   Do you usually anticipate finishing your work ahead of time?

6. When you are tired, do you try to continue working, or do you quit working for a while?
7. Is there anything you spend more time doing than you think you should?
8. Do you mind being interrupted in the middle of your work?
9. Do you enjoy listening to music while working, or are you distracted by it?
10. What do you usually do after you have finished working?

B. Combine some of your answers to write a paragraph telling about your own work or study habits. How effective are they? Is there anything you would like to change?

Gerunds after go in Common Fixed Expressions

In conversational English, a gerund is sometimes used together with the verb *go* to talk about sports and a few other activities.

go . . . bowling, camping, dancing, jogging, fishing, hiking, mountain climbing, (roller / ice) skating, sailing, (water) skiing, shopping, swimming.

Examples

I like to *go skiing* in the winter.

I *went shopping* for a birthday present last weekend.

ASK AND ANSWER

Take turns asking and answering questions in small groups about sports and other activities. Use *go* + gerund.

Has anyone in the group ever *gone skiing, mountain climbing*, etc.? If so, tell about it. When was the last time you went _____? How often do you go _____?

■■■■■■ *Infinitives Used as Objects of Verbs*

Note the use of the infinitive as an object after *decide, plan, hope,* and many other verbs.

Subject	Verb	Infinitive (Object)	
My sister	*decided*	*to work*	for a while.
She	*plans*	*to earn*	enough money to finish college.
She	*hopes*	*to start*	school again next fall.

Familiarize yourself with the following verbs, all of which can be followed by infinitives, before doing the exercises that follow.

(can) afford	hesitate	plan
arrange	hope	pretend
attempt	intend	propose**
decide	learn	refuse
demand	manage	seem
deserve	mean (intend or plan)*	tend
fail	offer	try (attempt)

PRACTICING YOUR SKILLS

Complete the sentences, using the gerund or infinitive form as appropriate. You may use the verbs given in parentheses or substitute your own.

1. I can't afford (spend) *to spend any more money on rent*.
2. I might finish (write) *writing my report this afternoon*.

---

*When *mean* is followed by an infinitive, its meaning is similar to *intend* or *plan*.

Did you *mean to say* something rude, or was it accidental?

When *mean* is followed by a gerund, its meaning is similar to *signify* or *involve*.

Marriage *means changing* a lot of your habits.

**Propose* followed by an infinitive means *intend*.

If elected, the candidate *proposes to cut* taxes significantly.

When propose is followed by a gerund, the meaning is similar to *"suggest."*

A university committee has *proposed changing* the date of registration.

3. I don't know how you manage (work) . . .
4. I think we should delay (go) . . .
5. I will arrange (come) . . .
6. It's worth (know) . . .
7. I'm going to attempt (take) . . .
8. I can't imagine (find) . . .
9. I hesitate (ask) . . .
10. Over the years, I've learned (think) . . .
11. Most of all, I miss (see) . . .
12. Moving to a new place means (change) . . .
13. I've worked hard, so I deserve (relax) . . .
14. To be a good guitar player you have to practice (play) . . .
15. I spend a lot of time (dream) . . .
16. Did you mean (behave) . . . ?

Verbs That Can Be Followed by a Gerund or Infinitive Without Changing Meaning

The following common verbs can be followed by either a gerund or an infinitive without any difference in meaning.

begin	hate	neglect
continue	like	prefer
can't stand	love	start

Gerund		*Infinitive*
I *began spending* my summers in Mexico a few years ago.	*or*	I *began to spend* my summers in Mexico a few years ago.
I *like traveling*, but I *can't stand flying*.	*or*	I *like to travel*, but I *can't stand* to fly.

ASK AND ANSWER

Working with a partner, ask and answer questions about traveling. Answer in complete sentences using an infinitive or a gerund. In some cases either form is possible.

1. Do you like to travel? Is there anything you dislike? Is there anything you can't stand?
2. Do you try to read about the places you are going to visit?

3. How far ahead of time do you begin making plans for a trip?
4. Do you enjoy traveling with friends?
5. Do you mind traveling alone?
6. Do you try to meet new people when you travel?
7. Do you appreciate getting advice from other travelers?
8. Do you prefer to travel to familiar or unfamiliar places?
9. Do you tend to choose places where there are many (few) tourists?
10. Have you ever started to take a trip you were unable to continue?
11. Do you usually manage to travel on a budget?
12. Have you ever gone camping?
13. Do you sometimes arrange to stay with friends for part of the trip, or do you prefer staying in a hotel?
14. Do you hope to take a trip soon? If so, where are you planning to go?

USING YOUR SKILLS

How important is traveling to you? Write or tell about the kind of traveling you have done or would like to do.

Verbs That Change Meaning When Followed by a Gerund or Infinitive: forget, remember, and stop

Examples	*Comments*
I didn't *remember to put* my keys in my coat pocket this morning.	Meaning: I didn't remember and didn't do it.
I don't *remember putting* my keys in my coat pocket this morning.	Meaning: I may have put my keys in my pocket, but I have no memory of the action.
I *forgot to write* the letter.	Meaning: I forgot and didn't write it.
I *forgot (about) writing* the letter. It was a long time ago.	Meaning I wrote the letter but I don't remember writing it.
She *stopped to smoke* a cigarette several times.	The infinitive tells *why* she stopped: (in order) to smoke a cigarette.
She *stopped smoking.*	The gerund shows *what* she stopped doing: smoking.

PRACTICING YOUR SKILLS

Answer the questions in full sentences, using either a gerund or infinitive after the verb as appropriate.

1. Are there many things you need to remember to do every day? Do you often forget to do things? What do you do to help yourself remember?
2. Which birthday of yours do you remember most vividly? What do you remember doing on that day?
3. By the time they grow up, most people have forgotten events from their early childhood. Have your parents told you things about your early childhood that you have forgotten doing? What is the earliest event you remember? What do you remember doing at that time?
4. When you are working, do you like to stop to take a break from time to time? What do you generally stop to do?
5. Many people have stopped or cut down on habits that they felt were harmful to their health, such as smoking, drinking too much coffee, eating too much sugar or salt. Have you ever tried to stop a harmful habit? Were you successful?

■■■■■■■ *Verbs That Must be Followed by a Noun or Pronoun Before the Infinitive*

Some verbs must be followed by a noun or pronoun before an infinitive can be used.

Subject	Verb	Noun or Pronoun	Infinitive	
My father	told	me	to learn	several languages.
I	convinced	my parents	to let	me study abroad.

advise*	enable	invite	persuade	teach
allow*	encourage*	instruct	remind	tell
convince	forbid*	order	require	urge
cause*	hire	permit*	select	warn

*These verbs are followed by a gerund when no direct object is used.

The teacher advised *reading* the chapter again.
The teacher advised me *to read* the chapter again.

Do you permit *smoking* in class?
Do you permit students *to smoke* in class?

■■■■■■■■ *Verbs That May Be Followed by a Noun or Pronoun Before the Infinitive*

Some verbs can be followed by either a noun or pronoun + infinitive or directly by an infinitive.

Subject	Verb	Noun or Pronoun	Infinitive
He	asked	me	to go.
She	expected	him	to finish.

Subject	Verb	Infinitive
He	asked	to go.
She	expected	to finish

ask	need	want
choose	promise	wish
expect	request	would like

Familiarize yourself with the preceding two lists of verbs before doing the following exercises.

PRACTICING YOUR SKILLS

Complete these sentences with the remainder of the infinitive and additional words as necessary.

1. The university advises new students to *make an appointment with an adviser before classes begin*.
2. An academic adviser will ask students to . . .
3. The adviser will allow students to . . .
4. An adviser may urge a student to . . .
5. Students may request their advisers to . . .
6. Scholarships enable students to . . .

7. A scholarship committee selects candidates to . . .
8. Does the university require each student to . . .
9. Does the university expect each student to . . .
10. It's difficult to persuade my parents to . . .
11. I never have persuaded my mother to . . .
12. Before I left home, my parents warned me not to . . .
13. I promised them to . . .
14. One of the things they expect me to . . .
15. They don't want me to . . .
16. They have never asked me to . . .
17. My whole family would like me to . . .
18. I hope the company will hire me to . . .
19. It needs several new employees to . . .
20. I hope someone will choose me to . . .
21. The company may order me to . . .

CHECK YOURSELF

A. Without looking at earlier pages, indicate whether the second word in each set of words should be a gerund or an infinitive. (In a few cases either may be used.) Then, construct a short sentence about yourself or a classmate. Use a variety of tenses. Check your answers on page 438 or work with a partner, checking each other's work.

   1. talk about / go.

     I've talked about going out of town this weekend.

   2. decide / move.

     Akmed has decided to move to a new apartment.

3. mean / say.	**12.** enjoy / use
4. arrange / stay.	**13.** refuse / listen
5. hate / wait	**14.** seem / be
6. order (someone) / do	**15.** offer / lend
7. look forward to / see	**16.** keep on / walk
8. tell (someone) / study	**17.** cause (something) / happen
9. can't help / want	**18.** dream about / become
10. concentrate on / finish	**19.** start / work
11. want / buy	**20.** need / choose

B. Construct sentences using either the infinitive (*to go*) or the gerund (*going*). Mention a specific place on campus or in the city in each of your sentences. Check your answers on page 438.

   1. think about / go

     I've thought about going to the public library after class.

   2. would like / go

     I'd like to go to the Art Institute this weekend.

3. hope / go	**11.** try / go
4. be in favor of / go	**12.** manage / go
5. quit / go	**13.** plan / go
6. forget / go	**14.** advise (someone) / go
7. intend / go	**15.** choose / go
8. postpone / go	**16.** can't stand / go
9. convince (someone) / go	**17.** decide / go
10. regret / go	

C. Work with a partner. Construct questions for your partner to answer using either an infinitive (*do*) or a gerund (*doing*). (In a few cases either choice is possible.) Use a variety of tenses in your questions. Check your answers on page 438.

   1. need / do

     What did you need to do last week?

   2. avoid / do

     Is there anything you will avoid doing next year?

3. think about / do	**12.** encourage (someone) / do
4. stop / do	**13.** attempt / do
5. ask / do	**14.** be used to / do
6. ask (someone) / do	**15.** anticipate / do
7. miss / do	**16.** expect / do
8. put off / do	**17.** hate / do
9. be worth / do	**18.** begin / do
10. remember / do	**19.** learn / do
11. approve of / do	**20.** teach (someone) / do

■ *Using the Passive Voice with Infinitives*

Sentences with direct objects + infinitives may be put in the passive voice, especially when we want to emphasize the action rather than the person(s) who initiated the action.

	Examples	*Comments*
(Active)	My family taught me to work hard.	Notice that in the passive voice the infinitive follows the first verb. A *"by* phrase" is seldom used.
(Passive)	I was taught to work hard. (by my family)	
(Active)	My parents didn't allow me to date until I was 18.	
(Passive)	I wasn't allowed to date until I was 18.	

PRACTICING YOUR SKILLS

A. Change these active sentences to passive ones.

1. My family expected me to succeed.

I was expected to succeed.

2. They encouraged me to apply to a university.
3. They persuaded me to study English.
4. They allowed me to study abroad.
5. My mother warned me not to forget my own culture.

Continue, adding sentences of your own in the passive voice. Talk about your own family's influence on your educaton and choice of career.

B. Use the passive voice to answer questions about a job you have had. (If you have not worked, tell as much as you can about the job of a family member or friend.)

1. What were you hired to do?

I was hired to type reports.

2.   Had you been trained to do the work in school? On a previous job?
3.   Were you expected to do other jobs besides the one you were hired to do?
4.   Were you ever required to do work you didn't like?
5.   Were you given information about everything you needed to do?
6.   Were you permitted to make some decisions on your own? Which ones?
7.   Was your employer required to provide benefits / insurance / sick leave?
8.   What did earning a salary enable you to do?

■ *Gerunds as Subjects of Sentences*

Gerunds, like nouns, can serve as the subject of a sentence.

Friendship   is   important to me (noun)
Having friends is   important to me. (gerund)

Subject	Verb	
Traveling	is	expensive.
Meeting new people	can be	stimulating.
Learning a new language	takes	time.

Note that the verb after a gerund is singular.

PRACTICING YOUR SKILLS

All of the following sentences have a gerund subject. Complete them in your own words.

1.   Getting used to unfamiliar surroundings *takes time* .
2.   Meeting people from all parts of the world *is fascinating* .
3.   Understanding a new culture . . .
4.   Reading newspapers in a new language . . .
5.   Speaking English all the time . . .
6.   Not speaking my own language . . .
7.   Tasting new foods . . .
8.   Finding an apartment / job . . .
9.   Living (at home / away from home) . . .
10. Worrying about things you can't help . . .

LITTLE WORDS

Separable Verb-Preposition Combinations*

Some verb + preposition combinations may be separated by noun objects and *must* be separated by pronoun objects.

Examples

(a) You need to *look up* the word in a dictionary.

or

(b) You need to *look* the word *up* in a dictionary.

You need to *look* it *up*.
Not
~~You need to look up it.~~

Comments

A noun object such as *word* can follow the verb + preposition combination (a), or it can come between the verb and the preposition (b).

When the object is a pronoun, the pronoun *must* separate the verb and the preposition.

Some Common Separable Verb-Preposition Combinations

cut . . . out = stop an activity
cut . . . down = reduce or lessen an activity

call . . . up = use telephone
call . . . off = cancel

look . . . up = search for information in a reference work
look . . . over = examine

put . . . on = put clothes on body
put . . . off = postpone, delay

think . . . up = invent
think . . . about = consider

try . . . on = try clothing to see if it fits
try . . . out = try other items to see if they are suitable

*Inseparable verb + preposition combinations are discussed in Chapter 9, pages 342–344.

turn . . . on = start flow of electricity, water, etc.
turn . . . down = reduce volume
turn . . . down = reject
turn . . . off = stop flow of electricity, water, etc.
turn . . . out = extinguish light
turn . . . up = increase volume

PRACTICING YOUR SKILLS

In pairs, take turns constructing imperative sentences by adding an appropriate preposition. Your partner should reply to the sentences in the negative using a pronoun and, whenever possible, adding a reason for the refusal.

1. Cut _____ the noise. (reduce)

   A: Please cut down the noise.

   B: I'm sorry, I can't cut it down. I have to use this machine.

2. Look _____ the next chapter. (examine)
3. Cut _____ the talking. (stop)
4. Turn _____ the radio. (lower volume)
5. Call _____ the meeting. (cancel)
6. Put _____ your coat. (get dressed)
7. Think _____ your plans. (consider)
8. Turn _____ the light. (extinguish)
9. Look _____ the word in the dictionary. (search)
10. Call _____ the members. (telephone)
11. Turn _____ the TV. (increase volume)
12. Put _____ the meeting. (postpone)
13. Turn _____ the water. (stop flow)
14. Think _____ a new idea. (invent)
15. Turn _____ the job offer. (refuse)

▄▄▄▄▄▄ *Additional Separable Verb-Preposition Combinations*

do . . . over = do again

fill . . . in = give information
fill . . . out = complete form

hand . . . out / pass . . . out = distribute to students
hand . . . in / turn . . . in = give work to teacher
hand . . . back = return work to students

look . . . over = read quickly

make . . . up = complete missing work

read . . . over = read again

take . . . out / check . . . out = borrow books from library
take . . . back = return books to library

PRACTICING YOUR SKILLS

Imagine that a friend of yours is going to enroll in your school for the first time next semester and is planning to take some of the courses you are taking now. Below, in scrambled form, are some of the questions your friend might want to ask you about classroom and library procedures. First, unscramble the questions. Then provide answers. Use the pronoun form in your answers.

1.   how often / teachers / do / homework / assignments / hand out / ?

   How often do teachers hand out homework assignments?

   Many teachers hand them out every day.

2.   students / at the beginning of class / their work / do / or / hand in / at the end of class?

3.   their work / what happens / students / on time / don't turn in / when?

4.   many teachers / do / to read over / ask you / your assignments / you / before / hand them in?

5.   usually have / a few minutes / at the end of class / the next day's assignment / to look over / do you / and / about it / ask questions?

6.   mistakes / cross out / of your papers / can you / on the final copy?

7.   the teachers / do / hand back / with corrections / assignments?

8.   supposed to / are you / all / on tests / the answers / fill in?

9.   make up / can you / missing work / you are / absent / if?

10.   do / over / assignments / can / you / your grade / to improve?

11.   have to / a form / fill out / a library card / to get / do you?

12.   books / students / take out / can / how many / at one time?

13.   you / can / dictionaries / check out?

14.   took out / a book / today /, would I / have to / bring back / when?

SENTENCE SENSE

Noun Clauses: Direct and Reported Speech

A noun clause is used the same way a noun is. It can be either the subject, the object, or the complement of a sentence. Noun clauses occur frequently when we present our own thoughts or report on the ideas of others.

These words introduce noun clauses.

1. *That* (sometimes omitted) introduces clauses derived from statements.
2. *Whether / if* introduce clauses derived from *yes / no* questions.
3. The question words—*when, where, why, how, who(m), what, which, whose*—introduce clauses derived from information questions.

Noun Clauses with that

Examples

I think *(that) smoking is a dangerous habit.*
S   V   O

Doctors say *(that) smoking is the leading cause of lung cancer.*

Many people believe *(that) cigarette advertising should be banned.*

I've noticed *(that) cigarette advertising is not permitted on TV.*

Comments

In these sentences a noun clause serves as the object of the verb.

That is often omitted.

Noun clauses often follow the verbs *say* and *think* or other verbs with related meanings: *ask, mention, remark, reply, tell, believe, know, hope, notice, realize, understand, wish.*

PRACTICING YOUR SKILLS

Complete the following statements with a noun clause stating your beliefs about an issue or problem you feel strongly about. (Teachers' note: You may want to suggest some suitable topics or elicit them from the class.)

1. I think (that) . . .
2. I have come to realize (that) . . .

3. Many other people believe (that) . . .
4. People sometimes tell me (that) . . .
5. I often answer (that) . . .
6. I know (that) . . .
7. I realize (that) . . .
8. I regret (that) . . .
9. In the future I hope (that) . . .

▬▬▬▬ *Telling about the Ideas of Others: Direct and Reported Speech*

When we want to quote someone's words or thoughts we have two choices.

1. We can use quotation marks to enclose the exact words that someone said or wrote.

Galileo once said, "I have never met a man so ignorant that I couldn't learn from him."

Quotations are a good solution when (a) we know or can remember the exact words, (b) the quotation is short, or (c) the exact words are important or striking.

2. We can use reported speech to restate the speaker's or writer's ideas in our own words.

Galileo once said (that) he had never met a man so ignorant that he couldn't learn from him.

Reported speech is a good solution when (a) we cannot remember the exact words that were said or written, or (b) we want to summarize or include only the most important parts of someone's speech or writing.

When we use reported speech, the tenses, word order, and pronouns and time words are often different than in the original.

▬▬▬▬ *Sequence of Tenses in Reported Speech*

When we report on a written text or words that were said at another time or place, we usually use the past tense for the reporting verb.

He *said* . . .
I *thought* . . .

In most cases the ideas that are reported will be shifted one step back in the past to harmonize with the time given in the reporting verb.* Compare the verb tense in the reported speech and direct speech version of each sentence below. What other changes do you notice?

	Direct Speech	*Reported Speech*
Present Tense	She said, "I'm busy right now."	She said (that) she was busy.
Present Progressive Tense	She said, "I'm trying to finish my paper before dinner."	She said (that) she was trying to finish her paper before dinner.
Present Perfect Tense	She said, "I've already written ten pages."	She said (that) she had already written ten pages.
Past Tense	She said, "I wrote seven pages yesterday afternoon."	She said (that) she had written seven pages yesterday afternoon.
Past Progressive Tense	She said, "I was writing all last weekend."	She said (that) she had been writing all last weekend.
Modals	She said, "I'm sorry I can't have lunch with you."	She said (that) she was sorry she couldn't have lunch with me.
	She said, "I'll call you next week. I may have some free time then."	She said (that) she would call me next week. She might have some free time then.**
	She said, "You may call me later."	She said (that) I could call her later.**
	She said, "I must get back to work."	She said (that) she had to get back to work.***

*Shifting to a tense that is farther back in the past is more common in written English and in formal speaking styles than it is in everyday conversations.

   Formal English: She said (that) she was busy.

   Conversational English: She said (that) she is busy.

In addition, shifting frequently does not take place even in formal style when the reported sentence deals with a timeless fact or idea, or with scientific or technical information.

   He said that knowledge *was / is* power.

   Francis Crick and James Watson stated that the genetic code *is / was* found in DNA.

**May* is changed to *might* when it expresses possibility and to *could* when it expresses permission.

***Must* is changed to *had to* when it expresses necessity.

PRACTICING YOUR SKILLS

Read over the following quotations on the subject of education and learning. Change them to reported speech. If you feel the statements can be true at any time, include both present and past forms.

1. B. F. Skinner, the psychologist, said, "Education is what survives when what has been learned has been forgotten."

   B. F. Skinner, the psychologist, said that education was what survived when what had been learned had been forgotten.

   B. F. Skinner, the psychologist, said that education is what survives when what has been learned has been forgotten.

2. David Cecil, the English biographer and critic wrote, "The first step in knowledge is to know that we are ignorant."
3. Henry Ford, the industrialist, believed, "Anyone who keeps learning stays young."
4. Winston Churchill, the statesman, said, "I am always ready to learn, although I do not always like being taught."
5. Dwight Eisenhower, general and former president of the United States, once stated, "An intellectual is a man who takes more words than necessary to tell more than he knows."
6. Robert Hutchins, the former president of the University of Chicago, once wrote, "The object of education is to prepare people to educate themselves throughout their lives."

■■■■■■■■■ **Say** *and* **tell** *in Reported Speech*

Say is immediately followed by the noun clause. When *tell* is used, a noun or pronoun object precedes the noun clause.

She *said* (that) she would be late.

She *told me* (that) she would be late.

Not

~~She said me that she would be late.~~

■■■■■■■■■ *Imperatives in Reported Speech*

Imperative commands and requests can be reported in two ways: (1) using a noun clause, (2) using an infinitive.

DIRECT SPEECH

Examples

Comments

She said, "Listen carefully to my instructions."

She told us, "Write your name in the upper right-hand corner of your papers."

REPORTED SPEECH USING A NOUN CLAUSE

She said (that) *we should* listen carefully to her instructions.

She told us (that) *we should* write our name in the upper right-hand corner.

A noun or pronoun subject and *should* or another modal expressing necessity are added to the request or command.*

REPORTED SPEECH USING AN INFINITIVE

She said *to listen* carefully to her instructions.

She told us *to write* our name in the upper right-hand corner.

The infinitive version is more common.

PRACTICING YOUR SKILLS

A. The following are instructions that a teacher might give to the students before they hand in the final draft of their essays. Imagine that you are repeating the teacher's instructions to a student who was absent from class. Change each imperative to (a) reported speech with a noun clause, (b) reported speech with an infinitive phrase. (Teacher's note: Change these instructions in accordance with your own requirements for the presentation of written work.)

---

*Have to or *must* can be used for strong commands.

She told us in a firm voice, "Write your name in the upper left-hand corner."

She told us (that) we *have to / must* write our name in the upper left-hand corner.

1.   Type or write neatly in ink.

S/He said (that) we should type or write neatly in ink.
S/He said to type or write neatly in ink.

2.   Double-space all typed papers.
3.   Leave margins of one inch or more on each page.
4.   Indent each new paragraph.
5.   Center the title at the top of the first page.
6.   Leave a space between the title and the first line.
7.   Number all pages except the first.
8.   Proofread one more time before handing in your papers.

B.   Work with a partner.
     Part I: Student A tells student B to do something, speaking as softly and quickly as possible. Student A pretends not to understand and asks for clarification. Student A repeats the original request using reported speech.

Example
A: Put your pencil in your left hand. (said softly and rapidly)
B: What did you say?
A: I said to put your pencil in your left hand.

Here are some sample commands. Add others.

1.   Pick up your book with your left hand.
2.   Open your book to page 100.
3.   Put your book on top of my book.
4.   Put your pencil on top of our books.
5.   Turn your head away from me.
6.   Look up at the ceiling.
7.   Touch the back of your chair with your left hand.
8.   Tap your foot twice.

Changing Questions to Noun Clauses

A question can be changed into a noun clause and combined with a statement or question to make a new sentence.

Do you know?
Is that course offered next semester?

main clause   *noun clause*

Do you know whether that class is offered next semester? (question)

I don't know.
How can I find out?

main clause   *noun clause*

I don't know how I can find out. (statement)

1. When a question is changed to a noun clause, the subject is placed *before* the verb. *Do, does,* or *did* is not used.
2. It is the main clause that determines whether the combined sentence is a question or a statement.

■■■■■■■■ *Noun Clauses Made from* yes/no *questions:* **if, whether**

Yes / no questions that are changed to noun clauses begin with *if* or *whether (or not). Whether* is more formal.

Compare the *yes / no* questions and sentences with noun clauses in the following examples. Note the order of subject and verb. Which sentences end in a period? Which end in a question mark? Why? (Clue: Look at the main clause.)

Yes / No Question	*Sentence with Noun Clause*
Will Math 380 be offered in the fall?	Do you know whether Math 380 will be offered next semester?
Is Professor Sims going to teach it?	I'd like to know if Professor Sims is going to teach it.
Did she teach it last year?	I wonder if she taught it last year.
Do I need a special permit to take it?	Could you tell me whether or not I need a special permit to take it?

PRACTICING YOUR SKILLS

Construct new sentences by combining the *yes / no* questions with the main clause statement or question stems. Remember that the subject will go before the verb in the noun clause of your new sentences.

1. I don't know. . . . Does the class meet on Friday?

   I don't know if the class meets on Friday.

2. Can you tell me. . . ? Does it meet three or four times a week?
3. Do you know. . . ? Are there any evening sections?

4. I'd like to know. . . ? Will I have difficulty getting in?
5. I wonder. . . . Can I look at the syllabus?
6. Someone asked me. . . . Has the text been chosen yet?
7. Could you find out. . . . Will it require a lot of homework?

Noun Clauses Made from Information Questions

The question words such as *when, who, what, how* are used to introduce noun clauses made from information questions.

Information Question	*Sentence with Noun Clause*
When is the class?	I'm not sure when the class is.
Who is going to teach it?	I don't know who is going to teach it.
What books will be used?	Do you know what books will be used?
How can I get more information?	Can you tell me how I can get more information?

PRACTICING YOUR SKILLS

A. Construct new sentences by combining the information questions with the main clause statement or question stems. Remember that in the noun clause the subject will come before the verb in your new sentences, and *do, does,* or *did* is not used.

1. We don't know . . . . When does the class end?

   We don't know when the class ends.

2. I don't know . . . . Who is teaching the class?
3. I'm not sure . . . . What classroom is it in?
4. Could you tell me . . . ? Where is the building?
5. Does he know . . . ? How much do the books cost?
6. I need to find out . . . . When does the class end?
7. I can't tell . . . . How many students are in the class?
8. Do you have any information about . . . ? Why isn't it offered in the summer?

B. (Teachers' note: You may want to divide large classes into groups of six to ten students for this exercise. If possible, arrange chairs so students face one another.)

Part I: One student begins by asking a question of any other student in the group. That student rephrases the question as reported speech and immediately continues by asking a new question of another group member. Stop when everyone has had a turn asking and rephrasing questions.

Example

Student A: What courses are you taking next semester?
Student B: Tomas asked me what courses I am taking next semester.
      Are you going to summer school? (addressed to student C)
Student C: Anna asked me if I was going to summer school.

Part II: Working as a group, try to remember the questions everyone asked.

First Tomas asked Anna what courses she was taking next semester.
Then Anna asked Ahmed if he was going to summer school.

USING YOUR SKILLS

A.   (Teachers' note: You or a student should present a well-prepared two- to three-minute demonstration of how to do something, using imperatives to give step-by-step instructions.)

Possible Topics

How to load film in a camera: Be sure to load film in dim light. Unlock the back of camera and transfer empty film spool to the opposite side, etc.

How to pack a suitcase well.
How to change a bicycle tire.
How to check the oil in your car.
How to make an excellent cup of coffee.

Students should take careful notes during the demonstration. Afterwards, they should write out instructions for an absent classmate.

Example

Munir warned us to be sure to load film only in dim light, not in the sunshine. He said that you should unlock the back of the camera and transfer the empty film spool to the opposite side . . .

B.   If English-language newspapers are available to you, examine with the class news reports of speeches and interviews. Look for use of direct quotation and reported speech.

C. Teacher's note: If possible, invite a guest speaker to give a five-to-ten-minute talk to the class and to participate in a brief question-and-answer period. The speaker can describe a job, hobby, trip, or a topic of current interest. Teachers can also prepare a talk themselves or use videotapes of speeches or press conferences.

Students should take notes during the talk and prepare to write an accurate account similar to one a reporter for a local newspaper would write. Teach and encourage students to use a variety of reporting words as appropriate: *explained, mentioned, noted, remarked, believed, stated, showed, added, concluded*, etc.

The Subjunctive Mood

Using the Base Form after Certain Adjectives that Express Importance

Examples	*Comments*
It is *essential* that all children *get* an education.	The base form of the verb is used after certain adjectives that show that something is essential or very important.
It is *vital* that we *build* new schools immediately.	
It is *important* that classes *not be* too large.	

Other common adjectives that require the base form in formal style are *advisable, best, crucial, imperative, necessary, preferable, urgent.*

Reducing Noun Clauses to Infinitives

Many subjunctive noun phrases can be rephrased as infinitives. The infinitive form is more common.

Examples	*Comments*
It is vital *that we build new schools.* (noun clause)	
It is vital *to build new schools.* (infinitive)	
It is essential *for all children* to get a good education.	*For* introduces a subject other than the subject of the noun clause.

PRACTICING YOUR SKILLS

The following sentences give ideas for reforming public education on the elementary and high school level. Add your own ideas.

Rephrase each sentence to begin with *It is important / essential / necessary / urgent*, etc. Then, complete the sentence with (a) a noun clause in the subjunctive mood, (b) an infinitive phrase.

1. The government must improve elementary and secondary education.

   It is essential that the government improve elementary and secondary education.

   It is essential for the government to improve elementary and secondary education.

2. We must provide equal educational opportunity for all members of society.
3. We must attract new teachers to the profession and train them well.
4. We must retrain older teachers in current teaching methods.
5. High schools should be furnished with modern equipment, including computers.
6. Every high school should have a good library.
7. Students should begin learning languages as early as possible.
8. We must provide a good physical education program.
9. Schools should sponsor a variety of clubs, sports teams, and other extracurricular activities.

███████ *Using the Base Form after Certain Verbs that Indicate Importance*

A base form is also used in the noun clause after certain verbs that indicate importance. An infinitive phrase can be substituted after some verbs.

NOUN CLAUSE OR INFINITIVE

Examples

Comments

A congressman *asked* that the secretary of education *visit* city schools. (noun clause)

He *asked* the secretary of education *to visit* city schools. (infinitive)

A base form is required in the noun clause after the common verbs: *advise, ask, desire, require, urge*. However, after these verbs, noun clauses are usually reduced to infinitives.

NOUN CLAUSE

The citizens *demanded* that the government *build* new schools.

The base form is needed in the noun clause after the verbs *demand, insist, propose, request,* and *suggest*. Infinitives cannot be used.

PRACTICING YOUR SKILLS

A.   Imagine that you want to be your country's secretary of education. You have a program that you believe will improve the educational system and have made a list of the major steps you want the school authorities to take. Tell about your program, beginning with one of the verbs below. Complete your sentences by converting imperatives into noun clauses or (whenever possible) infinitive phrases.

advise	insist	require
ask	propose	suggest
demand	recommend	urge
desire	request	

1.   Begin research on effective educational programs immediately.

   I advise that we begin research on effective educational programs immediately.

2.   Provide free kindergartens and nursery schools for all children.

   I propose to provide free kindergartens and nursery schools for all children.

3.   Institute a program of informal education and job retraining for adults who have left school.
4.   Change the high school curriculum to include more science and math courses.
5.   Change the high school curriculum to include more humanities* courses.
6.   Revise / abolish / institute competitive exams for entry into university programs. ·
7.   Encourage good students to become teachers by giving them scholarships.
8.   Raise teachers' salaries.
9.   Give parents more influence over their children's education.
10.   Give high school and college students a greater / smaller role in planning their own education.
11.   Lengthen / shorten the school year.
12.   Lengthen / shorten the school day.

   Continue the exercise by adding proposals of your own.

USING YOUR SKILLS

A.   In country Y, prosperity from increased tourism has allowed the education budget to be increased by 30 percent. How do you think the money should be spent?

B.   Many people believe that education is a lifelong pursuit and that people should continue to learn after they have left school. In your opinion, what are the most

---

*Humanities courses include courses in language, literature, philosophy, and history.

effective ways of insuring that adults continue to learn? Consider the role of public libraries, television and radio, community adult education programs, etc.

C.   In country X, 100,000 students complete high school every year, yet there is room for only 5,000 new students in the universities. What is the fairest way of selecting those students? Of insuring that the most talented people will be able to contribute to their country's future?

CHECKING IT OVER

Reviewing Passive Voice, Infinitives and Gerunds, Subject-Verb Agreement, and Articles

PRACTICING YOUR SKILLS

In the following selection from Russell Baker's column in *The New York Times*, the author takes a humorous view of the trouble inanimate objects cause him.

THE PLOT AGAINST PEOPLE

1   Inanimate objects are classified scientifically into three major categories—those that don't work, those that break down and those that get lost.

The goal of all inanimate objects is to resist man and ultimately to defeat him, and the three major classifications are based on the method each object uses to achieve its
5   purpose.

As a general rule, any object capable of breaking down at the moment when it is most needed will do so. The automobile is typical of the category.

With the cunning typical of its breed, the automobile never breaks down while entering a filling station with a large staff of idle mechanics. It waits until it reaches a downtown
10   intersection in the middle of the rush hour, or until it is fully loaded with family and luggage on the Ohio turnpike.

Thus it creates maximum misery, inconvenience, frustration and irritability among its human cargo, thereby reducing its owner's life span.

VOCABULARY

inanimate: not alive
cunning: cleverness, shrewdness
breed: usually means type of animal, here applied to an inanimate object—a car
idle: not busy

1. Sentence 1 is in the passive voice. If you changed it into the active voice it might read, "Scientists classify inanimate objects into three major categories . . ." Do you prefer the active or passive?

2. Find an example of the passive voice in paragraph 2. Try changing it to the active voice. Which version do you like better?

3. There are three examples of infinitives in paragraph 2 and one example of a gerund in paragraph 3. Find them.

4. In paragraph 4, change *automobile* to *automobiles*. Make all other necessary changes in paragraphs 4 and 5. Check your answers to **2.**, **3.**, and **4.** on page 439.

5. Without looking at the preceding passage, fill in the blanks with *a*, *the*, or ∅. Check your answers against the original after you have finished.

1   As _____ general rule, any object capable of breaking down at the moment when it is most needed will do so. _____ automobile is typical of _____ category.

   With _____ cunning typical of its breed, _____ automobile never breaks down while entering _____ filling station with _____ large staff of idle mechanics. It

5   waits until it reaches _____ downtown intersection in _____ middle of _____ rush hour, or until it is fully loaded with _____ family and _____ luggage on _____ Ohio turnpike.

Review of Tenses

USING YOUR SKILLS

In a story by John Updike, a contemporary American writer, a young man remembers his grandmother at various stages in her life. Updike uses several different tenses to refer to different times in the past. Examine the tenses used in each sentence. Discuss the author's choices with your classmates and teacher.

MY GRANDMOTHER

1   At the time I *was* married, she *was* in her late seventies; crippled and enfeebled. She *had fought* a long battle with Parkinson's disease; in my earliest memories of her she *is* touched with it. Her fingers and back *are* bent; there *is* a tremble about her as she *moves* about through the dark, odd shaped rooms of our house in the town where

5   I *was* born.

   My grandmother *would hover* near me, watching fearfully, as she *had* when I *was* a child, afraid that I *would fall* from a tree. Delirious, humming, I *would swoop* and *lift* her, *lift* her like a child, crooking one arm under her knees and cupping the other behind her back. Exultant in my height, my strength, I *would lift* that frail brittle body weighing

10   perhaps a hundred pounds and *twirl* with it in my arms while the rest of the family *watched* with startled smiles of alarm. *Had* I *stumbled*, or *dropped* her, I *might have broken* her back, but my joy always *proved* a secure cradle. And whatever irony *was* in the impulse, whatever implicit contrast between this ancient husk, scarcely female, and the pliant, warm girl I *would embrace* before the evening *was done*, direct delight

15   *flooded* away: I *was carrying* her who *had carried* me, I *was giving* my past a dance, I *had lifted* the anxious caretaker of my childhood from the floor, I *was bringing* her with my boldness to the edge of danger, from which she *had* always *sought* to guard me.

VOCABULARY

enfeebled: without strength
Parkinson's disease: nerve disease characterized by shaking
a tremble: a shaking
hover: remain nearby
delirious: very excited, confused
exultant: very, very happy
cradle: rocking bed for a small child
implicit: not stated
husk: shell or outer covering of a fruit or nut; old body
pliant: flexible

APPENDICES

APPENDIX 1: VERB FORMS: REGULAR AND IRREGULAR FORMS

Verb Forms

Except for the verb *be* all verbs in English can have no more than five different forms.

	Base	Past	Past Participle	Third Person Singular Present	Present Participle
Regular Verbs	talk	talk*ed*	talk*ed*	talk*s*	talk*ing*
	learn	learn*ed*	learn*ed*	learn*s*	learn*ing*
	add	add*ed*	add*ed*	add*s*	add*ing*
Irregular Verbs	give	gave	given	give*s*	giv*ing*
	let	let	let	let*s*	lett*ing*
	go	went	gone	go*es*	go*ing*

If you know the base form you can determine all the other forms of regular verbs and the present participle and third person singular present of both regular and irregular verbs.

1. Regular verbs end in *-ed* in both the past and past participle.
2. To form the third person singular present of both regular and irregular verbs add *-s/es*.
3. To form the present participle of both regular and irregular verbs add *-ing*.

Note: small spelling changes are sometimes needed when adding the verb endings *ed*, *-s/es*, or *-ing* to the base form. See Appendix 2 for a summary of these rules.

Pronunciation of *-ed, -s/es,* and *-ing* Endings

Pronouncing -ed

There are three different ways to pronounce *-ed*. The choice depends on the final sound of the base.

1. Pronounce -*ed* as a separate syllable when the base ends in -*t* or -*d*.

    waited, needed, rested, added

2. Pronounce -*ed* as /t/ (no extra syllable) when the base ends in a voiceless sound /p, k, s, f, sh, ch/.

    jumped, worked, kissed, laughed, pushed, watched

3. Pronounce -*ed* as /d/ (no extra syllable) for all other regular verbs.

    called, believed, judged, worried, played

Pronouncing -s/es

There are three different ways to pronounce -*s/es*. These rules apply to the plural endings of nouns as well as the third person singular ending of verbs.

1. Pronounce -*s/es* as a separate syllable /iz/ after "hissing" sounds such as /s, z, sh, ch/ or the "g" sound in change.

    misses, buzzes, fixes, pushes, watches, changes, judges

2. Pronounce -*s/es* as /s/ (no extra syllable) when the base ends in a "non-hissing" voiceless sound /p, t, k, f/.

    jumps, hates, kicks, laughs

3. Pronounce -*s/es* as /z/ (no extra syllable) after all other sounds.

    fills, studies, goes, wins, agrees

Pronouncing -ing

Always pronounce -*ing* the same way.

talking, learning, adding, giving, letting, going

Irregular Verbs

Be

The most common verb in the language, *be*, is very irregular. It has eight different forms.

Base	Present	Past	Past Participle	Present Participle
be	am/is/are	was/were	been	being

Other Common Irregular Verbs in English

Irregular verbs are verbs whose past and past participles do not end in *-ed*.

There are about 250 irregular verbs in English. Many of them are not used often and do not need to be memorized. You can look them up when you encounter them in examples of older written English.

On the other hand, one hundred or so irregular verbs, including some of the most common verbs in English, are used frequently. As an intermediate/advanced student of English you should know how to say and write these common irregular verbs without hesitation. Check yourself by covering up all but one of the columns with a sheet of paper and writing the forms in the other columns. Check with your teacher to see that you can pronounce each form correctly. Practice saying the verbs you are working on in sentences.

	Base	Past	Past Participle
1.	be	was/were	been
2.	beat	beat	beaten
3.	become	became	become
4.	begin	began	begun
5.	bend	bent	bent
6.	bet	bet	bet
7.	bite	bit	bitten or bit
8.	bleed	bled	bled
9.	blow	blew	blown
10.	break	broke	broken
11.	bring	brought	brought

12.	build	built	built
13.	burst	burst	burst
14.	buy	bought	bought
15.	catch	caught	caught
16.	choose	chose	chosen
17.	come	came	come
18.	cost	cost	cost
19.	cut	cut	cut
20.	deal	dealt	dealt
21.	dig	dug	dug
22.	do	did	done
23.	draw	drew	drawn
24.	drink	drank	drunk
25.	drive	drove	driven
26.	eat	ate	eaten
27.	fall	fell	fallen
28.	feed	fed	fed
29.	feel	felt	felt
30.	fight	fought	fought
31.	find	found	found
32.	fit	fit	fit
33.	fly	flew	flown
34.	forbid	forbade	forbidden
35.	forget	forgot	forgotten
36.	forgive	forgave	forgiven
37.	freeze	froze	frozen
38.	get	got	gotten
39.	give	gave	given
40.	go	went	gone
41.	grow	grew	grown
42.	hang	hung	hung*
43.	have	had	had
44.	hear	heard	heard
45.	hide	hid	hid
46.	hit	hit	hit
47.	hold	held	held
48.	hurt	hurt	hurt
49.	keep	kept	kept
50.	know	knew	known
51.	lay	lay	lain

*Used for things:

He *hung* his diploma on the wall.

The regular form hang/hanged/hanged is used for persons.

They hanged the criminal.

Base	*Past*	*Past Participle*
52. lose	lost	lost
53. make	made	made
54. mean	meant	meant
55. meet	met	met
56. pay	paid	paid
57. put	put	put
58. read*	read**	read**
59. ride	rode	ridden
60. ring	rang	rung
61. rise	rose	risen
62. run	ran	run
63. say	said	said
64. see	saw	seen
65. seek	sought	sought
66. sell	sold	sold
67. send	sent	sent
68. set	set	set
69. sew	sewed	sewn/sewed
70. shake	shook	shaken
71. shine	shone	shone***
72. shoot	shot	shot
73. show	showed	shown
74. shrink	shrank	shrunk
75. shut	shut	shut
76. sing	sang	sung
77. sink	sank	sunk
78. sit	sat	sat
79. sleep	slept	slept
80. speak	spoke	spoken
81. spend	spent	spent
82. split	split	split
83. spread	spread	spread
84. spring	sprang	sprung
85. stand	stood	stood
86. steal	stole	stolen

*Rhymes with *seed*.

**Pronounced the same as the color *red*.

***Irregular only when used as an intransitive verb:

The moon shone brightly last night.

The transitive form is regular.

He *shined* his shoes yesterday.

87.	stick	stuck	stuck
88.	sting	stung	stung
89.	stink	stank	stunk
90.	strike	struck	struck
91.	swear	swore	sworn
92.	sweep	swept	swept
93.	swim	swam	swum
94.	swing	swung	swung
95.	take	took	taken
96.	teach	taught	taught
97.	tear	tore	torn
98.	tell	told	told
99.	think	thought	thought
100.	throw	threw	thrown
101.	understand	understood	understood
102.	wake	woke	woken
103.	wear	wore	worn
104.	win	won	won
105.	write	wrote	written

Practice forming sentences using the verbs you need to learn.
Sample contexts:

Present Tense (base/and base + e/es)

I usually *choose* clothes that are comfortable.

My best friend *knows* me well.

Water *freezes* at 32° F.

Past Tense

My mother *chose* my clothes when I *was* a child.

He *knew* me when we were in elementary school.

The wet roads *froze* when the temperature dropped suddenly last night.

Past Participle (perfect tenses and passive voice)

I *'ve chosen* my courses for next semester.

My friend *has known* me for fifteen years.

The streets *have been frozen* since last night.

English *is spoken* throughout the world.

APPENDIX 2: SPELLING RULES FOR ADDING WORD ENDINGS

Adding *s/es* to Nouns and Verbs

Add *s/es* to form the plural of most countable nouns.

> book   book*s*   bus   bus*es*

Add *s/es* to form the third person singular present form of verbs.

> talk   talk*s*   wash   wash*es*

Add *-es* to nouns and verbs ending in *s, x, z, ch, sh,* and usually *o*.*

> class   class*es*   fix   fix*es*   fizz   fizz*es*   match   match*es*
> wish   wish*es*   tomato   tomato*es*   go   go*es*   do   do*es*

For nouns ending in a consonant** + *y*, change the *y* to *i* and add *-es*.

> bab*y*   bab*ies*   family   famil*ies*

For most words ending in *f,* or where *f* is the last letter pronounced, change the *f* to *v* and add *-es*.

> hal*f*   hal*ves*   shel*f*   shel*ves*   wi*fe*   wi*ves*   li*fe*   li*ves*

Exceptions:

> belief   beliefs   proof   proofs   roof   roofs   chief   chiefs

Adding *-ed, -ing, -er, -est*

Add *-ed* to form regular past and past participle verb endings.

> talk   talk*ed*   wash   wash*ed*

*Some common words ending in *-o* add *-s*:
> *piano   pianos   radio   radios   studio   studios*

**Vowels are *a, e, i, o, u*. All other letters are consonants with the exception of *y*, and *w* when they appear at the end of a word and form part of the vowel sound:
> stay, grow, new

Add *-ing* to form the present participle.

    talk talk*ing*   walk walk*ing*

Add *-er* to adjectives (comparative).

    quick quick*er*

Add *-est* to adjectives (superlatives).

    quick quick*est*

In most cases the appropriate ending is added without any change in the base form. However, small spelling changes in the bases are needed in several instances. The chart below summarizes the changes you need to know about.

	Base	-ed	-ing	-er	-est
For words ending in *e*, drop the final *e* before adding *ed, er, est,* or *ing.*	hope dance nice late	hoped danced	hoping dancing	 nicer later	 nicest latest
Exceptions: *be + ing* verbs ending in *ee + ing*			being seeing agreeing		
For verbs ending in *ie,* change *ie* to *y* before adding *ing.*	lie die tie		lying dying tying		
For words ending in a consonant + *y,* change the *y* to *i* before adding *-ed, -er* or *-est.* Keep the *y* when adding *-ing.*	study carry happy lonely	studied carried	 studying carrying	 happier lonelier	 happiest loneliest
For all one-syllable words and multi-syllable words that end with one vowel and one consonant and are stressed on the final syllable, double the final consonant before adding *-ed, -er, -est,* or *-ing.* but	stop plan beGIN preFER hot thin LISten	stopped planned preferred listened	stopping planning beginning preferring listening	 hotter thinner	 hottest thinnest

APPENDIX 3: CONTRACTIONS (SHORT FORMS)

The verbs *be* and *have* and most of the modal auxiliaries are almost always contracted in speech. Contractions after personal pronouns are also common in informal writing.

An apostrophe takes the place of one or more missing letters.

I *a*m = I'm   He *would* = He'd

■ *Contractions with Personal Pronouns*

Affirmative

I'm = I am

He's = "He is" or "He has"*
She's = "She is" or "She has"
It's = "It is" or "It has"

You're = You are
We're = We are
They're = They are

I've = I have
You've = You have
We've = We have
They've = They have

I'd = "I had" or "I would"**
He'd = "He had" or "he would"
(also: She'd, you'd, we'd, they'd)

Negative

isn't = is not
hasn't = has not

aren't = are not

haven't = have not

hadn't = had not
wouldn't = would not

---

*Look at the context to determine if 's = *is* or *has*.

She's my sister. = She *is* my sister.

She's gone home. = She *has* gone home.

**Look at the context to determine if 'd = *had* or *would*.

I'd studied English in elementary school. = I *had* studied. . . .

I'd go if I were you. = I *would* go.

I'll = I will
(also: he'll, she'll, it'll, you'll, we'll,
they'll)

won't = will not

wasn't = was not
weren't = were not

don't = do not
doesn't = does not
didn't = did not

can't = cannot
couldn't = could not
mustn't = must not
shouldn't = should not

▄▄▄▄▄▄ *Contractions after Nouns, Question Words,* that, there, *and* here

The contractions *'d*, *'s* and *'ll* are used after question words (*who/what/where*) and after *that/there* in speech. They are written only in very informal style.

Where's the nearest drugstore? (= Where *is*)

What's happened (= What *has*)

Who'd know the answer? (= Who *would*)

That'll be soon. (= That *will*)

The contraction *'s* is used with *here* and after nouns in speech. It is written only in very informal style.

Here*'s* the money I owe you. (= Here *is*)

Blanca*'s* leaving early. (= Blanca *is*)

My friend*'s* coming later. (= My friend *is*)

ANSWERS TO SELECTED EXERCISES

Chapter 1

p. 9

is, misses, is living, hopes, will come, can share, is taking, wants, will be returning, was born

p. 13

Marta Castro, language, she, She, She, she, She, She, English, it, She, she, Marta, parents, she, they, Marta, she, I, you, she, she, Marta, she, she, She, sister, they, Marta, She, she, she

p. 13

2. has, controls, helps, stands up, stands up, says, bows 3. answers, stands up, uses 4. come, open, arrives, close, leave, leaves 5. is, try 6. say, ask, is 7. are, talks, are

pp. 14, 15

calls, gives, is, means, belong, applies, lives, live, face, nurtures

p. 19

1. He must try 2. She should talk 3. He must not be embarrassed 4. She might have got help 5. How can he study 6. Who should he talk to He must find out 7. He will not stop trying 8. He should listen 9. He can't expect to learn

pp. 22, 23

child, kitchen, rooms, mother, home, dressmaker, workshop, kitchen, dressmaking, Poland, dresses, women, sense, design, eye, subtleties, fashions, boldness, dollars, fashion magazine, customer, customer, remnants, store, Belmont, Avenue, material, owner, remnants, stores, reason, owners, goods, days, apartment, women, housedresses, kitchen, table, fitting, bedroom, kitchen, room, machine, nut, Singer, scrolls, arm, tiers, drawers, needles, thread, side, treadle, window, coal, stove, year, college, source, heat, December, bedrooms, bottles, milk, cream, borscht, calves, feet.

Note: Nouns can be used to modify other nouns: remnant stores, home dressmaker. Noun + adjective combinations can also modify nouns: coal-black stove, nut-brown Singer.

p. 27

1. babies   2. feet   3. duties   4. wives   5. phenomena   6. series   7. libraries   8. stimuli
9. fish   10. hypotheses   11. women   12. nuclei   13. teeth   14. analyses   15. men
16. crises

p. 33

1. An egg has approximately 80 calories.   2. She is a lawyer.   3. Carrots are my favorite
vegetable.   4. I'm not afraid of insects.   5. We live in a small apartment.   6. How did you
like the movie we saw last night?   7. Shut the door right away.   8. Brazil is the largest
country in South America.   9. Football is my favorite sport.   10. Money can't buy happiness.

p. 36

2. CHILDREN CRY   3. VOCABULARY GROWS   4. BABIES STAND

pp. 37, 38

HOW BABIES LEARN LANGUAGE

Long before *they* enter school, *children know* the sounds of *their* mother tongue, and the
rhythm and melody unique to that language. *They understand* many of the words *they hear*
adults say. More amazingly, young *children know* how to put the words *they know* together
to form completely new sentences. We can say that *children* of four or five already *know*
the grammar of *their* own language. Of course *they* cannot talk about the rules of grammar, but *they are* already able to do something much more important. *They are* able to use
the grammar of *their* language to express *their* thoughts.

Children go through certain predictable stages in learning *their* first language. The stages
are the same for *children* who *hear* Chinese spoken around *their* cribs as they are for *babies*
who *hear* English, Spanish or any other of the world's 4,000 or more languages. *Babies* in
Beijing *learn* Chinese in the same way and at about the same age as *babies* in New York
City *learn* English or *babies* in Mexico City *learn* Spanish.

In the first few months of life, *babies* growing up anywhere in the world *make* the same
kinds of sounds. *They cry* and *make* sounds to show happiness and displeasure. The very
first noises *babies make* are not related to the language *they hear their* parents speaking.
Even deaf *children make* these same sounds. But soon *children begin* to distinguish between
the sounds that are part of *their* language and those that are not. *They keep* the sounds *they
need* and *discard* those that *they do* not need. Even though *babies* may not say *their* first
word until around the time of *their* first birthday, by that time *they* already *are* beginning
to sound like *speakers* of *their* native language.

Chapter 2

p. 44

1. sitting   2. coming   3. tying   4. boiling   5. running   6. planning   7. trying   8. arguing   9. choosing   10. offering   11. starting   12. sobbing   13. helping   14. dreaming   15. opening

pp. 46, 47

1. am studying   2. study   3. is raining   4. rains   5. is ringing   6. leave, am working, am doing   7. am taking, take, runs

pp. 50, 51

understand, hate, love, miss, think, am, am making, discovering, is, appear, understand, recognize, know, say, sound, look, forget, remember, is, am trying, know, is improving, spend, speak, try, am living, am thinking, is, is, has, study, is, is hopping, is watching, see, reminds.

p. 55

1. I don't like it when people don't look at me when they are talking.   2. Do you like it when people look directly at you?   3. In some cultures people stand very close to one another when they are talking, don't they?   4. I can't understand why people move their hands like that when they are talking.   5. What gestures do people in your country use frequently?   6. At what time is "Good afternoon" said?   7. He doesn't wave his hand at me when he sees me in the halls.   8. Can you show me the way people greet an acquaintance in your country?   9. In my country a person doesn't talk like that to a stranger.   10. It can be difficult to understand other people's customs, can't it?

pp. 60, 61

2. No, they aren't. Dolphins are mammals, but they live in water.   3. No, it isn't. A dolphin's brain is larger but simpler than a human brain.   4. No, they don't. Most babies say their first word around the time of their first birthday.   5. No they don't. Most North Americans show they are listening by maintaining intermittent eye contact.   6. No they don't. There are many different ways of greeting.   7. No, it isn't. Canada is the 2nd largest country in the world in area.   8. No, they don't. Most Canadians live within a hundred miles of the southern border.   9. No, they don't. "Stationery" means "writing paper", and "stationary" means "not moving".   10. No, it isn't. Smith is.

pp. 76, 77

1. correct   2. Newspapers in the region publish a little news about industrial development.   3. There is not any information about the economy in the foreign press, however.   4. Many new factories were built near the major cities recently.   5. There is a great deal (a lot) of research on pollution and other undesirable effects of industrialization.   6. correct   7. Unfortunately, several areas in the north and a few places near the border are still underdeveloped.   8. There aren't many natural resources in all parts of the country.   9. A great deal (A lot) of equipment is scarce in rural areas.   10. correct   11. However, transportation is still a problem in isolated sections.

p. 79

The occurs 24 times in the paragraph. Before singular countable nouns: the kitchen, the (largest) room, the center, the household, the customer. . . . Before plural countable nouns: the (local) women, the subtleties, the (latest) fashions, the (fashion) magazines. There are no examples of *the* before mass nouns in this paragraph.

p. 82

2. *A/An* followed by singular countable nouns: a (rare) manner, a hedgehog, a (large) cortex, an ("advanced") trait. There are no examples of *a/an* followed by plural nouns or mass nouns.   3. *The* followed by singular countable nouns: the organization, the (dolphin's) brain, the cortex, the brain. *The* followed by plural countable nouns: the (most "primitive" living land) mammals, the researchers.   4. Yes. "The researchers" and "the scientists" refer to people already mentioned or known to the reader. If no article were used, it would mean any group of researchers or scientists.   5. Yes. *The* "advanced" trait would refer to the only trait associated with higher intelligence.

pp. 82, 83

Americans have a sense of ∅ space, not of ∅ place. Go to an American home in ∅ exurbia and almost the first thing you do is drift toward the picture window. How curious that the first compliment you pay your host is to say how lovely it is outside his house! He is pleased that you should admire his vistas. The distant horizon is not merely a line separating the earth from ∅ sky, it is a symbol of the future. The American is not rooted in his place, however lovely: his eyes are drawn by the expanding space to a point on the horizon, which is his future.

p. 83

By contrast, consider the traditional Chinese home. Blank walls enclose it. Step behind the spirit wall and you are in a courtyard with perhaps a miniature garden around a corner. Once inside his private compound you are wrapped in an ambience of ∅ calm beauty, an ordered world of ∅ buildings, ∅ pavement, ∅ rock and ∅ decorative vegetation. But you have no distant view: nowhere does ∅ space open out before you. Raw nature in such a home is experienced only as ∅ weather, and the only open space is the sky above. The Chinese is rooted in his place. When he has to leave, it is not for the promised land on the terrestrial horizon, but for another world altogether along the vertical, religious axis of his imagination.

pp. 85, 86

2. PEOPLE TOUCH HANDS. 3. THEY INCLINE BODIES 4. PEOPLE SHAKE HANDS
5. MAN EXTENDS HAND 6. WOMAN HUGS FRIENDS. 7. MEN TOUCH FRIENDS

p. 90

1. The rooms in the back of the house next to the kitchen are small. 2. The furniture seems old but comfortable. 3. correct 4. She doesn't usually shake hands when she meets someone. 5. correct 6. The brain of a dolphin is not divided into specialized areas. 7. correct.

Chapter 3

p. 110

B. Phrases 4. "my sisters' friend" and 5. "my sister's friend" should sound the same. No phrases should look exactly alike. Check the position of the apostrophes.

p. 113

1. The Nile in Africa is the longest river in the world, more than a hundred miles longer than the Amazon in South America. 2. Lake Superior, between the US and Canada is the largest lake in North America. It is, however, much smaller than the Caspian Sea, which borders on the Soviet Union and Iran. 3. The Sonoran and the Mohave are the two largest deserts in North America. 4. Greenland, the largest island in the world, has the largest ice mass outside of Antarctica. 5. New Orleans is on the Mississippi River about one hundred miles north of the Gulf of Mexico.

pp. 118, 119

1. yours 2. hers 3. their 4. its 5. himself 6. themselves 7. herself 8. themselves
9. my friend and me. 10. Carlos and I.

pp. 119, 120

their, them, their, their, they, their, they, them, them, they, they, their, its, his, they, She, him, you, your, she, them, its, their, his, they, them, them, it, them, they.

p. 123

2. MAN BECOMES FATHER 3. INCUMBENT SEEMS TO BE VICTOR 4. MAN REMAINS MANAGER 5. PRESS SECRETARY IS SPOKESPERSON 6. SQUARE IS RECTANGLE 7. SUCCESS IS WORD 8. DIABETES IS DISEASE

pp. 124, 125

A. 1. A rectangle is a figure with four straight sides and four right angles.

2. A square is a figure with four equal sides and four right angles.

3. A right angle is an angle that has ninety degrees.

4. A triangle is a figure with three straight sides and three angles.

5. An isosceles triangle is a triangle that has two equal sides (that has two equal angles).

6. A pentagon is an enclosed, straight-sided figure with five sides and five interior angles.

7. A hexagon is an enclosed, straight-sided figure with six sides and six interior angles.

8. An octagon is a figure with eight sides and eight interior angles.

All squares are rectangles but not all rectangles are squares.

B. 1. The radius of a circle is the straight line that goes from its center to its outer edge.

2. The diameter of a circle is the straight line that goes from one edge of a circle to the other and that passes through its center.

3. The circumference of a circle is the length of its outer edge.

4. A semicircle is half a circle.

5. Two parallel lines are lines that run side by side at an equal distance from each other.

6. Two perpendicular lines are lines that are at right angles to each other.

7. A horizontal line is a line parallel or roughly parallel to the horizon.

8. A vertical line is a line (roughly) perpendicular to the ground or horizon.

Parallel lines never meet. Perpendicular lines may meet.

pp. 126–128

1. (nouns are underlined): a <u>lawyer</u>, many valuable <u>things</u>, his <u>home</u>, a <u>lifetime</u>, <u>indifference</u>, his most prized <u>possession</u>, the <u>interviewer</u>, the <u>basement family room</u>, an old <u>chest</u>, a <u>trombone</u>, the <u>instrument</u>, <u>college</u>, a middle-aged <u>lawyer</u>, a <u>life</u>, <u>freedom</u>, <u>spontaneity</u>, <u>nostalgia</u>, <u>responsibilities</u>, the <u>basement</u>, the old <u>trombone</u>

2. Singular countable nouns: lawyer, home, lifetime, possession, interviewer, basement, family, room, chest, trombone, instrument, college life; plural countable nouns: things, responsibilities; mass nouns: indifference, freedom, spontaneity, nostalgia

3. valuable things, prized possession, old chest, middle-aged lawyer, old trombone

Chapter 4

pp. 133, 134

A.

/əd/ (extra syllable)	/t/	/d/
recommended	passed	achieved
exceeded	asked	transferred
completed	looked	preferred
accumulated	finished	planned
admitted	discussed	studied

B. The regular past tense ending (-*ed*) is pronounced /əd/ (extra syllable) when the base ends in the sounds /d/ or /t/. It is pronounced /d/ after all other voiced consonants and after all vowel sounds. It is pronounced /t/ after all other voiceless consonants.

Remember that you must pay attention to the sound, not the spelling. Sounds like the first sound in *p*ie, *s*ink, and *c*ould are voiceless. Sounds like the first sound in *b*uy, *z*inc, and *g*ood, are voiced.

p. 136

1. saved   2. hoped   3. helped   4. tried   5. controlled   6. hopped   7. carried   8. started   9. worried   10. planned   11. dried   12. referred   13. succeeded   14. loved   15. visited

pp. 137, 138

painted, drew, put, was, parted, rose, called, saw, pointed, looked, talked, did not understand, spoke, did not ask, flunked, said, were, got, did, enjoyed, did not occur, was, talked, made, made.

Learn any past tense forms you did not write correctly.

p. 139

found, said, were, said, called, was, was, glanced, looked, looked, hoped, opened, wasn't, wasn't, hoped, sounded, didn't pause, stop, kept on, said, sat, was, came, was, was, didn't whisper, was, whispered

pp. 147, 148

1. at   2. in   3. in   4. in, on   5. on, on   6. at, at   7. on   8. on, on   9. on   10. on, in

p. 150

1. ~~through~~   2. ~~on~~   3. ~~through~~, ~~in~~, ~~in~~, ~~in front of~~   4. ~~facing~~   5. ~~over~~   6. ~~in front of~~
7. ~~behind~~   8. ~~at~~, ~~into~~   9. ~~by~~, ~~on~~   10. ~~through~~   11. ~~onto~~   12. ~~out from~~

pp. 151, 152

2. REVIEWERS ARE DISAPPOINTED   3. REVIEWERS ARE DISTURBED   4. AUDIENCES SEEM HOSTILE   5. AUDIENCES APPEAR ENTHUSIASTIC   6. FAILURE IS SURPRISING

pp. 152–154

A. lived, considered, made, was, witnessed, began, were, was, were, gave, died, lived, were, lived, used, saved, used, used

Chapter 5

pp. 164, 165

is, make, come, seem, find, put, want, be, want, want, means, want, want, double, add, have written, forget, do, ends, suppose, know, remember, is

pp. 166, 167

have looked, am, know, pause, think, has made, know, am, are, look, am, are, have looked, check, are, strikes, use, sound, do, think, is, catch, is, find, be, is, make, want

p. 181

1. After each class she did each assignment thoroughly.   2. The week before the test, she reviewed all previous assignments carefully.   3. The evening before the test, she studied her notes briefly.   4. correct   5. She ate a good breakfast calmly.   6. She entered the room confidently.   7. Because she was so well prepared, she was able to answer most of the questions rapidly.

p. 183

1. aggressively   2. angrily   3. arrogantly   4. audaciously   5. boastfully   6. capably
7. casually   8. courageously   9. cynically   10. generously   11. lazily   12. mischievously
13. naively   14. normally   15. patiently   16. sensitively   17. shyly   18. sincerely
19. skeptically   20. thoughtfully   21. timidly

p. 184

1. completely   2. completely   3. complete   4. solemnly   5. solemn   6. carefully   7. serious, completely   8. loud   9. loudly

p. 185

1. lively   2. friendly   3. hard   4. Surprisingly   5. successfully, good   6. nervous, silent, quickly, anxious

p. 187

1. On, in, in, at   2. On, at, at, at, On, in   3. on, at, in, on   4. in, in, in, on

pp. 188, 189

1. by, in time, for, on time   2. through, until   3. around   4. at, till   5. for, during   6. in a little while   7. For the time being   8. at once, in no time

pp. 189, 190

A. 2. COUNSELOR SHOWS THEM BOOKS   3. WORKSHOP TEACHES THEM TECHNIQUES   4. STUDENTS WRITE COMPANIES LETTER   5. FRIEND LENDS HER MAGAZINE   6. STUDENTS SEND COMPANIES RÉSUMÉS
B. 1. The placement office at the university gives a booklet about finding jobs in the computer industry to the students.   2. A counselor in the placement office shows several books about employment opportunities for computer science majors to them.   3. A workshop teaches several techniques useful in writing good résumés to them.   4. The students write a short letter to several large software companies on the West Coast asking for information about job opportunities.   5. The student's friend lends a magazine with several ads for computer programming jobs in California to her.   6. At the beginning of their senior year, the students send their résumés to software companies.

pp. 194–196

A. a, an, the, a, the, the, a, A, the, a, the, the, the
B. Of the 165 books cited, the *Bible* got the most votes: 15. No other book came close. Among the few books mentioned more than once were *The White Company*, by Arthur Conan Doyle, *Markings* by Dag Hammarskjold, *The Power of Positive Thinking* by Norman Vincent Peale, and *Walden* by Henry David Thoreau. A few authors — among them Homer, Aristotle, Erich Fromm — were named for more than one book.
C. Other authors ranged from Shakespeare to Lawrence Ferlinghetti, from Dale Carnegie to Virginia Woolf, from Benjamin Spock to Mark Twain. Almost no one in the survey cited a current best-seller.

The Sabines concluded that there was no way to predict which book would make a difference to whom, at what ages or in what kinds of life situations. In fact, they say: "The reading experience is so personal it borders on the intimate. And in a time when identity increasingly is lost the reading of books may remain as one of the few truly personal acts left to us ."

Chapter 6

p. 205

1. What have you been doing lately?   2. They will ask you how long you have been living at your present address.   3. My daughter has been watching soap operas for three hours.   4. I have been trying to get a driver's license for a year.   5. Our family has been living in the same town for a hundred years.   6. I have known my husband's parents since I was a child.   7. My mother has worked in my family's business since my youngest brother started school.   8. She has just left.   9. Recently I have been trying to speak English with my friends.   10. Have you ever seen the beautiful mountains in my country?

p. 214

The Color Purple — Alice Walker; Robie House — Frank Lloyd Wright; "Appalachian Spring" — Aaron Copland; *A Farewell to Arms* — Ernest Hemingway; Nighthawks — Edward Hopper; Let It Be — John Lennon and Paul McCartney; *Citizen Kane* — Orson Wells; *Ulysses* — James Joyce; "Mood Indigo" — Duke Ellington; "Fancy Free" — Jerome Robbins; *The 39 Steps* — Alfred Hitchcock

p. 217

Mandarin Chinese is spoken by approximately 750 million people in China and other Far Eastern countries. Other varieties of Chinese are spoken in China and elsewhere. Spanish is spoken as a first language by approximately 200 million people in Spain, South America, Central America, Mexico, and in many parts of the United States. Russian is spoken as either a first or second language by approximately 190 million people in the Soviet Union. Hindi is spoken by about 180 million people in India. Bengali is spoken by nearly 120 million people in northeastern India and Bangladesh. Arabic is spoken by about 115 million people throughout the Middle East and Northern Africa. Japanese is spoken by over 100 million people in Japan. German is spoken by approximately 100 million people in Germany, Austria, and Switzerland. Portuguese is spoken by more than 100 million people in Portugal and Brazil.

pp. 223, 224

1. in, in, in, in, in   2. by, by, by   3. by, by   4. with, with, without   5. for, for, for   6. by, by, by   7. as, as   8. by, by   9. with, with   10. as, by

p. 225

2. HE APPOINTS GOVERNOR AMBASSADOR (S-V-O-NC)   3. SENATORS CALL APPOINTMENT UNWISE (S-V-O-Adj.C)   4. PEOPLE CALL SELECTION MISTAKE (S-V-O-NC)   5. LEADERS CONSIDER CHOICE EXCELLENT (S-V-O-Adj.C)

p. 000

2. FIRE DESTROYED BUILDINGS, 2   3. PEOPLE ARRIVE, 1   4. CARDIOLOGIST IS DOCTOR, 3   5. UNIVERSITY GIVES STUDENTS BOOKLET, 5   6. PEOPLE SPEAK

LANGUAGE, 2 7. GIRL SEEMS UNHAPPY, 4 8. UNCLE LENDS HER MONEY, 5 9. JURY FINDS DEFENDANT GUILTY, 6 10. TEAM REMAINS WINNER, 3 11. NETWORKS DECLARE INCUMBENT LOSER, 6 12. WOMAN TEARS LETTER, 2 13. ABILITY INCREASES, 1

p. 228

A. I know that I *will hate* jogging. Every dawn as I *will thud* around New York City's Central Park reservoir, I *will be reminded* of how much I hate it. It *will be* so tedious. Some *will claim* jogging is thought conducive; others *will insist* the scenery *will relieve* the monotony. For me, the pace *will be* wrong for contemplation of either ideas or vistas. While jogging, all I *will be able to* think about *will be* jogging — or nothing. One advantage of jogging around a reservoir is that there *will be* no dry shortcut home.

B. I *have hated* jogging for three weeks. Every dawn as I *have been thudding* around New York City's Central Park reservoir, I *have been reminded* of how much I *have hated* it. It *has been* so tedious. Some *have claimed* jogging is thought conducive; others *have insisted* the scenery relieves the monotony. For me, the pace *has been* wrong for contemplation of either ideas or vistas. While jogging, all I *have been able to* think about *has been* jogging — or nothing. One advantage of jogging around a reservoir *has been* that there *has been* no dry shortcut home.

C. For six months I jogged every morning and *hated* it. Every dawn as I *thudded* around New York City's Central Park reservoir, I *was reminded* of how much I *hated* it. It *was* so tedious. Some *claimed* jogging *was* thought conducive; others *insisted* the scenery *relieved* the monotony. For me, the pace *was* wrong for contemplation of either ideas or vistas. While jogging, all I *could* think about *was* jogging — or nothing. One advantage of jogging around a reservoir *was* that there *was* no dry shortcut home.

p. 229

A. the, a, ∅, a, ∅, a, an, a, the, the, the, a, a, ∅, the, the, a, ∅, a, a, the, the

Chapter 7

p. 253

1. for, for, of, about, for   2. for, at, of, at, with   3. of, for, of, of, for, of   4. to, at, of, to, for   5. about, with

p. 270

Aldo Cimino <u>was</u> an employee of the Campbell Soup Company, a large manufacturer of canned soups. <u>In 1986</u> Cimino <u>had</u> 44 years of experience with Campbell. He <u>was</u> one of the few employees who <u>knew</u> everything there <u>was</u> to know about one important stage in the manufacture of canned soups. He <u>was</u> an expert on the 72-foot-high "cookers" that <u>filled</u> up to 850 soup cans a minute.

   Mr. Cimino <u>retired in 1987</u> and Campbell <u>worried</u> that when he <u>left</u> they <u>would lose</u> all his years of experience. <u>Previously</u> when one of the maintenance workers <u>had</u> a problem with the cookers, he <u>would</u> usually <u>ask</u> Mr. Cimino. Problems in this stage <u>of</u> the canning process <u>needed</u> to be fixed in a short time or the soup <u>had to</u> be thrown away. Cimino, because of his experience, <u>could</u> generally determine the trouble and find a solution very quickly after asking the worker a few questions.

In order not to lose valuable information when Cimino <u>retired</u>, Campbell <u>was going</u> to put his expertise into a computer program. Dozens of software engineers <u>were going</u> to interview Mr. Cimino and the workers and attempt to organize and codify a lifetime of experience about canning. Their idea <u>was</u> to capture his expertise in an inexpensive computer system. The computer <u>would</u> contain answers to thousands of questions that workers in the plant <u>asked</u> Mr. Cimino. Campbell <u>hoped</u> that after 1987, workers who <u>had</u> questions about what to do <u>could</u> turn to the computer for answers.

p. 271

2. Nowadays jeans are worn everywhere.   3. Jeans are worn to the opera.   4. Jeans are worn to the theater.   5. "Designer jeans" that cost more than $50 are worn.   7. Blue jeans were invented in California in the middle of the nineteenth century.   8. They were first worn by gold miners.   9. Gold was discovered in California in the 1840s.   10. A few years later gold was being searched for by thousands of people in the American West. 11. The first blue jeans were made by a seventeen-year-old tailor named Levi Strauss. 12. They were made from heavy canvas.   13. Canvas was being used to make tents. 14. Canvas was being used for covered wagons.   15. Before Strauss, canvas was not being used for clothes.   16. Later, another fabric was used by Strauss to make his popular overalls.   17. This softer and lighter fabric was made in Italy and France.   18. In France, it was called *serge de Nîmes*.   19. *De Nîmes* was pronounced "denim" in the United States. 20. The denim thread was made in the Italian town of Genoa.   21. That town was called Genes by French weavers.   23. Later, clothes made from denim were called jeans.

Chapter 8

p. 275

2. had prepared, were   3. had been, got   4. had been, got   5. became, had . . . had 6. hadn't worked, started   7. felt, had . . . studied, didn't understand   8. understood, were, had learned

p. 276

1. had completed   2. haven't eaten, have had, haven't called, have been, had . . . started 3. haven't . . . seen, had . . . seen

pp. 322, 323

encouraged, became, bought, refused, built, was, had believed, was, was, seemed, entertained, were, would dismantle, move, could be used, would cook, brought, played, were, ate, drank, danced, covered, brought, hung, prepared, went, were

Chapter 9

p. 357

2. simple present: continue, see, believe; will + verb: will marry, will have, will remain, will be; going to + verb: going to affect; future progressive: will be remarrying; future perfect: will have learned

p. 358

of, Into, of, into, from, of, in, of, of, in, of, into, of, into

Chapter 10

p. 366

1. possible   2. nonfactual   3. nonfactual   4. possible   5. nonfactual   6. possible   7. nonfactual

p. 368

2. factual, present or future time   3. factual, future time   4. nonfactual, present or future time   5. factual, present time   6. factual, present time   7. nonfactual, present or future time   8. nonfactual, present time   9. nonfactual, past time   10. factual, future time

pp. 391, 392

A. 3. mean to say   4. arrange to stay   5. hate to wait (or hate waiting)   6. order him to do   7. look forward to seeing   8. tell her to study   9. can't help wanting   10. concentrate on finishing   11. want to buy   12. enjoy using   13. refuse to listen   14. seem to be   15. offer to lend   16. keep on walking   17. cause it to happen   18. dream about becoming   19. start to work (or start working)   20. need to choose

B. 3. hope to go   4. be in favor of going   5. quit going   6. forget to go (or forget going)   7. intend to go   8. postpone going   9. convince him to go   10. regret going   11. try to go (or try going)   12. manage to go   13. plan to go   14. advise her to go   15. choose to go   16. can't stand to go (or can't stand going)   17. decide to go

C. 3. think about doing   4. stop to do (or stop doing)   5. ask to do   6. ask him to do   7. miss doing   8. put off doing   9. be worth doing   10. remember to do (or remember doing)   11. approve of doing   12. encourage her to do   13. attempt to do   14. be used to doing   15. anticipate doing   16. expect to do   17. hate to do (or hate doing)   18. begin to do (or begin doing)   19. learn to do   20. teach him to do

p. 411

2. Passive: "and the three major classifications are based on the method each object uses to achieve its purpose." Active: "People base the three major classifications on the method each object uses to achieve its purpose." The passive voice is preferable.   3. to resist, to defeat, to achieve, breaking down   4. With the cunning typical of <u>their</u> breed, <u>automobiles</u> never <u>break</u> down while entering <u>filling</u> <u>stations</u> with large <u>staffs</u> of idle mechanics. <u>They</u> <u>wait</u> until <u>they</u> <u>reach</u> downtown <u>intersections</u> in the middle of the rush hour, or until <u>they</u> <u>are</u> fully loaded with <u>families</u> and luggage on the Ohio turnpike.

Thus, <u>they</u> <u>create</u> maximum misery, inconvenience, frustration and irritability among <u>their</u> human <u>cargoes</u>, thereby reducing <u>their</u> <u>owners'</u> life <u>spans</u>.

INDEX